Approaches to Teaching the Works of Primo Levi

Approaches to Teaching World Literature

For a complete listing of titles, see the last pages of this book.

Approaches to Teaching the Works of Primo Levi

Edited by

Nicholas Patruno

and

Roberta Ricci

The Modern Language Association of America

New York 2014

Library of Congress Cataloging-in-Publication Data

Approaches to teaching the works of Primo Levi / edited by Nicholas Patruno and Roberta Ricci.
pages cm. — (Approaches to teaching world literature, ISSN 1059-1133 ; 133)
Includes bibliographical references and index.
ISBN 978-1-60329-147-7 (cloth : alk. paper) —
ISBN 978-1-60329-148-4 (pbk. : alk. paper) —
ISBN 978-1-60329-179-8 (EPUB) —
ISBN 978-1-60329-180-4 (Kindle)
1. Levi, Primo—Criticism and interpretation. 2. Levi, Primo—Study and teaching. I. Patruno, Nicholas, editor. II. Ricci, Roberta, editor.
PQ4872.E8Z5625 2014
853'.914—dc23 2014020776

Approaches to Teaching World Literature 133
ISSN 1059-1133

Cover illustration of the paperback and electronic editions:
Auschwitz III. Photograph by Jonathan Wilson, 2004.

Published by The Modern Language Association of America
26 Broadway, New York, NY 10004-1789
www.mla.org

Meditate che questo è stato:
Vi comando queste parole.
Scolpitele nel vostro cuore

Consider that this has been:
I commend these words to you.
Engrave them on your hearts

Dedicated to the memory of

Nancy Dersofi
Samual Tobias Lachs
Bice Cacialli-Rossi
Giampiero Ricci

CONTENTS

ACKNOWLEDGMENTS

As editors of this volume, several years in the making, we are deeply appreciative to all those who have been connected, directly or otherwise, with this project. We are most grateful to the Publications Committee and our editors over the course of the years, Joseph Gibaldi, Sonia Kane, James Hatch, and Sara Pastel. Their steadfast interest and patience in seeing to the completion of this volume, a commitment clearly indicative of their respect and admiration for Primo Levi and his legacy, are heartwarming and deeply appreciated. We thank also the MLA's anonymous readers for their encouragement and generous advice along the way. The perspicacity of their comments has provided keen insights to this research, and we are grateful for their care and attention in the editing and rereading of the earlier drafts. We are also beholden to those who responded to the initial questionnaire circulated in the opening stage of this project. With the importance of Levi as an indisputable given, their views confirmed the validity of this volume as an invaluable additional tool for classroom use in the teaching of his works. We are equally appreciative of our Bryn Mawr College students, particularly Didem Uca and Mary Blumenfeld, for their sensitive, bright, and well-articulated input. And there would not have been a book without the first-rate essays of all the contributors, many of them internationally recognized experts on Levi and on Holocaust literature. To them, our most fervent thanks for their unremitting cooperation, patience, and goodwill. Our unending thanks go also to Oliva Cardona, whose technical expertise and extreme good sense has been crucial to the completion of this volume.

No thanks are complete without the acknowledgment of support from colleagues, friends, and relatives. Their encouragement and understanding, especially in moments of uncertainty and self-doubt, cannot go unheeded. To this end, we thank our colleagues and friends, Azade Seyhan and Susan Adelmann among them, and the members of our respective families for their tireless support: Emma Ricci De Lucca, Maria Paola Rossi, Emilio Ricci, Harsh Grewal, Leah Grewal, Ryan Grewal, Edwina Patruno, and the other members of the Patruno family.

Part One

MATERIALS

Editions

Editions in Italian

Einaudi, one of the few Italian publishing houses to oppose the fascist regime, has played a key role in bringing forward Primo Levi's large and diverse body of literary production. All of Levi's writings, including subsequent editions of the titles mentioned below, have been published by Einaudi, with the exception of the original 1947 edition of *Se questo è un uomo* (pub. De Silva); his 1975 collection of poems, *L'osteria di Brema* (pub. Scheiwiller); his later and complete collection of poems, *Ad ora incerta* (pub. Garzanti); and *Racconti e saggi* (pub. La Stampa).

Between 1987 and 1990 Einaudi published *Opere*, three volumes containing the entire collection of Levi's works in the series Biblioteca dell'Orsa. Volume 1, with an introduction by Cesare Cases, includes the autobiographical accounts (*Se questo è un uomo*, *La tregua*, *Il sistema periodico*, *I sommersi e i salvati*); volume 2, with a commentary by Cesare Segre, contains Levi's novels (*La chiave a stella*, *Se non ora, quando?*) and his collection of poems (*Ad ora incerta*); volume 3, with an introduction by Pier Vincenzo Mengaldo, consists of Levi's tales and essays. In 1997, in commemoration of the tenth anniversary of Levi's death, Einaudi introduced an impressive two-volume collection of Levi's complete oeuvre, also entitled *Opere*, as a Nuova Universale Einaudi edition. Edited by Marco Belpoliti, this 3,200-page compilation contains a chronology gathered by Ernesto Ferrero and a bibliography of all Levi's writings and interviews. Fortunately for students, Einaudi has also published, at modest prices, Levi's major works—including *Se questo è un uomo*, *La tregua*, *La ricerca delle radici*, *"Lilit" e altri racconti*, *Vizio di forma*, *Storie naturali*, *L'altrui mestiere*, *Racconti e saggi*, and *Dialogo*—in paperback, reprinted several times and all still available. *Se questo è un uomo* and *La tregua* are usually combined into a single volume. These works are also available, as single volumes, in a scholastic, slightly abridged version, effectively and extensively annotated by the author. In such a format, these two volumes are especially helpful to students who have a limited knowledge of Italian and who are reading Levi for the first time.

A complete listing of Levi's works in Italian, with dates, content descriptions, and other relevant data, is available on the Web site for the Centro Internazionale di Studi Primo Levi (http://www.primolevi.it/Web/Italiano/Contenuti/Opera/110_Edizioni_italiane).

Anthologies

Instructors who cover Levi in survey courses of Italian literature will find selections from his works included in most twentieth-century anthologies of Italian literature. *Il filo rosso. Antologia e storia della letteratura italiana ed europea*, edited by Marco Santagata, Laura Carotti, Alberto Casadei, and Mirko Tavoni, deserves special mention, since it contains the most extensive number of excerpts taken from Levi's complete works. *Profili Novecenteschi*, edited by Luciano Niri, is another source that warrants consideration. As for Levi's poems, a brief collection is included in volume 8 (*Novecento*) of the *Antologia della poesia italiana*, edited by Segre and Carlo Ossola.

Levi's Holocaust narratives are also included in several Holocaust anthologies. Edited by Lawrence Langer, *Art from the Ashes*, which includes the essay "Shame" from Levi's *The Drowned and the Saved*, is among the most important. Also deserving consideration are Langer's *The Holocaust and the Literary Imagination* and Berel Lang's *Writing and the Holocaust*.

Translations

As Levi wrote in "Tradurre ed essere tradotti" ("Translating and Being Translated"), "Tradurre è opera difficile perché le barriere fra i linguaggi sono più alte di quanto si pensi comunemente" 'Translation is difficult work because the barriers between languages are higher than is generally thought' (110; qtd. in Mendel, "Primo Levi and Translation" 11). Despite his demonstrated personal concern, Levi's works have been prodigiously translated into English. Those interested in the issue of translation as it relates to Levi's works and to Levi as translator will find David Mendel's "Primo Levi and Translation" indispensable to their investigation.

Whereas Levi's principal works have been reprinted by various publishers over the years, the original translations have remained unchanged. The translations of *Se questo è un uomo* and *La tregua* in use today, *Survival in Auschwitz* and *The Reawakening*, contain the original Stuart Woolf translations. The 1987 and ensuing Macmillan reprints of *Survival* also include, as an afterword, the engaging "Primo Levi and Philip Roth: A Conversation." Raymond Rosenthal's translation *"The Sixth Day" and Other Tales*, a selection of tales taken from Levi's *Storie naturali* and *Vizio di forma*, is out of print. No translation is ever perfect, and reservations have been voiced on occasion. Clive James, for example, takes issue with the accuracy of William Weaver's selection of certain expressions in the *Drowned and the Saved* (*I sommersi e i salvati*). Nevertheless, Weaver has produced generally well-accepted translations of Levi, including *The Periodic Table* (*Il sistema periodico*), *Other People's Trades* (*L'altrui mestiere*), *The Mirror Maker* (selections from *Racconti e saggi*), *The Monkey's Wrench* (*La chiave a stella*), and *If Not Now, When?* (*Se non ora, quando?*). Ruth Feldman has translated a selection of stories from *"Lilit" e altri racconti* as *Moments of Reprieve* and, with Brian Swann, has applied a keen sensibility to the edition *Collected Poems*, taken from Levi's *Ad ora incerta* ("At an Uncertain Hour"). The collection of Levi's short stories now available to the

English-language reader has been broadened further with the recent publication of *A Tranquil Star: Unpublished Stories*, translated by Ann Goldstein and Alessandra Bastagli.

The twenty-first century has seen English translations of Levi's interviews, opinions, lectures, and other writings. *The Search for Roots: A Personal Anthology*, Peter Forbes's translation of *La ricerca delle radici*, is a primary source for those interested in learning about the writers and works that have been fundamental and most influential to Levi's literary persona. Advanced students interested in carrying out extensive research will want to consult *The Black Hole of Auschwitz* (*L'assimetria e la vita*), whose title is suggestive of the metaphorical expression often used by a disappointed and disheartened Levi during the last years of his life. Edited by Marco Belpoliti and translated by Sharon Wood, this volume, in addition to gathering together several of Levi's writings on the Holocaust, provides a significant insight on his wide range of interests and testifies to the skill, thoughtfulness, and sensitivity he applied to his subject matter. Judith Woolf's *The Auschwitz Report*, edited by Robert Gordon, is a translation of a report written by Levi with Alberto De Benedetti that was originally published in an obscure medical journal soon after the end of the war; it provides readers with a firsthand account of the harsh conditions in Auschwitz, although it contains no mention of Levi's work in the chemical laboratory in Buna-Monowitz. Ferdinando Camon's *Conversations with Primo Levi* (*Autoritratto di Primo Levi*), translated by John Shepley, is one of Levi's last and most penetrating interviews. The English translation includes a compelling essay in which Camon questions whether Levi's death was a suicide.

Very few bilingual editions of Levi's work are available. Feldman's translation of Levi's short story "Lilith" is included, however, in *Short Stories in Italian*, a volume in the series New Penguin Parallel Texts.

The Instructor's Library

Reference Works

Those who wish to become better acquainted with Jewish traditions and culture will find the following sources particularly helpful: Rabbi Joseph Telushkin's *Jewish Literacy*, Herman Wouk's *This Is My God*, and Raphael Patai's *The Jewish Mind*. On how Judaism influences Levi, suggested readings include David Mendel's "Primo Levi and the Jews," Joseph Sungolowsky's "The Jewishness of Primo Levi," and Sergio Parussa's "A Hybridism of Sounds: Primo Levi between Judaism and Literature."

Much has been written about the Holocaust, and the brief list that follows serves mainly as an initial and introductory reference for those with little prior knowledge of the Holocaust. The four volumes of Israel Gutman's *The Encyclopedia of the Holocaust* and Walter Laqueur's *The Holocaust Encyclopedia* provide a good start. Readers will appreciate immensely the renowned *Encyclopedia of Holocaust Literature*, edited by David Patterson, Alan L. Berger, and Sarita Cargas. This source, in addition to presenting the lives and works of over one hundred writers whose contributions have provided a greater appreciation of the complexities surrounding the Holocaust, contains two useful bibliographies: one of primary works and the other of book-length studies of Holocaust literature. David Szonyi's *The Holocaust: An Annotated Bibliography and Resource Guide* is a valuable resource that includes, along with coverage of standard topics associated with the Holocaust, a list of audiovisual materials, names of research institutes and archival centers, religious services, oral history projects, and traveling exhibits. Two other important sources are David M. Crowe's *The Holocaust: Roots, History, and Aftermath* and *The Holocaust: An Annotated Bibliography*, compiled by Harry James Cargas. This volume contains numerous annotations and the very well-organized and extremely helpful chapter "Researching the Holocaust: Guidance for Students, compiled by Dan Sharon" (165–72). Abraham Edelheit and Hershel Edelheit's *Bibliography on Holocaust Literature* and its two-volume supplement are also excellent resources. In addition to references to periodicals, books, documents, and eyewitness accounts, they comprise a wealth of material absent in other sources.

Historical and Literary Studies

There is no dearth of information regarding Jews and the Holocaust. For a succinct general overview of the culture and history of the Jews in Europe in the years preceding and during the Second World War, instructors of students of all levels will want to consider Ian Dear's *The Oxford Companion to World War II*, Martin Gilbert's *The Holocaust: A History of the Jews of Europe during the Second World War*, and Vera Laska's *Nazism, Resistance, and Holocaust in World War II: A Bibliography*. Additional sources for understanding the historical context of the Holocaust include Yehuda Bauer's *The Holocaust as Historical Experience*, Gilbert's *Atlas of the Holocaust*, Michael Marrus's *The Holocaust in History*, and Raul Hilberg's *The Destruction of the European Jews*.

Two important guides for an appreciation of the history and condition of the Jews in Italy are Cecil Roth's *The History of the Jews of Italy* and Barbara Garvin's *The Jews of Italy: Memory and Identity*. Renzo De Felice's *The Jews in Fascist Italy* gives an extremely detailed account and history of the Italian Jews during Italy's twenty-three-year history of fascism and its involvement in World War II. Also useful for understanding the historical and political circumstances of Jews in Italy under fascism are Meir Michaelis's *Mussolini and the Jews* and Michele Sarfatti's *The Jews in Mussolini's Italy: From Equality to Persecution*. The collection *Italian Fascism and Anti-fascism: A Critical Anthology*, edited by Stanislao G. Pugliese, presents various perspectives of fascist Italy in essays by the most prominent Italian writers, historians, philosophers, and political figures of that period. *The Italians and the Holocaust: Persecution, Rescue, and Survival*, by Susan Zuccotti, provides an abundance of valuable material and data and is one of the most in-depth accounts of the events surrounding the plight of the Jews and of active antifascist groups in Italy during the years of fascism and the subsequent German occupation.

Stuart Hughes's *Prisoners of Hope* supplies a significant and concentrated analysis of the literary contributions of prominent Italian Jewish writers, Levi among them. Levi is also included in the anthology *Jewish Writers of the Twentieth Century*, edited by Sorrel Kerbel (323–25), and in *Italian Novelists since World War II*, edited by Augustus Pallotta (162–70).

Monographic studies and conference proceedings have contributed significant bibliographic input since Levi's death, widening the spectrum of evaluation on the importance of his works. The reader of Italian will find extensive Italian reviews in Fiora Vincenti's *Invito alla lettura di Primo Levi*, an early valuable analysis of the life and works of Primo Levi up to 1982, and in Giuseppe Grassano's *Primo Levi* and Vania De Luca's *Tra Giobbe e i buchi neri*. For the reader of English, Nicholas Patruno's *Understanding Primo Levi*, a companion reader to Levi's works in English translation, provides an introduction for the English-speaking student and instructor; Mirna Cicioni's *Primo Levi: Bridges of Knowledge*, also published in 1995, further contributes to the knowledge base. A wealth of material that would fulfill the research needs of any student at any level may be found in the extraordinary bibliographies included in *Memory and Mastery: Primo Levi as Writer and Witness*, edited by Roberta Kremer; Gordon's *Primo Levi's Ordinary Virtues: From Testimony to Ethics*; and James T. Mellone's contribution to *The Legacy of Primo Levi*, edited by Pugliese. Whereas Gordon divides his bibliography between the works by Levi and publications on Levi, Mellone subdivides the biographical and critical studies on Levi and his work in books and in articles and essays. Mellone has updated his entries further in another of Pugliese's editions, *Answering Auschwitz: Primo Levi's Science and Humanism after the Fall*, by adding the category "edited collections of essays," which lists, by title and author, the many published proceedings from conferences on Levi ("Primo Levi"). Also indispensable is Gordon's *The Cambridge Companion to Primo Levi*, a stimulating overview of the works, life, and times of this important twentieth-century writer. Particularly for the Italian reader, *Primo Levi: Un'antologia della critica*, edited by Ernesto Ferrero, is also a valuable tool for a complete bibliography of criticism of Levi's works.

In terms of Levi's biography, Carole Angiers's *The Double Bond: Primo Levi: A Biography* and Ian Thomson's *Primo Levi: A Life* are by far the most complete in providing valuable information on Levi's life and cultural surroundings. The numerous photographs in Thomson's book are an added and most welcomed attraction.

Throughout his writing career, Levi constantly returned to the topic of his deep concern with language as a means of clear communication and in contrast to its abuse in the *Lager*. Among the many essays on this subject, students at the more advanced levels and capable of appreciating the nuances of language will benefit from reading Fabio Girelli-Carasi's "The Anti-linguistic Nature of the Lager in the Language of Primo Levi's *Se questo è un uomo*," Sander L. Gilman's "The Special Language of the Camps and After," Brian Cliff's "On Language and Violence," and Patricia Sayre and Linnea Vacca's "On Language and Personhood: A Linguistic Odyssey." Lina Insana's *Arduous Tasks: Primo Levi, Translation and the Transmission of Holocaust Testimony* focuses on translation taken in its original meaning of "translatio," or transposing, figuratively speaking, from one language to another, and examines how Levi's literary testimony marks a point of entry into his entire literary corpus. Another valuable source is Risa Sodi's chapter on Levi's linguistic choices, "Primo Levi's Holocaust Lexicon," in her *Narrative and Imperative: The First Fifty Years of Italian Holocaust Writing, 1944–1994* (39–85).

To address how Levi incorporates his scientific knowledge in his works, instructors might direct students to Nancy Harrowitz's "Primo Levi's Science as 'Evil Nurse,'" Mirna Cicioni's "Moral Snares and Parables: Between Science Fiction and Midrash," Jo Ann Cannon's "Chemistry and Writing in *The Periodic Table*," and Ilona Klein's "Humor, Science and Technology in Levi's *Storie naturali*."

Philosophical and ethical issues are another central topic in Levi's works related to the Shoah. Gian Paolo Biasin's "Till My Ghastly Tale Is Told: Levi's Moral Discourse from *Se questo è un uomo* to *I sommersi e i salvati*" and "The Haunted Journey of Primo Levi" provide a good initiation to this subject. "The Question of Ethical Discourse: Emmanuel Lévinas, Primo Levi and Giorgio Agamben," by Dan Leshem; "Primo Levi, Giorgio Agamben, and the New Ethics of Reading," by William McClellan; and *Primo Levi and Humanism after Auschwitz: Posthumanist Reflections*, by Jonathan Druker, each address Levi's positions on the philosophical and ethical dilemmas of the Holocaust. In Druker's exceptionally insightful study, accompanied by a wealth of valuable notes, the theories of Adorno, Lévinas, Lyotard, and Foucault are brought forward to raise the question of whether Levi, reasoning through the lens of the Enlightenment, "risks complicity with the murderous master narratives of Nazism" (2). Also worthy of notice are Lucie Benchouiha's *Primo Levi: Rewriting the Holocaust*, Sam Magavern's *Primo Levi's Universe: A Writer's Journey*, and Charlotte Ross's *Primo Levi's Narratives of Embodiment: Containing the Human*. Benchouiha, in her examination of the themes present in Levi's writings, singles out stylistic and linguistic nuances that contribute to making Levi the unique writer that he is. Magavern offers the reader a portrait of Levi's multifaceted creative persona along with a well-presented biographical profile. Of particular interest is Magavern's analysis of Levi's novels about blue-collar workers. Ross, relying considerably on a philosophical discourse, presents an engaging, innovative reading of Levi's works, focusing on the interpretation of bodies and embodiment as presented or alluded to in the wide breadth of his narrative, ranging from testimony and journalism to essays and science fiction stories.

Testimony remains the central theme in many, if not most, of Levi's works, and thus receives the most critical attention. Notable essays are Franca Molino Signorini's "The Duty and Risk of Testimony: Primo Levi as Keeper of Memory," Timothy Campbell's "The Object(s) of Memory: Models of Remembering in Primo Levi's *Se questo è un uomo*," Isabella Bertoletti's "Primo Levi's Odyssey: *The Drowned and the Saved*," Jay Losey's "'The Pain of Remembering': Primo Levi's Poetry and the Function of Memory," and Antoine Philippe's "The Drowned as Saviors of Humanity: The Anthropological Value of *Se questo è un uomo*." Not to be overlooked is "Testimony: Primo Levi's Poetry: Darkness and Light," by Feldman, a personal friend of Levi and translator of his poems into English.

In recent years Levi's literary gift and creative ability have received a greater degree of attention than in the past, fulfilling Levi's own wish to be seen simply as a writer, without diminishing his reputation as memoirist of the Holocaust. Today, in addition to being regarded as one of Italy's greatest thinkers of the twentieth century (Giuliani), Levi has also emerged as one of the major literary figures of post–World War II Italy, as confirmed by the literary prizes and international acknowledgements conferred on him.

In literature classes for advanced students with limited knowledge of the Italian language, instructors might include Cicioni's *Primo Levi: Bridges of Knowledge* and Sodi's *A Dante of Our Time: Primo Levi and Auschwitz*. Sodi's study, of particular interest to students of comparative literature, examines the importance of the many references Levi makes throughout his writing to Dante's *Commedia*, and especially to the *Inferno*. In reference to Levi's short stories, Raniero Speelman's "Primo Levi's Short Stories" is recommended; for Levi's poetry, still deserving of more attention and appreciation, Patruno's "At an Uncertain Hour: The Other Side of Primo Levi."

The writings mentioned above are but a fraction of the voluminous critical output published following Levi's death. Instructors can direct students to more information on Levi by having them access analytic views from an abundance of essays, many of which are proceedings from conferences on Levi in Italy and elsewhere. To this end, readers of Italian will find valuable material in *Voci dal mondo per Primo Levi: In memoria, per la memoria*, edited by Luigi Dei; *Primo Levi: Scrittura e testimonianza*, edited by David Megnaghi; *Mémoire oblige: Riflessioni sull'opera di Primo Levi*, edited by Ada Neiger; and *Diffusione e conoscenza di Primo Levi nei paesi europei: La manutenzione della memoria*, edited by Giovanni Tesio. Likewise, for readers of English, the following collections will be helpful: *Primo Levi: The Austere Humanist*, edited by Joseph Farrell; *The Cambridge Companion to Primo Levi*, edited by Gordon; *The Legacy of Primo Levi* and *Answering Auschwitz: Primo Levi's Science and Humanism after the Fall*, edited by Pugliese; *Memory and Mastery: Primo Levi as Writer and Witness*, edited by Kremer; and *New Reflections on Primo Levi: Before and After Auschwitz*, edited by Millicent Marcus and Sodi.

Aids to Teaching

Films and Music

Films and videos are desirable and instructive tools for engaging students in classroom activities, whether viewed in class or outside classroom hours. Of the many films related to the Holocaust, Claude Lanzmann's epic *Shoah* and Steven Spielberg's *Schindler's List* remain among the most widely viewed. Roberto Benigni's *La vita è bella*, controversial as it may be, can be a useful point of reference in relation to Levi's narratives, particularly in courses taught in Italian. Francesco Rosi's motion picture *La tregua*, based on Levi's second book and released in the United States as *The Truce*, is often incorporated in courses on Levi. Although it takes blatant liberties with the book, it provides an interesting way of looking at that work and fuels lively discussions. Another film worth mentioning is Tim Blake Nelson's *The Grey Zone*, the title of which is suggested by an episode taken from the chapter "The Grey Zone" in Levi's *The Drowned and the Saved*. Students of Italian will also appreciate the episode of *Sorgente di vita*, a RAI documentary series, in which Levi revisits Auschwitz forty years after his liberation ("Primo Levi ritorna"). An inspiring addition to the material to be viewed is the DVD of the one-person play *Primo*, based on *Survival in Auschwitz* and starring Sir Antony Sher in his remarkable portrayal of Primo Levi (Wilson). Davide Ferrario and Marco Belpoliti's documentary *La strada di Levi*, released in English as *Primo Levi's Journey* and narrated by Chris Cooper, evokes Levi's spirit instead of recounting his experience as narrated in *La tregua* and takes the viewer from Auschwitz to Turin, following an up-to-date view of the same path delineated in the book.

Along with the critical recognition and appreciation of Levi's poetry, a musical component has emerged. Simon Bainbridge, in his Ad Ora Incerta*: Four Orchestral Songs from Primo Levi*, has created compositions for Levi's poems "Il canto del corvo," "Il tramonto di Fossoli," "Lunedì," and "Buna." A song cycle for voice, piano, and small instrumental ensemble with the title *Shemà: Hear: Five Poems of Primo Levi*, arranged by Simon A. Sargon, is based on Levi's poems "Shemà," "25 febbraio 1944," "Il canto del corvo," "Cantare," and "Congedo." Deserving of special notice is Ari Frankel's *To Scratch an Angel*, a chamber opera inspired by the life, writings, and death of Primo Levi. Without referring specifically to any of Levi's writings, Frankel expresses impressions and implications by way of tonal and modal orchestral lyricism.

Internet Resources

When used properly and judiciously, the Internet can prove to be a useful supplemental tool for both teachers and students. It facilitates quick and easy access to information, including much of the bibliographic information mentioned above. Used wisely, online resources can be a good starting point for students and can help them tailor their research to their particular interests.

Although virtually none of Levi's writings are available in readable form online, some articles on the man and his works are accessible, such as Diego Gambetta's "Primo Levi's Last Moments" and Michael Rothberg and Druker's "A Secular Alternative: Primo Levi's Place in American Holocaust Discourse." *YouTube* offers a sizable amount of material, especially useful for those who understand Italian and want to see and hear Levi speaking in his own words. Both parts of the documentary *Sorgente di vita* are available ("Primo Levi: Back to Auschwitz"), as are clips of interviews with the author on his book *La chiave a stella* ("Primo Levi: *La chiave*") and his experience in Auschwitz ("Primo Levi: La memoria"). *YouTube* also offers material for those reading Levi in English, including "Primo Levi: Periodic Table of Videos," Murray Baumgarten's lecture "Primo Levi: *Survival in Auschwitz* and the Meaningfulness of Everyday Life," and Patruno's lecture "Primo Levi: Auschwitz and After."

Part Two

APPROACHES

Introduction

Primo Levi is one of the most widely read post–World War II Italian writers, in Italy and abroad. He is still known primarily for his contributions to Holocaust testimony and theory, and it was the experience of Auschwitz and his need to tell that sparked his career as a writer and drove him to continue to write until his death. Among the most candid intellects of those writers who survived the Holocaust, Levi contributes an incisive, generally calm and sober voice as witness to Holocaust literature. His works, characterized by the lean and dispassionate style with which he approaches the experience of incarceration, are classics, and no course on Holocaust studies can be considered complete without them. *Se questo è un uomo* (*Survival in Auschwitz*), *La tregua* (*The Reawakening*), and *I sommersi e i salvati* (*The Drowned and the Saved*), his three major works related to his imprisonment by the Nazis, eloquently display the soul of the persecuted Jew undergoing a journey that encompasses both facts and events as well as psychological and philosophical considerations.

Levi has written ably and absorbingly about other subjects and in several genres. In addition to being a memoirist, he was a columnist, novelist, writer of short stories and fantasy tales (many of which touch on science fiction), literary critic, poet, and essayist; he even tried his hand as translator (of Kafka's *The Trial*) and playwright. He has also been the subject of countless illuminating interviews, many of which have been translated into English. Levi has been fictionalized as a character in Thane Rosenbaum's novel *The Golems of Gotham* and portrayed by the actor John Turturro in Francesco Rosi's controversial motion picture *La tregua* (*The Truce*), based on Levi's *The Reawakening*, and, on stage, by Antony Sher in *Primo*, a one-man play based on *Survival in Auschwitz*. The power of his creative vein and the originality of his writings have been recognized and appreciated worldwide; his works have been translated into more than twenty foreign languages, most commonly into English. Levi is one of most prolific writers of our time and has earned the right to be regarded simply as a well-respected writer, as he wished to be seen, with no other qualifications added.

Undoubtedly Primo Levi makes an outstanding candidate to be read, examined, and valued in the classroom. Because of their breadth and wealth, his writings can be taught in several fields, including Jewish studies and Holocaust studies, comparative literature, and Italian language and literature. Serving as points of reference, his principal works also enrich the study of twentieth-century European history; psychology, especially when discussing survivor's guilt; and philosophy, within the context of moral and ethical behavior.[1]

The compendium of essays collected in this volume reflects a limited cross section of Levi's literary interests, but it strives to amplify what is already known about the author and his works. The content is meant to provide additional material from which to draw when approaching the challenging and important work of teaching Levi's works in the classroom. Part 2 of this volume, "Approaches," is divided into three sections, the first of which is "Testimony, Autobiography, and the Holocaust." Nancy Harrowitz, who teaches Levi in a Holocaust studies course, acknowledges that students initially perceive Levi as a writer who writes in great detail and as a profound thinker, not as a literary stylist. But Levi's strength as a writer lies in his ability to make the reader see the brutality of the concentration camp by means of a language that deflects the reader from the path "toward paralysis and toxicity of knowledge about the Holocaust." According to Harrowitz, the task of the instructor is to help students recognize that how Levi articulates his observations and thoughts is as important as the message contained in his writings.

Jonathan Druker's essay offers pedagogical strategies for using *The Drowned and the Saved*, and especially Levi's "Gray Zone" concept, to teach moral ambiguity. Druker pushes his students to confront the ethical uncertainties of human action in times of crisis, leading them to ask themselves what they might have done in a similar situation, whether as a German soldier, a bystander to the Holocaust, or as a victim. There are no easy answers to such questions, but posing them helps students think more expansively and less rigidly about ethical questions.

No study of Levi's work can be deemed complete without taking into account his poetry. Even though at times poetry may complicate the testimony of the prose works, it enhances, rather than demeans, Levi's search for meaning in directions unexplored in the narrative prose. Massimo Lollini's essay presents a few textual analyses of the poems seen in relation to the prose works. In linking some of Levi's poems to sources of biblical and Greek lyric origins, Lollini demonstrates how poetry deeply affects Levi's testimony. He also points to the opportunity to introduce Levi's poems using the musical settings created by the English composer Simon Bainbridge in Ad ora incerta*: Four Orchestral Songs from Primo Levi*.

Levi's creative vein, although only recently acknowledged, has been present from his very earliest attempts at writing. Drawing from Levi's interviews, essays, and works of fiction, Nicholas Patruno seeks to eradicate the notion that the testimonial aspect of *Survival in Auschwitz* and *The Reawakening* prevents Levi from making use of his imagination. Fantasy is unavoidable, even when the prevailing purpose is to document the memory of the tragic events of Auschwitz. The juxtaposition of Levi's fantasy and his sacred commitment to speak on behalf of the victims who cannot may place Levi in a vexed position as a writer.

The essay by Massimo Giuliani focuses on Levi's interviews, fragmented conversations, short essays, and minor texts. Even through a short interview, Levi is capable of conveying important messages, subtle moral insights, and educational ideas. Levi's interviews expose readers to the complexity of his vision of history, his self-consciousness, his judgment, his educational writing and intellectual work, and the irony and the ethic of his "relative optimism."

The second section of part 2, "Language, Language Instruction, and Translation," begins with Pietro Frassica's essay on the plurality of language and the effect of cacophony of sounds in communication in the concentration camp. Adding to the atrocities and brutality the prisoners are subjected to, the language spoken in Auschwitz is a unique phenomenon designed by the Nazi machinery to reduce prisoners to a subhuman level. Frassica's observations speak to Levi's response to this situation and provide alternative ways of looking at *Survival in Auschwitz*.

Letizia Modena's essay, on her approach to Levi in an advanced Italian course, proposes to bridge the gap between language and content courses by focusing on selections from Levi's *Se questo è un uomo* and two stories in his *Storie naturali*. The solemnity and the historicity of *Se questo è un uomo* encourage students to articulate their thoughts and ideas, whereas the short stories facilitate pedagogical activities more typical of language classes, such as compositions and oral-comprehension and conversation exercises.

The act of translation, intended in the original sense of transporting, in this case from a state of incoherence to one of clarity, is at the center of the final essay in this section, by Lina Insana. She argues that translation studies can illuminate our understanding of Levi's testimonials and literary projects by recasting the survivor's task as a complex process of translation. Through an analysis of case studies ranging from Roberto Benigni's film *La vita è bella* (*Life Is Beautiful*) to Levi's *Survival in Auschwitz* to his poetic production, Insana demonstrates how translation can be a fruitful pedagogical framework for the Holocaust studies classroom.

The third section of part 2 is "Teaching Individual Works." Later in his writing career, Levi found his own "new" creative voice in *The Periodic Table*, the book considered by most critics to be his masterpiece. Millicent Marcus explores the shifting and evolving relation of scientific and literary thought in Levi's "chemical autobiography." As his journey through the periodic table of elements unfolds, the distinctions between hard and soft knowledge, reason and imagination, and fact and fiction break down, giving way to the continuity at the heart of his memorialist project. Elisabetta Properzi Nelsen sees in this work the basic elements that make it a classic, if one relies on Italo Calvino's definition of a classic: it is "personal, intellectual, and historical memory but also the written form of an individual psychological consciousness that contains desires, fears, phobias and complexes; social, ethical, and religious norms; and taboos." With Jewishness—and all its ramifications—at the center of the work, its uniqueness lies in the way the author treats these aspects of human life in terms of the elements of the periodic table.

In her essay on Rosi's film based on Levi's *La tregua*, Gaetana Marrone calls on the function of cinema as a medium to tell stories through which we can learn how to judge events in the context of history. In acknowledging the differences that exist between Levi's book and the film, Marrone claims that Rosi intended to champion Levi as the progressive counterpoise to the "static" view of the Holocaust found in the established historical responses to the Nazi atrocities. The dramatic translation from text to film prompts the question of what are the relative benefits, uses, risks, and pitfalls of literary and cinematographic genres, styles, devices, and strategies to support Levi's mandate to remember.

Risa Sodi's contribution provides the backdrop for presenting Levi's only novel that does not center on Italy, *If Not Now, When?*, which is set in the Slavic and Germanic lands to the northeast. Unlike his other fictional works, this novel does not reflect Levi's personal war experience, nor is it directly linked to the *univers concentrationnaire* of the Holocaust. Sodi concentrates on Levi's knowledge of the Ashkenazi world, the factors that led him to write this novel, the creation of the novel's main characters, and the degree to which they function as Levi's alter egos.

In their essays the contributors have relied on different Italian editions, all published by Einaudi. With the exception of the 1947 De Silva edition of *Se questo è un uomo*, of which most copies were lost during the 1965 flood in Florence, all other editions and several reprints that have followed have remained faithful to the Italian version being read today, published for the first time in 1958. It should be noted that there exists a scholastic and slightly abridged Italian-language version of *Se questo è un uomo* and of *La tregua*, with commentaries by the author. The printings of the available English translations by Stuart Woolf are identical, even though they carry different titles: *Survival in Auschwitz* and *The Reawakening* in the United States, and *If This Is a Man* and *The Truce* in the United Kingdom. In referring to *Survival*, scholars and teachers exchange one title for the other rather loosely, often favoring the British title, which is more accurately related to the Italian title and more fitting, for instance, in the analysis of the line "Consider if this is a man" in the work's epigraphic poem, "Shemà."

We offer here comments from two of our former undergraduate students at Bryn Mawr College. Mary Blumenfeld notes, "When reading the works of Primo Levi . . . you need to have time to invest in each of the author's words because each one alone speaks volumes. Levi put a great deal of thought into every mark he made on a page, which he made clear in 'Carbon,' the final story in *The Periodic Table*, when he explained the amount of history and contemplation that went into a single dot of ink." Didem Uca, a major in comparative literature, seconds these thoughts: "Levi's texts serve not only as a firsthand account of the events, but also a theoretical framework on which further study on the topics of trauma, memory, and representation can be based. . . . Levi is singular in his ability to combine dispassionate analysis, philosophical argumentation, and moments of sheer poetic beauty. Because Levi uses many interdisciplinary approaches in presenting his story, readers must also be able to work within and across several disciplines. This interdisciplinarity is, of course, the topic of his book *The Periodic Table*, but is evident in his other works, as well. Levi's memoirs are not only historical texts but also provide lessons in psychology, aesthetic theory, and philosophy. It is these combinations of unexpected facets of human life that make Levi's texts so compelling, and, without emphasizing this aspect, much of his depth as a writer would be lost."[2]

In closing, and echoing the views of the students above, the works of Primo Levi can be and are read and treated in reference to different fields of study. Even when translated into English, Levi's major works lose little of their vibrancy of language and none of their validity of content, as demonstrated by the fact that most of them are still in print and widely read and taught. Levi's free-flowing hypotactical style facilitates the task of the translator with a good grasp of the Italian language. Since there are no variations to speak of among the translations, the instructor can spend more time concentrating on the analysis of the text. And when teaching the works of Levi in Italian or in translation, the instructor who is also familiar with, even if not fluent in, the Italian language is rewarded with the added gratification of appreciating and sharing with the students the subtle nuances embodied in the wide range of linguistic choices of an extraordinary writer who, by all accounts, is regarded as one of the major literary figures of the twentieth century.

NOTES

[1]Levi is included in the *Bibliographical Dictionary of Twentieth-Century Philosophers*.

[2]We are grateful to Didem Uca and Mary Blumenfeld for their valued opinions.

Levi and the Question of Style: The Challenge of Teaching the Holocaust

Nancy Harrowitz

When teaching the works of Primo Levi, some of the first comments made by students involve the question of style or, rather, the perception of an absence of it. Students (like many critics) describe Levi as a dispassionate, scientific observer who writes with great detail and profound thought. They do not, however, perceive Levi as a great literary stylist, or as any kind of stylist. Not only do critics and readers see Levi as a transparent writer, for whom style is irrelevant, but Levi himself furthered this notion as much as possible in his discussions about writing and in his self-representation as a writer.[1]

This situation generates some interesting questions that are relevant for the teaching of Levi and for the representation of the Holocaust. Why would a Holocaust survivor-writer want to downplay the issue of style? Why would a writer of Levi's talent attempt to hide that skill? And what is there about Holocaust literature that would result in a largely style-blind readership when it comes to Levi? I am going to address these questions from three points of view: how the perceived absence or presence of style affects students' understanding of Levi's texts; what their reactions say about received notions regarding the relation of testimony, writing, and Holocaust literature; and what challenges the Holocaust presents to teachers.

Reviews and critical analyses of Levi's texts often rely on a traditional and very limiting understanding of expository writing and on some prevalent myths regarding the manner in which Levi says what he wants to say in his texts. The basic presuppositions are the following: Levi knew exactly what he wanted to say; Levi was in full control of everything he wanted to say; and Levi said what he wanted to say in a prose that Irving Howe called "unadorned and chaste" ("Writing" 186) and that Cynthia Ozick described as "lucid and calm," demonstrating "magisterial equanimity" (37, 46; see also Harrowitz, "Autobiography"). These descriptions are accurate and meant to be very complimentary, but they can be quite limiting as well, for they infer that the content of what Levi wrote lies on the surface of his prose and that there are no obstacles to arriving at a full understanding of it. These notions depend on the assumption that an author is in complete control of his writing, a concept discarded by literary critics for good reason many decades ago. Yet this logic still prevails when it comes to the reception of Levi's texts and to the reception of Holocaust testimonies in general.

It appears to be a simple jump to arrive at the conclusion that if Levi wrote in an objective and unadorned fashion, there are no stylistic encumbrances to block or obfuscate a direct path between the reality he wants to convey and the ability of his writing to convey that reality. Students make this jump frequently, especially when studying Elie Wiesel's *Night* and Levi's *Survival in Auschwitz* in the same class. They do perceive Wiesel's writing as a style, but this perception leads them to slip up frequently and call the text a novel instead of a testimony. It is as if the category of fiction permits the author stylistic freedom and allows a figural laissez-faire not comfortable or permissible in testimony. Students are often caught up in the emotional and fast-paced intensity of Wiesel's text and its focus on the individual and on the father-son relationship. The text moves quickly through wrenching episodes to its grim conclusion, as Wiesel is liberated only to discover that what has happened has marked him forever ("and a corpse stared back at me in the mirror" [115]). Most students find that the text is hard to put down, and they often read it cover to cover in one sitting. I must admit that even after rereading it to teach it many times, I have the same experience. Wiesel's brilliance in drawing the reader into the story—many readers, from many different backgrounds—is attested to by the text's immense popularity in many different countries and cultures. It is the most often translated and published Holocaust memoir worldwide.

What Lawrence Langer names "durational time," the intensity of the experience for the Holocaust survivor and the existence of that time outside normal chronological boundaries ("Memory's Time" 14), also affects the reader of Wiesel's testimony. Chronological time, defined by Langer as that time that lies outside Auschwitz and defines the life outside as well, rather than durational time typically reigns over the reading of Levi. Never have I had a student tell me that they read many chapters in one sitting or that they did not want to put the book down. Students also typically define their reading experience with Levi as intense, but in a different way: they become caught up in Levi's description of that incomprehensible *univers concentrationnaire*, but they need to put the book down, to reflect on and think about what Levi says. They remain outside the text, looking in through the opportunities that Levi presents, whereas readers of *Night* are drawn into the temporal condition of the narrative and stay there for the duration of the reading.

When students begin to read Levi's *Survival in Auschwitz*, comparisons to *Night* are inevitable. Some students resist the complexity of the reading; they are by now accustomed to having the emotion of the testimony served to them with powerful and elegant prose that moves them deeply. Reading Levi's text requires a very different concentration: instead of sweeping away readers in a flood of poetic images and emotions, the text challenges them to use their intellectual faculties. The reader of Levi's text can imagine, can almost see, the scenes that Levi describes because of the detail he provides. Once the student is engaged on this level, the empirical tends to govern the more subjective aspects of the narrative. The typical student wants to understand the text as the deliverer of what it was really like in the *Lager* and Levi as the great communicator of these messages. Partly responsible for this reaction from students is Levi's insistence on removing himself from the text as much as possible. Note, for example, his frequent use of the pronoun *we* instead of *I*; his deferring to the communal experience suggests that the experience of the group is more important than the experience of the individual.

One of the greatest challenges in teaching *Survival in Auschwitz* is explaining the horrors to a group of students largely unschooled in Holocaust history: answering their pained questions as to how this event could have happened, how governments could have ignored the massacres, how members of a civilized society could have been bystanders and not protesters. Teaching the Holocaust to a group of uninformed students is like shooting their loved pet in front of them. The spectacle is painful and frightening and destroys their innocence about civility and humanity suddenly and with accompanying trauma. To use Langer's terminology once again, the experience of learning about the Holocaust through Levi's text, as reported by my students over the years, is both durational and chronological. The students are drawn into the time period, experiencing the shock of the massacres while becoming more aware of (and guilty about) their subject position as safe and secure in their world. But the durational affects the chronological, as students become increasingly aware of the fragility of their own security. This recognition poses a great challenge and an enormous risk at the same time, since many students are traumatized by the readings and quite literally do not know how to integrate what they are learning with their current worldview and perspective on humanity, to say nothing of their religious views. Reading Levi helps students with their abruptly changing notions of the world, since his thoughtfulness in understanding and exploring the question of humanity speaks to them on a deep level. It helps them partially heal—perhaps deceptively—the rupture caused by what they are learning and gives them tools for how to reflect on it. Levi's distance from the text and his emphasis on thinking as deeply as possible often serves as an emotional defense for students as well: they take their cues from how Levi handles trauma and its recounting.

Yet to take Levi's text at face value and define his role as a mediator and explicator diminishes an understanding of *Survival in Auschwitz* as a literary text and misses much of the complexity and nuance of Levi's thought. Another challenge for instructors, therefore, lies in teaching students how to read Levi's Holocaust text as literature and as testimony at the same time. This pedagogical step may seem obvious, but it generates several questions and reactions: Does this literariness interfere with a student's ability to accept the text as historical reality? What are the consequences of separating one's empirical notions of history from a testimony, and should these ever have been seen as inseparable? Does this perspective throw the empirical evidence of the text into question? Does it undo the benefit of the often cool analytic tone they see in the text that explains to them and protects them at the same time?

Once it is established that testimony needs to be understood as a literary form, the question of style can become an obstacle lying between students and the truth they wish to extract from the text. The evocative poetic style of Wiesel works to deliver an emotional truth about suffering, and so they see no conflict between his style and what he does with it. For Levi, however, although students may appreciate the skill and beauty of his writing, they resist his writing's calling attention to itself, potentially distracting the reader from what he is describing. Part of the problem lies with an embedded set of assumptions regarding Holocaust literature and rules regarding its writing. In general, students (and other readers) want Holocaust testimony to be more than a record of an individual's experience; they want it to be solidly historical as well. Despite my teaching the testimony as literature—by demonstrating through close readings Levi's consummate and underestimated power as a subtly nuanced and complex writer—the students still want the text to present a clearly articulated set of historical facts. Of course, literature and history are not mutually exclusive, but neither is their relation simple. Berel Lang discusses the thesis that "Holocaust writing aspires to the condition of history" (*Holocaust Representation* 20); he argues as well that realism "has served the literary imagination as a figurative or stylistic 'choice' with no place for truth or falsity among its criteria. . . . The assessment of style, in other words, involves many but always other factors than the standard of truth or falsity" (*Post-Holocaust* 121). Irving Howe believes that "Holocaust writings make their primary claim . . . through facts recorded or remembered" ("Writing" 182).

These assumptions or beliefs affect the reception of another genre of Holocaust writing: Holocaust fiction. I find that much of the students' unease about and often outright rejection of Holocaust fiction is related to their desire that Holocaust writing and historical fact be inseparable. The noted historian Raul Hilberg comments, "The question is not confined to *what* we should describe, it is also a matter of *how* we should write. Are there any rules?" ("I Was" 21). The rules, spoken or unspoken, are driven by demands that any writing about the Holocaust must function as historical representation. Testimony in particular is the most vulnerable form of Holocaust writing when it comes to these rules. The authority of testimony comes from an insistence that it be an unvarnished—or unstylized—truth. As Michael André Bernstein argues:

> One of the most pervasive myths of our era, a myth perhaps even partially arising out of our collective response to the horrors of the concentration camps, is the authoritative authority given to first person testimony. Such narratives . . . are habitually regarded as though they were completely unmediated, as though language, gesture and imagery could become transparent if the experience being expressed is sufficiently horrific. (339)

The attitude, often unwitting, that testimony is unmediated and transparent has deeply affected the ways in which Levi's writing is viewed, even those writings that are not testimonial. Issues such as point of view and differences between individual experiences are glossed over in favor of empirical truth, as if the testimony was not a literary text, with all that implies regarding the use of language and the personal perspective of the writer.

A close reading of a passage of *Survival in Auschwitz* illustrates some of these issues regarding style, transparency, and Levi and demonstrates as well the consummate skill with which Levi writes. The passage in question ends the chapter entitled "Die drei Leute vom Labor." The placement of the chapter in the text is notable: it occurs right before the text addresses the last episodes of Auschwitz, told with urgency, in which the camp is abandoned by the Nazis and the ill and dying prisoners are left to wait for the Russian Army to stumble on them. The chapter concerns Levi's winter spent in the laboratory with other slave laborers and three civilian workers. This is the period that Levi often attributed to his being able to survive the camp: a winter spent inside in the laboratory rather than outside in the impossible cold.

The civilian workers, three young German women who assist the prisoner chemists, are firmly rooted in the world outside the *Lager*. Indifferent to their meaningless jobs, they openly demonstrate their intolerance and bigotry toward the prisoners working in the lab. Their attitude embodies the opposite of empathy: it demonstrates an utter lack of concern and lack of curiosity about the camp that borders on the inhumane. After Levi asks one of them a question, she responds instead to the Kapo, and Levi hears her refer to him as "*Stinkjude*"; after this incident, the Kapo asks the prisoners not to speak to the women directly but to make all requests through him (143).[2] In this scene, Levi reveals the complicity of civilians that made them effortlessly able to accept the Nazi assertion that the Jews were less than human and to react to this assertion with hatred. The scene emphasizes as well how vast the divide was between their world and his and allows students to view these women through Levi's eyes and therefore through his reduced condition.

Consider also the following segment, which begins with a discussion between two of the women and then reverts to Levi's thoughts about the statement that one of them makes, "This year has gone by so quickly":

> "Are you going home on Sunday? I am not, travelling is so uncomfortable!"
>
> "I am going home for Christmas. Only two weeks and then it will be Christmas again; it hardly seems real, this year has gone by so quickly!"
>
> . . . This year has gone by so quickly. This time last year I was a free man: an outlaw but free, I had a name and a family, I had an eager and restless mind, an agile and healthy body. I used to think of many, far-away things: of my work, of the end of the war, of good and evil, of the nature of things and of the laws which govern human actions; and also of the mountains, of singing and loving, of music, of poetry. I had an enormous, deep-rooted, foolish faith in the benevolence of fate; to kill and to die seemed extraneous literary things to me. My days were both cheerful and sad, but I regretted them equally, they were all full and positive; the future stood before me as a great treasure. (143)

Levi normalizes his pre-Auschwitz existence through recounting his past state of physical and intellectual freedom, by recounting what he used to think about and ponder over. The topics range from the pleasurable (love, music) to the philosophical (the "nature of things," the "laws which govern human actions"). The list that Levi makes of his thoughts and activities constitutes a definition of what makes a person human and civilized. Through a contrapuntal strategy, the English translation of the Italian title of the book, *If This Is a Man*, is brought into play. In the implied query of his title, Levi is referring to what has been done to humankind in Auschwitz. He challenges the reader to contemplate dehumanization with our commonly held notions of what is human and what is humanity and to think about the line that demarks humanity and the lack thereof. In this portrait of himself as a naive young man, Levi presents parameters of what is human, or rather what was human for him, before Auschwitz, giving us a microcosm of untainted, innocent humanity.

When Levi writes, "I had an enormous, deep-rooted, foolish faith in the benevolence of fate," he expresses the same innocence shared by students who have little experience of the world, an innocence that is severely shaken by the study of the Holocaust. The students may know of the existence of mass murder and tragedy, but reading Levi brings it to their doorstep. For the most part, they share in Levi's faith in the benevolence of fate, but before reading his account, they probably have not thought of that faith as foolish. They are close in age to the Levi of this text, they can find common ground in the life that he describes in this passage, but they are also forced to confront the destruction of dreams and hope in the future that Levi is now experiencing. The passage functions as a mirror for young readers, reflecting their own experiences exploring the world, but it is the evil of Snow White's stepmother that they see reflected as a backdrop, not the implicitly promised fairness of the civilized world in which their youthful naïveté has led them to believe. The very word *civilized* must now exist with qualifications for them. The future seen as a "great treasure" has become a painful ironic parody, as Levi confronts the ashes of the destruction of his future.

Levi, in writing "to kill and to die seemed extraneous literary things to me," underscores the literariness of his own text by emphasizing and perhaps even mocking the difference between reading about such events in literature and actually living them and then writing about them. His story of Auschwitz ensures that student readers cannot conceive of killing and dying as "extraneous literary things," even though they are reading it in a literary text. But what exactly is extraneous, the "things"—that is, killing and dying—or the literature that has rendered them such? Levi has called into question literature as the great yet deceptive mediator between a reality and its representation. In doing so, has he made it impossible to view his text of Auschwitz as literature, if literature makes murder extraneous through its very representation? The use of the word *extraneous*, meaning outside the discussion, establishes that killing and dying were outside the realm of his experience and only dubiously knowable through literature. Killing and dying are literary things precisely because they only existed in literature for him: they had no intrinsic reality. He also defines literature as extraneous, by virtue of its agency in the exile, the removal, of the concepts of killing and dying from reality.

Where does that leave the status of his text? Perhaps Levi is negotiating precisely that transparency that Bernstein asserts is the desired effect in testimony: a gesture toward undermining or even removing the literary quality of the text so that experiences can appear unmediated. At the same time, however, Levi calls attention to that very literariness through the consummate skill and subtlety of the writing of this passage. The last part of the segment turns sharply in another direction:

> Today the only thing left of the life of those days is what one needs to suffer hunger and cold; I am not even alive enough to know how to kill myself.
>
> If I spoke German better I could try to explain all this to Frau Meyer; but she would certainly not understand, or if she was so good and intelligent as to understand, she would be unable to bear my proximity, and would flee from me, as one flees from contact with an incurable invalid, or from a man condemned to death. Or perhaps she would give me a coupon for a pint of civilian soup.
>
> This year has gone by so quickly. (143–44)

When Levi baldly states, "I am not even alive enough to know how to kill myself," the intensity and meaning of his words are like a slap in the face for the reader. The downward spiral has now reached its bottommost point: the despair is physical and palpable, and its extremity is surprising coming from Levi, who typically shows more reticence about his personal feelings. And what could be more personal and more shocking than a statement about his inability to kill himself because of his demoralized and weakened condition, the origins of which he has so painstakingly detailed for us a paragraph earlier? He abruptly makes clear what is at stake in the *univers concentrationnaire*: he cannot carry out what he states to be his own free will, even in dying.

Holocaust testimonies always carry the specter of the potential and seemingly imminent death of the subject with them; at times it appears implausible, given the circumstances, that the author has actually survived to write the narrative. Positing a death wish toward the end of the text throws into crisis this already delicate negotiation between a suspension of disbelief on the reader's part and the empirical, textual evidence of survival. It also underscores the fragility of the relationship between Levi's previous claim of a marginalized literature that reports "extraneous . . . things" and a testimony whose literariness is severely undermined in this moment by a too-close brush with his death wish.

The passage in its entirety is very tightly constructed, as Levi repeats "this year has gone by so quickly" three times: once at the beginning, repeating what the young woman has said entirely without irony; the second time with heavy irony to underscore the tremendous difference between his past year and hers; and the third time to end a bridge narrative that has demonstrated the incivility and barbarity of the bigotry and hatred that has led to the disparity between his last year and hers, of the meaning of the passing of this time for the two of them. The notion of potential good is also bracketed here: he asserts that proximity to the condemned is unbearable, so that even if intent to do good is possible, its execution is impossible. This chapter ends on a very pessimistic note; in fact, it is one of the most low-spirited moments anywhere in Levi's writing. His experiences with the civilian workers foreshadow the kind of rejection and hostility that many survivors encountered after they were freed from the camps. The bridge narrative that Levi creates between the experiences and attitudes of the workers and his own, so close to the end of the text, takes on a much larger perspective.

To conclude, I would like to return to a question I posed earlier: Does Levi's writing style, both his attitude toward it and his use of it, have anything to do with the dangers of acquiring knowledge regarding the Holocaust? Can we understand Levi's simultaneous adoption and denial of style as a shield between the knowledge necessary for commemoration and historical memory and the petrifying Gorgon that is the risk of too much exposure to evil? His strength as a writer lies precisely in this paradox: as Levi leads us directly to the Gorgon through his detailed and profound examinations of complex questions, he also deflects us from this path toward paralysis and toxicity of knowledge about the Holocaust, partly through his deft handling of a stylistic language that is evocative yet deeply personal, despite his frequent attempts to privilege the community's perspective rather than his own. The other part of the equation is our comprehension and reaction to Levi's deeply philosophical mind at work. His profound grasp of Western values and culture, apparent in his reflections, remind us of what was lost during the Holocaust. He uses our highest culture to try to understand the destruction done to civility, to humanity, and to what is humane, and his supremely intellectual and philosophical attempts to understand are ultimately the best defense against the Gorgon.

Teaching the Holocaust through Levi's works is a multifaceted challenge. In confronting the difficult and emotionally demanding issues presented, students struggle to make an uneasy peace with what they are learning of a wrenching history and Levi's articulation of the accompanying destruction of humanity. What emerges from their painful meeting with the text is well worth the effort, as students learn a deep, resonant, and universal empathy that serves them well in their encounters with other Holocaust texts and in their future encounters with the world at large.

NOTES

[1] See, e.g., Levi's chapter "Communicating" in *The Drowned and the Saved* (Summit, 1988), 89–104.

[2] All quotations from *Survival in Auschwitz* are from the 1996 Touchstone translation.

"What Would I Have Done?": Teaching *The Drowned and the Saved* to Confront Moral Ambiguity

Jonathan Druker

Primo Levi's volume of Holocaust essays, *The Drowned and the Saved*, is one of the truly indispensable books in a liberal arts or general education curriculum. If undergraduate degree programs are to serve as a passage to adulthood and citizenship—and not merely as specialized training in a particular discipline—college students ought to read this book, which dares to unsettle schematic definitions of victims and perpetrators in Auschwitz and, more broadly, confronts the moral ambiguities of human action in times of crisis. The strength of Levi's writing, very much in evidence in these essays written forty years after the defeat of Nazism, is that his historically specific discussion of what it means to be a Holocaust survivor, in both moral and psychological terms, is also a discourse on what it means to be human in the post-Holocaust world.

One of Levi's main tasks in *The Drowned and the Saved* is to discredit simplifications and stereotypes about the inhabitants of Auschwitz. The SS men were not the inhuman monsters of the popular imagination but, Levi insists, disturbingly human and "made of the same cloth as we" (202).[1] Newcomers to the camps did not find a clear distinction between friends and enemies. Rather, they encountered what Levi called "the Gray Zone," a morally ambiguous world where "the 'we' had lost its limits" (38), where privileged prisoners, having been drawn into a web of complicity with the SS, were the chief victimizers. In a broad sense, the concept of the gray zone is a meditation on the workings of power and privilege in all human societies. If the extremity of Auschwitz lays bare general truths that are normally buried, then Levi's analysis of moral ambiguity in the camps is relevant to every student, indeed to every person.

The Drowned and the Saved is a demanding read for undergraduates, and Levi knows why. "The young above all demand clarity," he remarks, adding that "they do not like ambiguity" (37). Nevertheless, Levi's ideal readers are the young. He writes for them out of duty, because what he witnessed in Auschwitz is "fundamental." Yet he does so in full awareness that he risks speaking without being heard (198). The book's epigraph, drawn from Samuel Coleridge's *The Rime of the Ancient Mariner*, positions Levi as the teller of a "ghastly tale," a hellish journey from which he is the lone survivor. In turn, his young reader is positioned as the wedding guest, as the reluctant listener to a hermetic story that defies easy explanation. In the classroom, the teacher's role is to mediate unobtrusively between this challenging text and students who have only just begun to confront "the non-credibility of what took place in the Lagers" (12).

To assist in this mediation, here I discuss strategies for using *The Drowned and the Saved* to confront moral ambiguity. One goal of this pedagogy is to lead students to ask themselves what they might have done in the same situation, whether as a German soldier, a bystander to the Holocaust, or a victim, and to consider whether the severe oppression in Auschwitz reduced the victims' space for moral choice to such an extent that no one can fairly judge their actions. Of course, there are no easy answers to such speculative questions, but posing them helps students understand the legacy of the Holocaust and contend with moral and political choices in the present moment. As passive bystanders, are we implicated in the attempted genocides of our era in Rwanda and Darfur? In our failure to take action, are we, too, participants in the gray zone?

In a liberal arts or general education curriculum, the instructor's main task is to make the classroom a site where students develop their sense of responsibility and learn to think for themselves instead of passively accepting received wisdom. *The Drowned and the Saved* is an ideal text for achieving these aims because it compels students to confront one of the saddest lessons taught by the Holocaust: that human beings "had the potential to construct an infinite enormity of pain, and that pain is the only force created from nothing, without cost and without effort. It is enough not to see, not to listen, not to act" (86).

I teach Levi's Holocaust essays in English translation in Holocaust Literature and Film, an interdisciplinary course I created for the general education curriculum at a large public university in the Midwest. My writing-intensive course is designed to make students aware of how diverse literary and cinematic genres, including memoir, documentary, fiction, theater, and poetry, may be employed to represent historical events such as the Holocaust. The students, majoring in everything from business to chemistry, have some knowledge of and interest in the Holocaust but almost no knowledge of Levi. I briefly orient students to the historical context in which the texts and films were produced. The rest of the class time is given over to discussions that oscillate between specific questions with factual answers and open-ended, speculative questions.

I always begin my course with Levi's remarkable *Survival in Auschwitz* because it gives such a clear and detailed account of what Auschwitz was like. It also raises issues that are crucial in any study of the Holocaust, such as how the Nazis dehumanized their victims and how the concentration camp functioned as a Darwinian world where solidarity among the prisoners was quite rare. I teach *The Drowned and the Saved* immediately after Levi's survivor memoir because it develops astutely many themes of the first book, especially the ethical issues encapsulated in the gray zone and the question of shame or survivor guilt. The idea of the drowned and the saved, for example, the fundamental binary that Levi employs in analyzing the concentration camps, is first presented in *Survival in Auschwitz* (87–100).[2] To describe "this world of negation" (122), Levi finds it necessary to invert the typical moral hierarchy of the damned and the saved. Thus, those who did not return from Auschwitz, the drowned, are largely innocent, and the survivors, the saved, are the sinners. In his essays, Levi extends this discussion, specifically linking the drowned/saved binary to the survivors' ubiquitous sense of shame.

> I might be alive in the place of another, at the expense of another; I might have usurped, that is, in fact, killed. The "saved" of the Lager were not the best, those predestined to do good, the bearers of a message: what I had lived through proved the exact contrary. Preferably the worst survived, the selfish, the violent, the insensitive, the collaborators of the "gray zone," the spies. . . . The worst survived, that is, the fittest; the best all died. (*Drowned* 82)

Passages like the one above help students set aside the conventional notion that the will and strength to endure confer nobility or goodness on the camp survivors. By definition, survivors are not wholly innocent, and Levi makes it clear that he is personally implicated in the moral ambiguity of the gray zone. In my experience, students always recognize that the ethical force of Levi's writing derives in part from his willingness to scrutinize unsparingly his past deeds (e.g., 79–82).

Every essay in *The Drowned and the Saved* is teachable, but it is not possible in a typical undergraduate course to cover all the topics Levi entertains in just two-hundred pages. I concentrate on two essays, "The Gray Zone" (36–69) and, to a lesser extent, "Shame" (70–87). For Levi, the passage of forty years demands a clear-eyed judgment of individuals' actions in the Holocaust. These evaluations are made neither easily nor with an evident sense of moral superiority: "For me judging is painful," he confesses (196). Still, he refuses to shirk this solemn obligation. In class, we discuss how, according to Levi, the ghettos and concentration camps were structured to break down the simple binary of victim/perpetrator with the consequence that many victims were not only deprived of their lives but also of their sense of innocence. My students prepare for this discussion by carefully reading the text and writing responses to the following study questions supplied in advance:

> What is "the Gray Zone" and how did it come about? Does Levi see any clear distinctions (call them "black lines") between victims and oppressors?
>
> What moral judgments does Levi offer regarding low-level functionaries, Kapos and others occupying commanding positions, and members of the *Sonderkommandos*?
>
> What continuities or analogies does Levi find between human behavior in Auschwitz and how we behave in everyday life?
>
> Do you think it is legitimate to judge human behavior under inhumane circumstances? Why or why not?

Students discover that Levi would "lightheartedly absolve . . . prisoners without rank [and] low-ranking functionaries" because they were not violent. He asserts, however, that judging the higher-ranking prisoners is more difficult. For one thing, "the greatest responsibility lies in the system" (44), and it encouraged depravity. Kapos had unlimited power to do violence to their charges; in fact, they were "deposed if they did not prove to be sufficiently harsh" (46). But among the members of Auschwitz's privileged classes, although often the most violent and murderous individuals, were a few political opponents of the Third Reich who used their privilege to undermine the camp system (45).

In regard to the *Sonderkommandos*, the special squads of prisoners that ran the crematoriums and maintained order among the new arrivals selected for the gas, Levi wisely abstains from offering judgment on those who themselves suffered so much: "I ask that we meditate on the story of 'the crematorium ravens' with pity and rigor, but that judgment of them be suspended" (60). The SS had developed a clever if temporary strategy for absolving themselves of the worst crimes: they did not push the victims into the gas chambers. It is clear, nevertheless, that the *Sonderkommandos* were victims, not executioners. Levi arrives at a similar inability to offer a definitive judgment, what he terms *impotentia judicandi*, in the case of Chaim Rumkowski, the president of Lodz ghetto who collaborated with the Nazis. His "story is so eloquent on the fundamental theme of human ambiguity fatally provoked by oppression" (60–61). That his moral compass failed in the face of Nazi subjugation and seduction should interest us, Levi suggests, because "we are mirrored in Rumkowski, his ambiguity is ours" (69). In short, Levi succeeds in persuading his reader that to judge human behavior during the Holocaust, in both moral and legal terms, is far from simple. He asks, "How would each of us behave if driven by necessity and at the same time lured by seduction?" (68).

A caution is in order. Once students grasp the morally ambiguous nature of the gray zone, where the simple binary victim/perpetrator breaks down, they are tempted to elide the actions of all the participants and think that no clear moral or legal distinctions can be drawn among them. The instructor can head off such misapprehensions by calling students' attention to passages in which Levi makes evident the black line in the gray zone that separated various types of victims from various types of perpetrators. When the film director Liliana Cavani asserted, "We are all victims or murderers, and we accept these roles voluntarily" (qtd. in *Drowned* 48), Levi responded acidly, "to confuse [murderers] with their victims is a moral disease or an aesthetic affectation or a sinister sign of complicity; above all, it is precious service rendered (intentionally or not) to the negators of truth" (48–49). In short, just because the SS and the prisoners shared a common humanity means neither that deep inside we are all murderers nor that victims choose their suffering.

As of way of reviewing and summarizing Levi's judgments of the different classes of prisoners and perpetrators, I use the blackboard to help students make a map of the gray zone that spans, along an axis of increasing power, from the *Muselmänner*, or "Muslims," the physically and mentally depleted prisoners deprived of all human agency, who are described at some length in *Survival in Auschwitz*, to the SS, who have voluntarily chosen to perform the work of genocide. In between, but in some cases floating on account of Levi's indecision, are the low-level functionaries, the *Sonderkommandos*, and the Kapos; on the other side of a clear line of responsibility are passive bystanders and the German industrialists and their employees who exploited slave labor provided by the camps.

Having dissected the prisoners' gray zone, the instructor may wish to focus next on Levi's attempt to judge the immoral actions and criminal guilt of the perpetrators of the Holocaust and their accomplices. While Levi asserts that all Germans share a measure of collective guilt (15, 203), he is more interested in personal ethics, pausing to reflect on the actions of men like Adolph Eichmann, the Auschwitz commandant Rudolph Höss, and Albert Speer. An important question for Levi is the extent to which the Nazi state truncated the ability of these individuals and others to make moral choices. To prepare to discuss this issue in class, students carefully read the text and write a response to the following study question, supplied in advance:

> In *The Drowned and the Saved*, Levi attempts to understand why individuals performed the work of genocide during the Holocaust. What does he conclude about the relative importance of individual moral breakdown versus the coercive power of totalitarian institutions in the performance of this work?

In reading the essays in which Levi touches on perpetrator guilt, students find that, while he recognizes the coercive power of institutions, his interpretation of the events consistently focuses on the failure of individual moral responsibility (29). He defends this position in a furious reply to a postwar German correspondent who suggested that the Germans were betrayed and victimized by Hitler:

> I might remind you that nothing obliged German industrialists to hire famished slaves if not for their profit; that no one forced the Topf Company (flourishing today in Wiesbaden) to build the enormous multiple crematoria in the Lagers; that perhaps the SS did receive orders to kill the Jews, but enrollment in the SS was voluntary. (179)

Students should be reminded that Levi was himself a slave laborer at a synthetic rubber factory owned by the huge industrial conglomerate IG-Farben, so his interest here is personal as well as historical. Elsewhere, Levi stresses that the SS were not generally sadists but "average human beings, averagely intelligent, averagely wicked," some of whom were fanatical Nazis, others merely opportunists who freely signed on (202). No great force of evil was necessary for the Holocaust to occur, merely a large number of diligent, ambitious, and unquestioning workers and businessmen. Yet whether one's devotion to the work of genocide was serious or cynical, Levi remains an unyielding judge, stating unequivocally that "one must answer personally for sins and errors; otherwise all trace of civilization would vanish from the face of the earth, as in fact it had vanished from the Third Reich" (178). Criminal acts cannot be excused, even if authorized by a state, nor can soldiers justify following immoral orders. Individual responsibility, Levi implies, is the last and most important deterrent to future genocides.

A significant point for students to grasp is that Levi does not ultimately apply the gray zone to the perpetrators. Like the victims, they were depersonalized by a totalitarian state, but Levi believes they had enough individual freedom to maintain at least some moral autonomy. For the sake of comparison, I suggest to my students that Hannah Arendt draws a different lesson from the Holocaust. She, too, saw the SS men as ordinary, but she credited the Nazi state with a greater ability to impair individual identity and responsibility: "The essence of totalitarian government, and perhaps the nature of every bureaucracy, is to make functionaries and mere cogs in the administrative machinery out of men, and thus to dehumanize them" (289). For Arendt, "the fearsome, word-and-thought defying banality of evil" lies precisely in the fact that state-mandated (i.e., legal) bureaucratic functions undertaken by thousands of normal people made the Holocaust possible (252). In modern societies, the fragmentation of labor allows individuals to perform their part in mass murder without feeling accountable. She believes the prevention of future genocides is less about individual responsibility than the creation of a system of international law that prohibits and punishes crimes against humanity perpetrated by states. Regardless of whether the instructor finds Levi or Arendt more compelling, an effective classroom strategy is to remain noncommittal and encourage students to decide for themselves.

In closing, I recommend several other texts and also films that complement my approach to *The Drowned and the Saved* and might be usefully included in courses where Levi is taught. In Tadeusz Borowski's *This Way for the Gas, Ladies and Gentlemen*, the narrator, a non-Jewish Pole who works alongside the *Sonderkommandos* and in the camp infirmary, candidly admits his gray zone status. The narrator and his peers live on the food and goods brought by the transports crammed with innocent victims. In describing openly his difficult position between victim and victimizer, he writes, "we are not evoking evil irresponsibly or in vain, for we have now become a part of it" (113). All six stories in *Smoke over Birkenau*, by Liana Millu, document the experience of women in the camps. With this book, originally written in Italian, students are able to consider the possible relation between gender and moral values in times of crisis. The question is whether female prisoners exhibited a degree of solidarity and caring that was lacking in the male prisoners described by Levi. Addressing the gray zone from the perpetrators' side, *The Reader*, a novel by Bernhard Schlink, tells the story of a former concentration camp guard who deserves condemnation but also, the author hopes, our understanding and even compassion. Students will need to decide for themselves whether this fictional character conveys general truths about how we ought to judge the perpetrators of genocide.

The Grey Zone, a film directed by Tim Blake Nelson, is perhaps most interesting in its unwillingness to leave the viewer stuck in the terrible moral dilemma the *Sonderkommandos* face at every moment. Instead, it narrates the tense planning for a revolt and the revolt itself (and it is true that the last of the twelve squads of *Sonderkommandos* at Auschwitz did revolt). As a result, the film provides its characters with a moral escape as they are redeemed through heroic action. This ending, however, misses the point of Levi's gray zone, where there is no redemption but only the unhappy choice between death and a tainted life. Claude Lanzmann's *Shoah* is perhaps the best cinematic investigation of moral ambiguity in the Holocaust. In one tragic scene, for example, a survivor describes digging up a mass grave for cremation only to find the bodies of his wife and young children. As the camera lingers on his face and he speaks in a choked voice, we, the viewers, can only pity those who suffered from such coerced collaboration. Finally, if prospective teachers have time to read only one secondary source to help students grasp more fully the moral ramifications of Levi's essays, I recommend Tzvetan Todorov's *Facing the Extreme*.

Studying Levi is rewarding for our students because he approaches his subject with both intellectual rigor and a highly engaged ethical faculty. But he also knows the limits of historical analysis and the practical outcome of seeking justice. Neither engaging in historical analysis or seeking justice can reverse the monstrous crimes or repair the millions of shattered lives, but they can make palpable the horror of genocide to our students, who urgently need to confront the legacy of the Holocaust and its moral implications for today.

NOTES

[1] All quotations from *The Drowned and the Saved* are from the 1989 Vintage translation.

[2] All references to *Survival in Auschwitz* are to the 1996 Simon and Schuster translation.

Poetry and Testimony in Levi

Massimo Lollini

I teach Primo Levi in different contexts, both in Italian and English. He is one of the most important writers I introduce in my course Literature and Testimony, in which I present different literary and testimonial accounts of the tragedies that have afflicted the history of the twentieth century, from World War I to the Holocaust. Besides reading Levi's most important testimonial works, from *Se questo è un uomo* (*Survival in Auschwitz*) to *I sommersi e i salvati* (*The Drowned and the Saved*), in this course I teach a unit on Levi's poetry. I focus here on this teaching unit and emphasize the importance of Levi's poetry to understanding his prose works and his testimony to the Holocaust.

Asked in an interview why he was writing poetry about the Shoah and what he thought of the German philosopher Theodor Adorno's famous statement that it is not possible to write poetry after Auschwitz, Levi responded that his experience was the opposite: for him, at the end of World War II, it was only possible to write poetry on Auschwitz (*Conversazioni* 137). To write about Auschwitz was not a choice available to the survivor; for Levi, the urgency to bear witness to what he experienced in the Nazi camp turned him to poetry as his first and most fundamental means of expression.

Levi did not consider himself a poet and wrote only a few poems, most of them directly related to his testimony as a survivor of the Shoah. He thought that poetry was connected to the irrational side of his soul and wrote poems only "at an uncertain hour," not knowing why, as though he had been visited by a mysterious muse with whom his rational and professional side as a chemist and prose writer was uncomfortable. However, the poems are intimately connected to his prose works and to his effort to make sense out of his experience as a survivor.

Poetry and Testimony in Levi's Early Works

Levi composed a first group of poems in 1945–46; these poems are strictly connected to his testimony as developed in *Se questo è un uomo* and *La tregua* (*The Reawakening*). Each of these prose works has a poem as an epigraph, "Shemà" and "Alzarsi," respectively, suggesting the agony and resentment of the survivor who has to tell his ghastly tale of violence and mass destruction witnessed in the Nazi camp and feels he has been marked forever by that experience. Levi wrote a second group of poems in the seventies and eighties, when he rewrote the testimony given forty years earlier in a collection of essays entitled *I sommersi e i salvati*, which represents his ultimate moral and spiritual message. Even in this last testimonial work Levi has a poetic epigraph, this time taken from Samuel Coleridge's *The Rime of Ancient Mariner*:

Since then, at an uncertain hour,
That Agony returns:
And till my ghastly tale is told
This heart within me burns.
(lines 582–85)

Levi draws the title of his entire collection of poems, *Ad ora incerta* ("At an Uncertain Hour"), from these verses. He also quoted them in one of his poems contemporary to the writing of *The Drowned and the Saved*, "The Survivor," whose title alludes to the fact that, as it happens in Coleridge's poem, the survivor has to tell his disquieting story, his "ghastly tale" of death and destruction, interspersed with the nightmares, the ghosts of the dead comrades that still visit him.

After having provided this preliminary information, I read with my students "Shemà," the poem that Levi inserted as an epigraph to *Se questo è un uomo*. This is also the word that begins the prayer "Shemà Israel": "Hear, O Israel, the Lord our God, the Lord is One." This scriptural verse (Deut. 6.1–4) is incorporated into Jewish daily life in both morning and evening prayers. It states Judaism's central belief in the unity of God. Levi's poem, however, has very little to do with the belief in the unity of God or in the related commandment of love. Levi is here concerned with bringing to the people the bad tidings related to the dehumanization experienced in the Nazi system:

Meditate che questo è stato:
Vi comando queste parole.
Scolpitele nel vostro cuore
Stando in casa andando per via,
Coricandovi, alzandovi. (3)[1]

Consider that this has been:
I commend these words to you.
Engrave them on your hearts
When you are in your house, when you walk on your way,
When you go to bed, when you rise. (9)

In the concluding lines of the poem we find abusive language unrelated if not opposed to the spirit of the commandment of love:

Ripetetele ai vostri figli.
O vi si sfaccia la casa,
La malattia vi impedisca,
I vostri nati torcano il viso da voi.

Repeat them to your children.
Or may your house crumble,

Disease render you powerless,
Your offspring avert their faces from you.

I suggest to my students that this last section of "Shemà" can be better understood if one thinks not only of Deuteronomy but also of ancient Greek lyric, in which one finds curses similar to those uttered here by Levi. Although Levi's poem uses a rhetoric of biblical curses, the curses have a different direction from those announced in Deuteronomy 28.15, which are directed at a nation that finds its sense of identity in its faithfulness to the Lord's command; those who are not faithful are cursed for their entire lives. In Levi's poem, however, the curse is directed to all the people who are unwilling to listen to the witness. The task of Levi's testimony is not to reiterate the Lord's command or to call for a religious or national unity but to tell a terrible story that no one wants to hear. Levi wants all human beings to meditate on the scale of violence that has been perpetrated in the Nazi camp without drawing any conclusion on human nature after Auschwitz. For this reason I suggest that in "Shemà" Levi is following an ancient model that emerged in archaic Greek lyric rather than merely paraphrasing biblical curses (Archilocos 77, 166; Arrighetti and Montanari; Slings).

In this perspective I lead the students to appreciate how Levi's position as a witness is not biased by any preconceived philosophical or religious assumption. Notwithstanding his famous statement neglecting survivors' testimony in favor of that of the *Muselmänner* (*Drowned* [Vintage, 1989] 83–84),[2] he has to be considered a true witness, precisely because he is aware of all the limits implicit in his testimony and expresses them in writing, in the act of bearing witness. For Levi, being aware of the limits of his testimony does not indicate "l'impossibilità di testimoniare" 'the impossibility of bearing witness,' as it does for Giorgio Agamben in his chapter on the witness in *Quel che resta di Auschwitz. L'archivio e il testimone* (*Remnants of Auschwitz: The Witness and the Archive*; 36; 39). The fact that writing does not convey the entire "truth" about any given event is evident not only in testimonial literature but also in any written attempt at representing the world of experience, and it should not lead to the contemplation of silence. When we read Agamben with Levi's poems, I point out to my students that Levi emphasizes not the impossibility of bearing witness but the limits and intersubjective dimension of testimony. Furthermore, I lead my students to recognize the importance that literature plays in Levi's testimony in general and in this poem in particular. I mention at least two other important intertextual sources for Levi's poem: the "Canto of Ulysses," by Dante (*Inferno* [1997] 26), and Elio Vittorini's *Uomini e no* (*Men and Not Men*). In "Shemà," the line "Consider whether this is a man" repeats the rhetorical structure of Ulysses's discourse challenging his sailors to explore the unknown, "Consider how your souls were sown." Moreover, the ethical reflection that lies at the core of "Shemà" and of *Se questo è un uomo* in key moments repeats and paraphrases paragraph 104 of Vittorini's *Uomini e no* and is in dialogue with Robert Antelme's *L'espèce humaine* (*The Human Race*).

In this intertextual context, I introduce two chapters of *Se questo è un uomo*, "Il canto di Ulisse" ("The Ulysses Canto") and the last chapter, "Storia di dieci giorni" ("The Story of Ten Days"), written as diary entries recording the last ten days Levi spent in the camp. As with many Holocaust testimonies, *Se questo è un uomo* has a hybrid form: the narrative is framed by a poem and a diary. It is important to acknowledge that the poem and the diary are the literary forms privileged by Levi to express his most profound ethical reflection in *Se questo è un uomo*. The ethical dilemmas announced in the poetic epigraph return in "The Story of Ten Days"—especially in the entry for 26 January, which needs to be read along with the poem "Shemà"—and remain unresolved in the diary entry. At this point I discuss with my students Emmanuel Lévinas's *Quelques réflexions sur la philosophie de l'hitlérisme* ("Some Reflections on the Philosophy of Hitlerism"), an early (1934) and profound reflection on the consequences of Hitler's ideology that helps students understand the problems related to humanism raised in the testimonies of Vittorini, Levi, and Antelme, among others. Lévinas holds that the philosophy of Nazism, in reducing the idea of humanity to pure biology, neglects what is considered essential in humanity in Christian and liberal traditions, namely the idea of human freedom.

In the discussion on Levi's idea of humanism, I emphasize that poetry does not play an ancillary and paratextual role to Levi's testimonial prose writing, and I show students how it deeply affects his testimony. Concluding the analysis of the poems that now stand as epigraphs to *Se questo è un uomo*, *La tregua*, and *I sommersi e i salvati*, I argue that Levi's testimony finds its first and most comprehensive expression in poetry.[3] In particular the poetic epigraphs to *Se questo è un uomo* and to *La tregua*, combined with the diaristic conclusions of these two testimonial works, deconstruct and destabilize the linearity of the narrative, emphasizing the radical dilemmas and ethical questions as the real core of Levi's early works.[4] In this respect, Levi's humanist philosophy differs from the interpretations that emphasize the unity and dignity of human kind open to the point of including the inhuman and the Nazi (Antelme and Vittorini) and, conversely, from those that see Auschwitz as marking the end and ruin of any ethics of human dignity (Agamben). Most of my students recognize Levi's testimony and ethical stance as profound and problematic in comparison with the assertive and conclusive answers given by the other critics we read.

The reading of another poem, "Il canto del corvo" ("The Crow's Song"), confirms the deep connection between the early poetic and prose works of Levi. The powerful, sinister, and disturbing image of the crow bringing news of death and destruction that we find in this autobiographical poem is present also in the final pages of the coeval prose work *Se questo è un uomo*. Moreover, the poem is announced in the concluding remarks of "Ka-Be," a chapter in *Se questo è un uomo* in which Levi gives voice to the despair of the prisoners in the *Lager*: "Nessuno deve uscire di qui, che potrebbe portare al mondo, insieme col segno impresso nella carne, la mala novella di quanto, ad Auschwitz, è bastato animo all'uomo di fare all'uomo" 'No one must leave here and so carry to the world, together with the sign impressed in his skin, the evil tidings of what man's presumption made of man in Auschwitz' (49; 55). In the poem the crow becomes the messenger of evil tidings; his singing and dancing is "turpe" 'vicious' on the snow, and his news of death robs Levi of sleep. Finally, the crow falls and dies, marking a cross on the snow with his beak.

This sinister image reappears in the diary entries that conclude *Se questo è un uomo*, in which Levi describes the death of friends and comrades during the interval between the flight of the Nazis and the arrival of Soviet troops to the camp: "Non ho mai capito come allora quanto sia laboriosa la morte di un uomo. Fuori ancora il grande silenzio. Il numero dei corvi era molto aumentato, e tutti sapevano perché" 'I never understood so clearly as at that moment how laborious is the death of a man. Outside the great silence continued. The number of ravens had increased considerably and everybody knew why' (167; 171). The crow here and in the poem refers to death in the Nazi camps and to the poet himself, who came from far away to tell us something so disturbing that his life has become unbearable. The fact that the crow at the end of the poem dies also points to the disappeared, who, according to Levi, are the true witnesses of the Shoah. They return in his dreams and in his thoughts and haunt his life. His subjectivity is forever interconnected to theirs. He speaks for them, because of them, and also to them. Levi insists in all his works that the survivors speak in their stead, by proxy.

At this point in the class discussion I read the poem "Voci" ("Voices"), which helps students realize the complexity of the subject position in Levi's poems. I emphasize the intersubjective dimension of Levi's poetry and how listening to the poem is crucial and necessary to creating the only possible conditions to perceive absent voices, the "voci mute" 'voices mute,' as Levi writes in a powerful oxymoron, that still speak through the voices of the survivors: "Voci mute da sempre, o da ieri, o spente appena; / Se tu tendi l'orecchio ancora ne cogli l'eco" 'Voices mute forever, or since yesterday, or just stilled; / If you listen hard you can still catch the echo' (*Ad ora incerta* 522; *Collected Poems* 46).

In the chapter "Cromo" ("Chromium") in *Il sistema periodico* (*The Periodic Table*), Levi recalls that writing poems after his survival made him feel that he was becoming a human being once again, "uno come tutti, né martire, né infame né santo" 'a person like everyone else, neither a martyr nor debased nor a saint' (871; 151). These same words are in the poem "Cantare" ("Singing"), which he wrote in 1946:

> Allora avvenne che tutte le cose
> Furono ancora com'erano state.
> . . . .
> Fummo di nuovo soltanto giovani:
> Non martiri, non infami, non santi
>
> (*Ad ora incerta* 522)

Then everything was again
As it always had been.
. . . .
Once more we were just young men:
Not martyrs, not infamous, not saints.
(*Collected Poems* 6)

Nevertheless, the peace created through writing could be but the "brief" and "cloudlike things" that constituted the subject matter of the singing:

Questo ed altro ci veniva in mente
Mentre continuavamo a cantare;
Ma erano cose come le nuvole,
E difficile da spiegare.

This and other things came into our minds
While we kept singing.
But they were cloudlike things,
Hard to explain.

I read this poem with my students to show how poetic discourse in general and Levi's poem in particular interrupts the linearity and clarity of the narrative discourse alluding to unresolved dilemmas in the account of the witness. Poetry adds a problematic dimension to Levi's testimony that does not demean the substance of his statements in the prose works but instead enhances his search for meaning in directions unexplored in the narrative prose. In the poems we find the doubts, passions, and questions that remain concealed in the monumental clarity of his prose. Reading "Singing" helps student put in perspective and contextualize Levi's claim that it is always possible to communicate (*Drowned* [Vintage, 1989] 89). Along these lines it is possible to better understand the limit of Levi's polemic against the obscurity of Paul Celan and of modern poetry in general (Lollini).

In the poems Levi expresses his experience in an extremely concentrated and powerful way that tests our capability to listen to his voice. To help the students learn how to listen, I use the British composer Simon Bainbridge's Ad ora incerta: *Four Orchestral Songs from Primo Levi*. This work is a convincing and effective effort to make Levi's poetic voice heard through music while preserving its lyricism. Bainbridge has created a work of art entering in a deep dialogue with Levi's voice. Listening to Bainbridge's arrangements helps students recognize the lyrical dimension of Levi's poetry and what it adds to his testimony. Bainbridge selected for his composition some lyrics from a first group of poems that Levi wrote in 1946. I usually have the students listen to "The Crow's Song," which opens Bainbridge's sequence, as a conclusion to the analysis of Levi's early poems. These poems render the feeling for truth we find in Levi's scientific and moral essays deeper, more vivid and alive. What in the prose works remains a general truth can in these musical settings of the poems become a powerful and individualized series of images addressing, in astonishing simplicity and authority, the human soul and the human feeling of compassion.

Poetry and Testimony in Levi's Late Works

The "cloudlike things" introduced by Levi in "Singing" return in crucial moments of his late poems. Among those I analyze with my students is "Autobiografia" ("Autobiography"; *Ad ora incerta* 558), written in 1980, which is very different from the poems Levi wrote in 1946 and represents the last stage of his reflection on himself as a survivor of the Shoah. As with the early poems, the late ones parallel a prose work, *I sommersi e i salvati*, which addresses the kind of reflection found in the late autobiographical poems. The lyric element of the early poems is preserved, but a philosophical dimension also appears, as if to emphasize the reflective and theoretical element of the lyric discourse. Levi assumes several identities in these late poems, but he identifies himself most often with ancient scientists and philosophers who have died or committed suicide in the attempt to discover the meaning of natural phenomena. In the poem "Plinio" ("Pliny"; *Ad ora incerta* 548), Levi wears the mask of Pliny the Elder, a Roman intellectual and author of the celebrated *Natural History*, an encyclopedic work that was authoritative on scientific matters up to the Middle Ages. When he was living in Naples, after learning of an unusual cloud formation (later found to have resulted from an eruption of Mount Vesuvius), Pliny went close to the volcano to discover the cause and to reassure the terrified citizens. He was overcome by the fumes resulting from the volcanic activity and died in 79 BCE. The poem begins with these words:

> Non trattenetemi, amici, lasciatemi salpare.
> Non andrò lontano: solo fino all'altra sponda;
> Voglio osservare da presso quella nuvola fosca
> Che sorge sopra il Vesuvio ed ha forma di pino.
>
> Don't hold me back, friends, let me set out.
> I won't go far; just to the other shore.
> I want to observe at close hand that dark cloud,
> shaped like a pine tree, rising above Vesuvius.
> (*Collected Poems* 33)

In "Autobiography," Levi attributes to himself the attempt to observe the clouds at close hand. This poem is inspired by a fragment from the ancient philosopher Empedocles: "Once I was already youth and maid, bush, bird, and mute fish that leaps out of the sea" (qtd. in *Collected Poems* 44). I give students background information on Empedocles, who, according to legend, was a self-proclaimed god who brought about his own death, by flinging himself into the volcanic crater atop Mount Etna to convince followers of his divinity. Empedocles assumed that all matter was composed of four essential ingredients—fire, air, water, and earth—and that matter neither comes into being nor is destroyed but is merely transformed from one form to another. Finally, he was a believer in the transmigration of souls and declared that those who had sinned must wander for thirty thousand seasons through many mortal bodies.

"Autobiography" draws on these references to Empedocles's life and philosophy; Levi writes that he has lived different lives as a fish, as a "cicala ubriaca" 'drunken cicada,' as a "fanciulla, esitante in danza" 'maiden, hesitating in dance.' This reference to the transmigration of souls that for Empedocles was a consequence of a sin alludes loosely to Levi's sin, expressed in the feeling of guilt as a survivor of the concentration camp. As Levi explains in *I sommersi e i salvati*, this feeling was widespread among survivors and is related to the self-accusation of having failed in terms of human solidarity or of having omitted to offer help in the concentration camp (78).

Levi's poem "Autobiography" ends with the following verses:

> Geometra, ho investigato il segreto del cerchio
> E le vie dubbie delle nubi e dei venti.
> Ho conosciuto il pianto e il riso e molte veneri.
> Perciò non irridetemi, uomini d'Agrigento,
> Se questo vecchio corpo è inciso di strani segni.
> (558)

> Surveyor, I probed the secret of the circle,
> The dubious paths of clouds and winds.
> I have known tears and laughter and much beauty.
> Therefore, don't mock me, men of Agrigento,
> If this old body is deeply and strangely marked.
> (*Collected Poems* 44)

The recurrent image of clouds confirms that in Levi's poetry the explorations both of natural phenomena and of the human soul end in the appreciation of the limits of any human pursuit and in the revelation of an "old body" that is "deeply and strangely marked." Through this revelation, Levi's poems bear witness to the horror experienced by the survivor of the camp of mass destruction constructed by Nazism. The image of a body "deeply and strangely marked" reminds us that Levi in the Nazi camp was stripped of his name and had a number tattooed on his left arm.

In the final discussion following the analysis of this poem I reiterate that in his poems Levi addresses a profound and crucial level of human experience, in which the poetic truth gives voice to the disquieting ethical problems of Western culture. Through his poetic testimony, Levi reminds us of the dangerous and discomforting nature of a culture that has lost its ethical dimension and follows the "dubious paths of clouds and winds."[5]

NOTES

Parts of this essay are adapted from my chapter "Primo Levi's Testimony, or Philosophy between Poetry and Science," in Evlyn Gould and George J. Sheridan's *Engaging Europe: Rethinking a Changing Continent* (Lanham: Rowman, 2005; 131–52; print).

[1] Unless otherwise noted, all quotations in Italian from Levi's works are taken from *Opere*, edited by Belpoliti (Einaudi, 1997). All references to *Survival in Auschwitz* are to the 1987 Collier translation.

[2] Both the German and English terms, Muselmänner and Muselmann, are used by Levi. He writes in a footnote, "This word 'Muselmann,' I do not know why, was used by the old ones of the camp to describe the weak, the inept, those doomed to selection" (*Survival* 88). There are different explanations of the origin of this word. Giorgio Agamben relates it to the literal meaning of the Arabic word *muslim*, indicating a person who submits unconditionally to the will of God (*Remnants* 45). Peter Kuon holds that the figure of the Muslim as a cultural stereotype was not part of the camps and suggests that the term derived from a similar expression in Yiddish, "*mis(er), mi us* (disgust), that had entered into current German, with a slight semantic shift, as *mies* (bad, poor, sick)," originating the word *miser Mann* or *Mieselmann*. The Yiddish term indicating a debilitated camp prisoner who has reached the ultimate state of exhaustion before dying "might have been (mis)understood by non-Yiddish speaking camp inmates as 'Muselmann'" (207–08).

[3] Levi wrote his first poem on Auschwitz, "Buna," on 28 December 1945. This work precedes the first pages of "The Story of Ten Days," which were written in January 1946.

[4] It is important to have the students realize that this problematic core of *Se questo è un uomo* is lost in the American translation of the title as *Survival in Auschwitz* (Patruno, *Understanding* 10).

[5] The instructor who would like to explore more of Levi's poems on scientific and philosophical discourse at the origins of Western culture may read with students "Nel principio" ("In the Beginning"), on the question of the scientific assumption of the origins of the universe with the Big Bang; "Le stelle nere" ("Black Stars"), on the scientific theory of black holes; and "*Sidereus nuncius*," which paraphrases Galileo's celebrated work and comments on the insurmountable difficulties in finding a rational meaning in the universe.

Levi's "Personaggi Ambigeni" and the Negotiation of Autobiography and Memory

Nicholas Patruno

In his introduction to the book *Primo Levi*, the editor, Marco Belpoliti, tells the reader that the work is dedicated not to Primo Levi the witness but to Primo Levi "scrittore . . . narratore e poeta" 'writer, . . . narrator, and poet' (6; my trans.).[1] By making this distinction, Belpoliti is acknowledging that our concern with seeing Levi primarily in the role of witness has tended in certain instances to undervalue his worth as a creative writer. Even though in more recent times there have been studies on the appraisal of Levi's creativity (see, e.g., Moliterni, Ciccarelli, and Lattanzio), this is not yet the case for *Se questo è un uomo* (*If This Is a Man*) and *La tregua* (*The Reawakening*), works that are still viewed almost exclusively as testimony of his Auschwitz experience, especially outside Italy. The sacredness of the subject matter demands to be treated with respect and dignity—the reader, understandably, is hesitant to acknowledge the possible presence of fiction in these works.

Thus, following the flow of Belpoliti's book, in my course Primo Levi, the Holocaust, and Its Aftermath, I engage those students taking the course for credit in comparative literature and Italian studies in a discourse that aims at exploring Levi's writings from artistic and literary points of view. I start by cautioning students to accept Levi's statement, in the preface to *Se questo è un uomo*, that his liberating and urgent need to tell precedes any stylistic intent with a grain of salt.[2] Secondary as it might have been at that point, his concern with style is not to be neglected. Levi makes this clear in his insistence, in an interview with Giuseppe Grassano, on wishing to be considered simply a writer, with no qualifications added:

> [U]n ex deportato, un testimone: lo sono, profondamente anche. Però non voglio essere solo questo, che significherebbe in qualche modo un iscatolamento, una clausura. E quindi mi ritengo libero di trattare qualunque tema, senza escludere il ritorno a questo medesimo tema del Lager. (*Conversazione* 167)

> [A] deportee, a witness: that I am, and profoundly so. But I do not wish to be only that, which would mean in some way being boxed in, a kind of closure. I consider myself free to treat any subject, without excluding the return to this same theme of the Lager.

With this statement in mind, I encourage students to explore further Levi's creative vein by reading some of his less familiar writings, essays and short stories among them. They soon discover that autobiography and memory are central features of his literary approach and that Levi uses these two components to shape his message. I ask students whether one has more validity over the other in reflecting the truth of the content matter and to what extent the author is compelled to adhere to true facts in their application. This dualism appears to take different tangents when we consider Levi as a Holocaust writer and simply as a writer. The question, then, is whether, not unlike many other writers, Levi is justified in taking liberties with his autobiography but compelled to being constrained when memory related to his Auschwitz experience comes into play. With this situation in mind I direct students to look at two interrelated stories from his *Vizio di forma*: "Lavoro creativo" (131–44; "Creative Work"), yet to be published in English translation, and "Nel Parco" (160–76), included in *A Tranquil Star* as "In the Park" (57–71). In these two stories students can appreciate Levi's message in dealing with autobiography as a literary genre and on the importance placed on the role of the writer in relation to memory when dealing with certain types of characters.[3]

In "Lavoro creativo," a story clearly evocative of Luigi Pirandello's "Tragedia di un personaggio" ("Tragedy of a Character") and his play *Sei personaggi in cerca d'autore* (*Six Characters in Search of an Author*),[4] a character named James Collins calls on Antonio Casella, the writer who had created him, to seek advice on some stories that he, Collins, has written, with Casella, his creator, as protagonist. In the course of their conversation, Collins tells Casella that he lives in a park with many other characters from different times and places and that many of them are "personaggi ambigeni" (140), or characters who, in addition to having a fictional existence on the printed page, were historically real at one time.[5] Collins also explains to Casella that characters continue to exist until the texts in which they appear are no longer read, at which point they become diaphanous and eventually fade away.

Years later, motivated in great part by the desire to visit and reside in the park, Casella, who has been in a creative slump for some time, gathers all his creative strengths to write his autobiography. Of Casella, Levi writes:

> Lavorò per tre anni, senza gioia, ma con diligenza e tenacia: si dipinse volta a volta audace e cauto, intraprendente e sognatore, arguto e malinconico, magnanimo ed astuto; accumulò insomma nel suo altro io tutte le virtù che non aveva saputo costruire dentro di sé nella sua vita reale. Creò un mondo più vero del vero, al cui centro stava lui, soggetto di avventure splendide, spesso e intensamente sognate, mai osate; pagina su pagina, pietra su pietra, si murò intorno un edificio armonioso e solido, fatto di viaggi, di amori, di combattimenti e di scoperte; una vita piena e molteplice, quale nessun uomo aveva mai vissuta. (143)

> He worked for three years, with no joy, but with diligence and tenacity: he depicted himself from time to time as audacious and cautious, sharp and sad, magnanimous and astute; in short, he accumulated in his other "I" all

> the virtues he had not been able to create within himself in his real life. He created a world more real than reality, at whose center he stood, the subject of splendid adventures, often and intensely dreamed but never undertaken; page after page, stone upon stone, he built around himself a harmonious and solid edifice, made of voyages, loves, fights, and discoveries; a life that was full and multifarious, such that no man had ever lived.

The students notice that Casella, in presenting the self's other, thus altering his real-life characteristics, makes a character of himself. And with this change, I suggest, Casella does not do anything different from what other autobiographers do, as Luis Gustave Vapereau notes: "Autobiography leaves a lot of room to fantasy, and the one who is writing it is not at all obliged to be exact about the facts, as in memoirs, or to tell the truth, as in confessions" (qtd. in Lejeune 123). The author-narrator-protagonist, having complete say over which facts to include and portraying the self as he or she wishes to be perceived by the reader, is at liberty to arrange, manipulate, and use facts, real or invented, in any way deemed most useful and convenient. "Lavoro creativo," published seven years after *La tregua*, suggests to readers that Levi expects to be allowed the same degree of creative flexibility in narrating his personal account. Levi, however, also deals with memory, which, as Vapereau underscores, demands accuracy of facts. Herein lies, then, the problem: committed as he is to write on behalf of those who cannot, Levi is compelled to rely on his memory and remain as truthful as he can to the facts and events, but since he sees himself as simply a writer, he counts on the same freedom enjoyed by any other creative writer.

At this point I refer students to the chapter "La memoria dell'offesa" in Levi's *I sommersi e i salvati* (*The Drowned and the Saved*), in which Levi, while deeming memory a "strumento meraviglioso" 'marvelous instrument,' also admits to its being "fallace" 'fallacious' (663).[6] Realizing, however, that this admission may be creating a caveat for his position, Levi feels the urge to insert an apology in the chapter's closing paragraph to insist that his memory of Auschwitz has remained clear and "indenne" 'unaffected' (673). Instead of reassuring the reader (and perhaps himself), this insistence leaves students wondering whether his memory is reliable. To corroborate this impression, I ask students to read the chapter "Levi and Memory" in Gillian Banner's *Holocaust Literature*, in which the author notes that Levi's "apology" for memory, especially "distant memory," a "suspect source," problematizes not only "the memory of the offence" but all his writings associated with memory (124). Levi, even if unconsciously, has to cope with this predicament and must come to grips with another and more viable way of handling memory. Following Banner's suggestion, I ask students to consider that the details of memory, as opposed to history—and Levi never considered himself a historian—must be accepted as varying as time goes on. This variation, however, does not mean that what memory recalls has not really taken place. The event has occurred, even if the details have become hazy with time. Under this light, students see that what applies to facts may also be extended to how individuals are remembered, seen, or presented. Memory and fantasy, then, even though they are generally distinct expedients, may act in unison in the mind of the writer. I suggest to students that this concept may also apply to Levi's combining memory and fantasy in his presentation of some of his characters.

"Nel Parco," which picks up where "Lavoro creativo" ends, helps clarify this connection. Casella, following the success he has had with readers of his autobiography, short-lived as it was, is admitted to the park and assigned a residence. (It bears remembering, however, that the Casella who is admitted into the park is the character or other version of himself.) With the help of Collins, Casella gets acquainted with the place and learns particulars he never knew about many of the other characters. He also learns that in this park the characters do either nothing or practice the trade or profession destined for them at birth.

In the presentation of the park and the characters, I call to the students' attention François Rabelais, whom Levi clearly had in mind and whom he greatly admired. Referring to Rabelais, Levi says in an interview, "se potessi lo sceglierei come padre" 'if I could I would choose him as a father' ("Per Primo Levi" 126), and in *L'altrui mestiere* he refers to the French writer as "mon maître" 'my teacher' (15).[7] Casella refers to Rabelais by name, book, and chapter (*Vizio*165; *Tranquil Star* 59). Of particular interest to students of comparative literature is the connection between this story and the episode in chapter 30 of Rabelais's *Pantagruel*, where Epistemon, whose head had been cut off in a battle and had been subsequently healed by Panurge, brings news from the land of the devils and tells of the various unexpected and surprising tasks and jobs held by characters and well-known historical figures he had seen there. Although Casella may be attempting to establish his literary validity by mentioning Rabelais, Collins responds by dismissing Rabelais, who, never having turned himself into a character, has never been in the park and thus must have learned from Pantagruel or some other charlatan what can only be false accounts (165; 60). In this instance it is the author who is learning from the character, just as Casella is the one who learns from Collins. This split between characters and their authors is also evident in "Lavoro creativo" when Casella finds Collins at his door and fails to recognize him. The author's remembrance of Collins's physical appearance differs from what it actually is, and his ignorance of what Collins has experienced after having been made to die in Casella's book further verifies that there is no close relationship between the two of them.

The separation between author and character and the limited interaction between the two parties is something to which Levi has given considerable thought. In *L'altrui mestiere* (*Other People's Trades*), for example, in the essay "Scrivere un romanzo" ("Writing a Story"), Levi addresses the author-character relationship:

> Quanto ai personaggi, il discorso si fa complesso. Su questo tema, il ménage a tre fra l'autore, il personaggio e il lettore, si sono scritti quintali

> di libri, ma essendo io ormai un addetto ai lavori, mi permetto di dire la mia, ossia di proiettare le mie diapositive. Anche per i personaggi si prova all'inizio l'impressione di una libertà senza limiti. In astratto, tu hai su loro un potere assoluto, quale nessun tiranno ha mai avuto sulla faccia della terra. Puoi farli nascere nani o giganti, puoi affliggerli, torturarli, ucciderli, resuscitarli; o donare loro la bellezza e giovinezza eterne, la forza, la sapienza che tu non hai, la felicità di ogni minuto (ma questa sarai capace di descriverla senza annoiare il tuo lettore?). (160)
>
> As far as characters go, the discourse gets more complex. On this topic, the ménage à trois among the author, the character, and the reader, tons of books have been written, but I, being addicted to such works, will have my say; that is, I will project my own slides. With the characters also, initially one has the impression of limitless freedom. In the abstract, you have over them absolute power, like no tyrant has ever had on the face of the earth. You can have them be born midgets or giants, you can afflict them, torture them, kill them, resuscitate them; or give them eternal beauty and youth, the strength, the wisdom that you don't have, the happiness of every minute (but will you be able to describe this without annoying your reader?).

Levi concedes, however, that the apparent control the author has over the character, although it may seem absolute, is short-lived at best. Characters are strange creatures who react to the author at times. They can hold grudges and also play tricks on the author. The freedom, therefore, that the author has is only apparent; the character has a will and rights of his or her own and is at liberty to exercise them, as Levi writes, again calling Pirandello to mind:

> Veramente i personaggi di un libro sono creature strane. Non hanno pelle nè sangue nè carne, hanno meno realtà di un dipinto o di un sogno notturno, non hanno sostanza che di parole, ghirigori neri sul foglio di carta bianca, eppure puoi intrattenerti con loro, conversare con loro attraverso i secoli, odiarli, amarli, innamorartene. Ognuno di loro è depositario di certi elementari diritti, e sa farli valere. La tua libertà di autore è solo apparente. Se, una volta concepito il tuo homunculus, tu lo contrasti, se gli vuoi imporre un gesto avverso alla sua natura, o vietargli un atto che gli sarebbe congeniale, incontri una resistenza, sorda ma indubbia: come se tu volessi comandare alla tua mano di toccare un ferro rovente, o, un oggetto che ti (che le) ripugna. Lui, il non-esistente, è li, c'è, pesa, spinge contro la tua mano: vuole e disvuole, silenzioso e testardo. Se tu insisti, intristisce. Si apparta, cessa di collaborare con te, di suggerirti le sue battute; perde corpo, diventa piatto, sottile, bianco. È carta, e ritorna in carta.
>
> Anche per un altro verso la tua libertà d'invenzione è apparente. Allo stesso modo che è impossibile trasformare una persona di carne in un

> personaggio, farne cioè una biografia obiettiva e non distorta, così è impossibile eseguire l'operazione inversa, coniare un personaggio senza travasargli dentro, oltre ai tuoi umori d'autore, anche frammenti di persone che tu hai incontrate, o di altri personaggi. (161)
>
> Truly, characters are strange creatures. They have neither blood nor skin, they are less real than a painting or a night dream, they have no substance other than words, black scribbles on a sheet of white paper, and yet you can entertain yourself with them, converse with them throughout the centuries, detest them, love them, fall in love with them. Each one of them is the depository of certain elementary rights and knows how to make them have weight. Your freedom as author is only apparent. If, once you have conceived your homunculus, you contradict him, if you want to impose on him a gesture contrary to his nature or forbid him an act congenial to him, you will encounter resistance, deaf but certain, as if you wanted to order your hand to touch a hot iron or an object that disgusts you. He, the nonexistent, is there, exists, weighs, pushes against your hand: he wants and does not want, [is] silent and stubborn. If you insist, he gets sad. He takes himself to the side, ceases to collaborate with you, to suggest his wit or quick replies; he loses his body, becomes flat, thin, white. He is paper and returns to paper.
>
> Your freedom of creation is apparent also on another level. Just as it is impossible to transform a real person into a character, to make, that is, an objective and nondistorted biography, it is equally impossible to perform the opposite operation, to coin a character without putting into him, in addition to whims as author, fragments of persons you have met or of other characters.

At this point, I return to Levi's notion of "personaggi ambigeni" and ask the students to consider how this characterization may manifest itself in his major works related to the Shoah. In "Nel Parco," Collins goes out of his way to point out to Casella the presence of characters who are "ambigeni," admitted to the park only after close scrutiny. Collins tells Casella, "Ci sono molti casi in cui il soggetto è persona e personaggio insieme. Noi li chiamiamo ambigeni, e c'è una commissione che decide se devono essere ammessi al Parco o no" 'There are many cases in which the subject is a person and character at the same time. We call them *ambigeni*, and there is a committee who decides whether to admit them to the Park' (140; my emphasis). The screening is quite onerous. In giving the examples, Collins tells Casella that there was no problem in admitting "Orlando, quello di Roncisvalle," whose prevalence as character over the historical reality was so overwhelming, but that it was controversial to admit Saint Peter and Richard III and, for the benefit of all, to deny admission to Napoleon, Hitler, and Stalin. In the light of the importance placed on these "personaggi ambigeni," most revealing in "Nel Parco" is that Casella identifies Mordo Nahum, one of the most important characters in *La tregua*. In admitting the character status of Mordo Nahum, Levi leaves no doubt as to this man's being the product of his imagination. Yet Levi reveals in a 1986 interview that Mordo is based on a real-life person, Leon Levi, a Greek Jew from Saloniki, whom he had met soon after his liberation from Auschwitz ("Conversazione con Anthony Rudolf"). Mordo, then, can clearly be characterized as a "personaggio ambigeno," as can Cesare, the other major character in *La tregua*, whose real name is Lello Perugia and who also appears, as Piero Sonnino, in the chapter "Ka-Be" in *Se questo è un uomo*.[8] In making them his mentors, Levi finds in Mordo and Cesare, both "personaggi ambigeni," the opportunity to measure himself against their actions and behavior. For Levi, they reflect the parameters within which to function, after Auschwitz, in his reentry into a "normal" life.

At this stage I ask students to focus on these two characters and their relationship with the author, looking at *La tregua*. Mordo, that exceptional man with suggestively devilish red hair and great curved nose, joins forces with Levi through mutual need: Mordo needs Levi for his ability to speak some German, and Levi needs Mordo for his superior ability in commerce and negotiations. During the unforgettable week they spend together in Cracow and then in Katowice, Levi learns valuable, albeit disconcerting, lessons in survival from Mordo, who never loses sight of the fact that the key to the game for survival is always the same: work. Work, to him, is anything, legal or otherwise, that brings a profit without loss of freedom. He accepts unconditionally the Hobbesian concept that man is a wolf-like predator who turns even against his own. Strangely but pointedly, after the war he never speaks of his experiences in the *Lager* because struggle is incessant and present everywhere. "Guerra è sempre" 'war is always,' as he often says, and it is foolish to believe otherwise, no matter where you are (189).[9]

With his rigidity, cynicism, and unwavering attachment to absolute practicality, Mordo is the author's opposite. But even though Levi may find Mordo callous and insensitive—or even someone who "potrebbe anche essere un uomo senza cuore" 'could also be heartless' ("Conversazione con Anthony Rudolf" 104)—he cannot help respecting him. In *La tregua*, Levi refers to Mordo as "grande greco," "supergreco," and "il mio Greco." Ironically, though, it is a respect that evolves from Levi's aversion to Mordo's principles, which at first seem hostile and harsh to the mild-mannered, urbane young man from Turin.

Mordo accuses Levi of foolishness and laziness: foolishness because he has no shoes, an item even more important than food in time of war; laziness because he does not share Mordo's work ethic. Mordo maintains that no one should expect anything for nothing, a belief that places the two men on a brief collision course. Levi, who is seeking warmth, comfort, and renewal of human contact, is reprimanded by Mordo, who accuses him of wanting to live off others. Unfortunately, Levi comes to realize that Mordo's cynical view of life is essentially spot-on. He experiences this cynicism in the Polish town Trzebinia when, just after his release from the camp, a lawyer with no anti-Semitic sentiment presents Levi to a curious crowd not as an Italian Jew but as a political prisoner. Wishing to be helpful, the lawyer explains to Levi that he avoids identifying him as a Jew because prejudice does not end with a war and because, echoing Mordo's words, in life, "la guerre n'est pas finie" 'the war is not over' (191). Levi discovers this to be the sad truth, once back home, as he contends with the war inside himself for the rest of his life.

Mordo, despite his cynical and pessimistic views on life, reveals himself as Levi's mentor, but there is a second mentor to balance the scale: Cesare. Levi first met Cesare in the infirmary in Auschwitz, when Cesare (then called Piero Sonnino), ill with dysentery during the last days in the camp, is assisted and possibly saved by Levi. Once they have been liberated, Cesare plays a crucial and therapeutic role in helping the author regain a taste for living. Cesare's colorful and lively personality, one with an almost childlike excitement and enthusiasm, counterbalances Mordo's grayness and his obsession with work. For Cesare, work is simply "una sgradevole necessità" 'an unpleasant necessity' (*La tregua* 212), though one that might lead to an unexpected and interesting encounter, thus turning into a happy experience. Motivated more by the enjoyment of his own craftiness than by the material profit he might gain from it, Cesare likes to perform with stylishness and virtuosity and to swindle someone, but without causing pain. In working a crowd, Cesare displays competence as a mime and as a skilled charlatan. He clearly enjoys delivering his sales pitch, accompanied by words and obscene expressions invented on the spot. With his consummate plebeian oratorical skill, Cesare lures Levi into wanting to imitate his words and expressions as closely as possible through the dialogue and the indirect discourse in his writing. I point out to students that the linguistic re-creation is a distinction Levi reserves only for Cesare, whose charm lies partly in his mastery of the colloquial Roman ghetto jargon, a combination of the Roman idiom interspersed with distorted Hebrew and Yiddish words. Symbolically, this slang language celebrates the natural harmony between the self and the surrounding environment, indicating Cesare's ability to assimilate everything into his own terms, a most valuable lesson in life. Thus, and this is indispensable for students to see, in his flexible use of language Cesare restores it to the dynamic and dialectical role it was intended to serve, reviving it from the static decay to which it had been reduced in the *Lager*. Levi celebrates this man by calling him "un figlio del sole, un amico di tutto il mondo" 'a son of the sun, a friend to the whole world' (212). He is described as foreign to hatred or contempt, variable like the sky, "festoso, furbo e ingenuo, temerario e cauto, molto ignorante, molto innocente e molto civile" 'festive, sly and simple, daring and cautious, highly ignorant, very innocent, and extremely civil' (212). In short, Cesare ranks among the most delightful and captivating personalities to cross Levi's path. More notably, Cesare almost single-handedly rekindles in the author, albeit briefly, "la gioia di vivere che Auschwitz aveva spenta" 'the joy of living that

Auschwitz had extinguished' (213). Cesare's exuberant and contagious vitality, combined with his unmatched ability to do and to perform, makes him an absolute ruler among these survivors and perhaps is what prompts Levi to reward him with this imperial name.[10] Cesare is the hero of this odyssey and, with his picaresque and roguish qualities, the embodiment of a Rabelaisian character. Considering the veneration Levi held for Rabelais, it is important for students to recognize this characterization as the highest compliment Levi can bestow on Cesare, whose attitude is not dissimilar from the one he sees in Rabelais, who "conosce la miseria umana; la tace perché, buon medico anche quando scrive, non l'accetta, la vuole guarire" 'knows human misery; he does not talk about it because, as the good doctor he is also when he writes, he does not accept it, he wants to heal it' (*Vizio* 19). Cesare has also come face-to-face with the basest of human suffering, and he rejects it and tries in his own way to heal it. Like Mordo, Cesare refuses to mention his experiences at Auschwitz.

While Mordo has taught Levi to stay alert and not to expect any rewards from life, Cesare shows him that there is still enjoyment that can be squeezed out of it. Mordo lectures the writer on the importance of having a good and comfortable pair of shoes, but it is in Cesare's shoes, figuratively speaking, that Levi feels more comfortable. Cesare helps Levi reenter the world of social relationships, as he molds him into a new man, much after Cesare's own image. It is a change that Levi willingly accepts, even if only for a short time, as evidenced by Cesare, who "baptizes" him with the nickname "Lapé," derived from the French *lapin* ("rabbit"), because Levi's new growth of soft hair reminds Cesare of a rabbit's fur (*La tregua* 257). The students understand that by accepting and taking the name of Lapé, Levi too turns himself into a "personaggio ambigeno." In *La tregua*, those so often referred to "picaresque" adventures in which Levi participates at the side of Cesare are actions that he performs under this newly acquired name and persona. As long as he is with Cesare, Primo/Lapé will be a different person and will do things so out of character for the straitlaced, sophisticated scientist named Primo Levi. This phase of carefree behavior reaches a culminating point in the chapter "Una curizetta" ("The Little Hen") where, with the author at his side, Cesare, driven by his strong desire to eat a chicken, activates an entire small community with words, sounds, mimicry, and gestures. Nowhere else in this book or in any of his other works does Levi reach the level of humor present in these delightful and entertaining passages.

Characterization, however, is strongest when the character reacts predictably, when he or she is not "out of character." Whereas Cesare and Mordo stay faithful to their persona, for Levi the Lapé figure constitutes a radical change, not destined to last. The German book on medicine he finds and absorbs with the keen intellectual curiosity of his previous life, as well as the sound of a train, an object now connected with pain and suffering but still, paradoxically, a symbol of a return to "civilization," are strong reminders of where he belongs. He simply cannot keep on existing as Lapé, who is nothing more than a diaphanous representation of himself.

Students come to the conclusion that Levi's "personaggi ambigeni" can be central to the plot and are reflective of a fertile creative mind. They see that Levi is a writer in the artistic and creative senses of the word, even if he needed the survivor experience to bring this to the fore. With his creation and coinage of a new character type, Levi is fully aware, as he also wants readers to be, that he is introducing into the literary landscape something that is uniquely his. In the light of his *Lager* experience, it is understandable that he may want to express himself through unconventional literary mechanisms. The "personaggi ambigeni," in their small but relevant way, bridge the gap somewhat between reality and art, between what is historically true and what is a reflection of the writer's creative frame of mind. By remembering the historical person behind the character, students appreciate Levi's ability to respect the memory of the event and its many victims while recognizing his fantasy, seen in the creation of his characters, as an active part of his being.

NOTES

[1] Henceforth, unless otherwise noted, translations are mine.

[2] It bears remembering that Levi made some revisions between the 1947 edition of this work and the present one. Among these changes, he added the chapter "Initiation." This revision indicates that even though style may not have been on the forefront of his concerns he was certainly aware of it.

[3] Levi comments at great length on characters in his essay "Scrivere un romanzo" (*L'altrui mestiere* 159–63).

[4] Levi acknowledges Pirandello's interest in characters in his comments on the characters in *Se non ora, quando?* (*If Not Now, When?*): "penso proprio di avere capito Pirandello ora" 'I really believe to have understood Pirandello now' ("Mendel" 134; my trans.).

[5] It bears pointing out that the term *ambigeno* does not appear in Italian dictionaries, including the most recent edition of the Devoto-Oli *Dizionario della lingua italiana* and Battaglia's multivolume *Grande dizionario della lingua italiana*. It would be safe to assume, then, that Levi has coined this term, one that finds its closest connection to *ambigenere*, a term applied primarily to nouns that have the same ending in the masculine and feminine singular form (e.g., *custode*, *musicista*, *pianista*).

[6] All references to *I sommersi e i salvati* are to the 1986 Einaudi edition.

[7] Levi has written on Rabelais and refers to him in several other writings (e.g., *Vizio di forma* and *La ricerca delle radici*). In the story "Le nostre belle specificazioni" ("Our Fine Specifications"), Levi has one of his characters quote Rabelais by heart and then adds, "Rabelais . . . è un vademecum indispensabile per ogni uomo moderno" 'Rabelais . . . is an indispensible vade mecum for all modern men' (*Vizio* 151). Perhaps Levi's attachment to the French writer is expressed best in an interview with Andreoli: "Proprio la mia simpatia per Rabelais è apparentemente incomprensibile. Eppure tra tutti è quello cui mi sento più legato in modo quasi filiale. Se potessi lo sceglierei come padre" 'My attachment [my sympathy] for Rabelais is not comprehensible. Yet, among all he is the one to whom I feel closest, almost in a filial way. If I could I would choose him as father' ("Per Primo Levi" 126).

[8] Levi provides this information about Piero Sonnino / Cesare / Lello Perugia in the scholastic edition of *Se questo è un uomo* and *La tregua* (Einaudi, 1989). See also Dini and Jesurum 46.

[9] All references to *La tregua* are to the joint edition of *Se questo è un uomo* and *La tregua* (Einaudi, 1989).

[10] Not to be overlooked is the likelihood that Levi may have adopted the name Cesare to pay tribute to his father, with whom, according to Angier, he was never close but who, like the character Cesare, had a zest for life (52–55).

The Complexity of Levi: Approaching Levi through His Interviews, Articles, and Short Essays

Massimo Giuliani

In two anthologies of Primo Levi's works, both edited by Marco Belpoliti and published by Einaudi, are collected interviews and essays originally disseminated in books, magazines, and newspapers. The first, *Conversazioni e interviste, 1963–1987*, appeared in 1997 and selections were translated by Robert Gordon as *The Voice of Memory*; the second, *L'asimmetria e la vita. Articoli e saggi, 1955–1987*, was published in 2002 and translated by Sharon Wood as *The Black Hole of Auschwitz*.[1] Both collections represent a shortcut to the mental and cultural universe of Primo Levi. Even though it is difficult to truly appreciate the depth of Primo Levi's persona without reading his major works, the short(er) works included in these collections convey the complexity of his personality as a human being, a writer, and a survivor of the *Lager*. In them, as in his longer works, Levi presents his ideas convincingly and demonstrates his ability as an author "who stays entirely inside his writings, . . . who said all he had to say, and who said it with great clarity" (Giuliani 2). He communicates his message lucidly, sparing the reader from obscure or unintelligible lines. Levi ably conveys something important, subtle, and educational even by way of a very brief interview, and in those interviews that turn into conversations, in which he is given the time and space to articulate more accurately his analytic thought, he engages his interlocutor with his own point of view.[2]

No longer limited to consideration as a memoirist or a witness of the largest collective tragedy of the twentieth century, today Levi figures justly among the classics. His writing style has *pondus*, weight, substance, and quality and is particularly suited to students, since it invites them to discriminate intelligently and to articulate judgments and opinions rationally and with discernment. Approaching Levi through his interviews and articles will motivate students, especially in advanced classes, to read Levi's other works. To de-construe a writer to better understand him entails a diachronic reading of his entire literary output. The interviews, as interesting and revealing as they are, narrate Levi synchronically, over and over, as in a game of mirrors: with each interview he is asked to describe himself anew, to focus one more time on his experience and consequently to retell his story both as a deportee-witness and as a writer. The process is a reminder of what takes place during a psychoanalytic session, where the story—one's own story—to be analyzed is always the same but needs to be narrated with different nuances and from different angles. Belpoliti writes:

> L'intervista è per Primo Levi un modo per prolungare l'arte del racconto, per aggiungere qualcosa di ulteriore, qualcosa che ha salvato all'oblio e di cui la sua "memoria meccanica" può restituire all'improvviso un nuovo

> frammento. Nelle conversazioni egli appare come l'archeologo di se stesso . . . [ma] l'arte del narrare è per lui anche un'arte di ripetersi, del rinnovare il medesimo racconto davanti a un nuovo pubblico di ascoltatori con qualche modesta ma necessaria variazione.
>
> ("Io sono un centauro" ix)

> For Levi, the interview is an extension of the art of storytelling, a way of adding something further, something that he has saved from oblivion, a fragment that his so-called "mechanical memory" can suddenly restore. Often in conversation he sounds like the archaeologist of his own past . . . [but the] art of storytelling, for him, is also the art of repeating oneself, of renewing the same old story for new listeners, with a modicum of necessary variation. ("I Am a Centaur" xix)

But the texts of interviews are usually taped and downloaded by the interviewer, not by the interviewed. To say, then, that the interviewed is the author of his or her interview is not totally accurate. At best, the result is de facto a joint venture, a coauthorship that automatically becomes a mediated, filtered communication. The distance between when the interview takes place and when it is transcribed allows time for revision, interpretation, and interrogation. In articles and short essays, the goal of the author is to say much in a brief space, a limitation that places the text into a tension between form and content, as well as between the universal message and the reference to current events. Thus the author's thoughts on specific issues, facts, people, and situations, which make sense only when put in their historical perspective, become somewhat refracted. The result is that when the author is read at a distance of years he or she is exposed, offering a snapshot of the self. Furthermore, a collection of articles is like a book of photographs taken by a professional who, with each shot, in addition to the particular image frozen in time, must also reveal the eye of the catcher of that image, the position from which the image was taken, the technique used to catch it, and above all the poetry expressed by that image caught in that specific way.

Lightning Self-Portraits

As evidence of his complexity, Levi sometimes responds to a simple, brief question with an extensive, carefully reasoned out, and enlightening reply, reflective of his mature acumen and self-consciousness. In response to a question regarding a comparison between himself and Kafka, whose *Il processo* (*The Trial*) Levi had translated in the first of a new Einaudi series dedicated to "writers translated by writers," Levi openly admits to much more than what he had been asked. With this confession, appearing a few years after the publication of the translation, readers and students can see how, in an introspective process, Levi expands the question into a fuller discourse. He candidly reveals, with some disappointment, his openness to self-criticism and to a change of view:

> Abbiamo avuto destini molto diversi. Kafka è cresciuto in un gravissimo conflitto con il padre. E' stato frutto di tre culture frammiste—quella ebraica, quella praghese e quella tedesca—infelice nei suoi rapporti sentimentali, frustrato nel lavoro, infine gravemente malato. E' morto giovane. Io, malgrado l'episodio del Lager, che mi ha segnato profondamente, ho avuto una vita diversa, meno infelice. Il lieto fine mio personale, il fatto di essere riuscito a sopravvivere al Lager, mi ha reso stupidamente ottimista. Oggi non sono più ottimista. A quel tempo lo ero. A quel tempo ho commesso un illogico trasferimento del mio personale lieto fine—che mi ha arricchito oltretutto, perché mi ha reso scrittore—a tutte le tragedie umane.
>
> *Se questo è un uomo*, benché parli di cose terribili, è veramente poco affine a Kafka. E' stato notato da molti, è un libro ottimista e sereno, in cui si respira questo cammino verso l'alto, nell'ultimo capitolo soprattutto. Sembrava assurdo pensare che dal fondo, dalla fossa, dal Lager non dovesse nascere un mondo migliore. Io penso tutt'altro oggi. Penso che dal Lager non possa nascere che il Lager, che non possa nascere che il male da quell'esperienza. Dopo aver verificato come uno Stato moderno, organizzato, tecnicizzato, burocratizzato abbia potuto partorire Auschwitz, non si può non pensare con spavento alla possibilità che quell'esperienza si rinnovi. Quell'esperienza può rinnovarsi, non dico che debba rinnovarsi, ma che può sì, questo lo vedo e lo temo. ("Un'aggressione" 191–92)

> We had very different fates. Kafka grew up in very serious conflict with his father; he was the product of three intermingled cultures, Jewish, German and the culture of Prague. He was unhappy in his emotional life, frustrated in his work, and in the end seriously ill. He died young. I, on the other hand, despite the episode of the *Lager* which marked me deeply, have had a different life, a less unhappy life. My own personal happy ending, that fact of having survived the camps, made me stupidly optimistic. Today, I am less of an optimist. At that time I was more so. At that time I committed an illogical transfer of my own personal happy ending—which enriched me, by making me a writer—on to all human tragedies.
>
> *If This Is a Man*, although it deals with terrifying things, has very little in common with Kafka. It has been noted by many that it is an optimistic and calm book in which you breathe the air rising up from the depths, especially in the last chapter. It seemed absurd to think that from those depths, from the ditch, from the *Lager* there might not be a better world to come. Today, my thoughts are quite different. I think that only another *Lager* can be born from the fact of the *Lager*, that only bad can come of this experience. After having witnessed how a modern, organized, technicized, bureaucratized state could give birth to Auschwitz, one cannot but

> think in terror of the possibility that it might happen again. That experience can recur, it does not have to recur, but it certainly can, and I see this and I fear it. ("Assault" 158)

Students may opt to search for other statements that flash self-portraits in just a few lines. In a conversation with the literary critic Giuseppe Grassano, for example, Levi admits to feeling like a centaur. It is one of his preferred metaphors to articulate his inner complexity, consisting of apparently conflicting and irreconcilable elements within him:

> Sono un liceale con un'educazione umanistica, ma insieme anche un chimico e infine un ex deportato. Quindi ho almeno tre fondi diversi di scrittura. Lo studio e le letture mettiamoli tutti insieme da una parte; c'è poi l'esperienza di Auschwitz. Lidia Rolfi dice che il Lager è stato la sua università e io le ho plagiato quest'affermazione. Anche per me Auschwitz è stata la seconda università. E finalmente il mestiere concreto, quello di chimico in fabbrica. Non voglio rinunciare a nessuna delle tre esperienze. Adesso se ne è aggiunta una quarta, se vogliamo, quella dell'aver scritto. ("Conversazione con Primo Levi" 179–80)

> I am a "liceo" student with a humanistic education, but also a chemist and an ex-deportee. So I have at least three different sources for my writing. If we put my studies and literature on one side together, then there's the experience of Auschwitz. Lidia Rolfi says that the camps were her university and I picked up this comment of hers. For me too, Auschwitz was a second university. And lastly, there's my career, a very concrete career as a factory chemist. I have no desire to abandon any one of these three experiences. Now there's a fourth experience to be added to them, if you like, the experience of being a writer. ("Conversation" 131)

He insists on this self-portrait with Giovanni Tesio:

> Io credo proprio che il mio destino profondo sia l'ibridismo, la spaccatura. Italiano ma ebreo. Chimico ma scrittore. Deportato, ma non tanto (non sempre) disposto al lamento e alla querela. . . . Forse è proprio questo il motivo che mi fa amare Rabelais, che era un uomo molto serio, studioso, colto, celebre medico, ma che provava giusto nel ridere e nel far ridere. ("Credo" 186)

> I truly believe that my most profound destiny is the hybridism, the rupture: an Italian but a Jew; a chemist but a writer; a deportee but not so much (and not always) ready to complain or to sue. . . . Probably this is the reason why I love Rabelais, who was a very serious man, an erudite scholar, a famous doctor, but ready to enjoy a laugh and able to make others laugh. (my trans.)

In each page, Levi exposes himself with great simplicity and intellectual honesty, sometimes not without a certain coquetry. This simplicity, however, is not to be taken as an intentional oversimplification or as a means to simplify reality. On the contrary, it is a method, a style of work, an effort aimed at facilitating the grasp of the complexity at hand. It can be said, then, that Levi is simple and complex at the same time. He is methodical in his arguments and is careful not to stray into any form of rationalism that would impede him from seeing the irrationalism that exists in human beings and history. To use a couple of current philosophical terms, Levi is simultaneously modern and postmodern. He is modern because he believes in reason, in the ability of every human to understand the rules and the values of society and communicate with all. His efforts to understand (through *ratio*) and to communicate (through *verba*) constitute the two essential movements of the *logos*, of human reason, as imparted by Dante through Ulysses's words: "Considerate la vostra semenza: / fatti non foste a viver come bruti, / ma per seguir virtute e conoscenza" 'Consider your origin: you were not made to live as brutes, but to pursue virtue and knowledge' (*Inferno* [1997] 26.118–20; my trans.); Levi resolutely adopts Dante's *logos* in the chapter "Il canto de Ulisse" ("The Canto of Ulysses") in *Se questo è un uomo* (*If This Is a Man*). And Levi is postmodern insofar as his trust in reason is critical and knows its limits. In an interview for the magazine *Storia illustrata*, he says, "Non ho mai avuto fiducia nell'istinto morale dell'umanità, nell'uomo buono 'naturaliter'" 'I never had a trust in the moral instinct of humanity, in a human being as *naturaliter* good' (qtd. in Belpoliti, "Nota" 260; my trans.). Such a statement leaves no doubt about his distance from any illuminist rationalism he may have had in his youth, when he was still being guided by "fantasmi cartesiani" 'Cartesian phantoms,' as he states in the opening pages of *Se questo è un uomo* ([Einaudi, 1989] 5; 13).

In addition, his vision of history, albeit global, always stays open to the hard work of comparison and therefore to relativity, thus never becoming a metaphysical or teleological vision. His vision is ethical, pedagogical despite itself, and evolutionary. It is, in other words, in full agreement with his scientific education. For Levi, therefore, the interview is a perfect tool to communicate in a synthetic but effective way, to share with his readers (especially through the pages of his numerous articles in the Turin daily *La stampa*) everything from occasional reviews of a movie or a book to his opinions on important events such as the 1982 Israeli military intervention of Lebanon (I encourage students to read the last section of *Conversazioni e interviste*, dedicated to the State of Israel). Levi's ability to make valuable use of the interview is evident when he interviewed himself in the appendix he added to the scholastic edition of *Se questo è un uomo*, a supplement defined by Marco Belpoliti as "l'autocommento più prezioso sul tema del Lager" 'the most precious self-commentary on the theme of the *Lager*' ("Nota" 260; my trans.).

Sharpness of Judgment

Distilled from the pages of his many interviews and brief essays, Levi's sharpness of judgment emerges as the most striking feature of his short works. Despite the widespread impression that his testimony is not judgmental but merely factual, Levi's texts offer extremely clear-cut and precise judgments, even when they are open to future and changing opinions. The sharpness of his judgments, always rooted in facts, be they material or psychological, and open for anyone to verify or test, is what surprises students the most.

Theodor Adorno's well-known and often quoted assertion that "nach Auschwitz ein Gedicht zu schreiben, ist barbarisch" 'to write poetry after Auschwitz [as it was written before Auschwitz] is barbaric' suggests that Auschwitz represents a watershed moment in the world of art and aesthetics, a paradigm change within the Western consciousness (30; my trans.). But like all expressions aimed at striking the public imagination, this one sounds paradoxical. When asked by the reporter Giulio Nascimbeni, of the daily *Il corriere della sera*, about Adorno's remark, Levi, unafraid of critically evaluating the authority of the philosopher, offers the following subdued, carefully reasoned response:

> La mia esperienza è stata opposta. Allora mi sembrò che la poesia fosse più idonea della prosa per esprimere quello che mi pesava dentro. Dicendo poesia, non penso a niente di lirico. In quegli anni, avrei riformulato le parole di Adorno: dopo Auschwitz non si può più fare poesia se non su Auschwitz. ("Levi" 137)

> My experience was the opposite. Then it seemed to me that poetry was more apt than prose to convey what weighed inside me. When I say "poetry" I do not think of anything lyrical. In those years I would have reformulated the word of Adorno: after Auschwitz, the only way to write poems is writing them about Auschwitz. (my trans.)

This perhaps surprising statement compels the reader to compare Adorno's and Levi's apparently conflicting positionings of Auschwitz as the measure of everything.

Another example of sharpness of judgment, in this case, sharpness of psychological judgment, is evidenced in Levi's commentary in a radio interview in 1986 with Milvia Spadi. Commenting on Pier Paolo Pasolini's disturbing movie *Salò o le 120 giornate di Sodoma* ("Salò; or, The 120 Days of Sodom"), a film evocative of the violence and depravity of the final days of the fascist regime in the Republic of Salò, and on Pasolini's statement, borrowed from the Marquis de Sade, that "absolute power is anarchy," Levi states:

> Le dirò che [*Salò* di Pasolini] mi è dispiaciuto molto come film, mi è sembrato un rigurgito, l'opera di un uomo disperato. Infatti Pasolini era

> disperato. E io non amo la disperazione. Mi pare che la disperazione paralizzi. Credo che sia un film che ha nuociuto, questo . . . non mi ricordo neanche più il titolo esatto. Credo di aver rimosso. Non era così, non è vero che fosse così. Questa ferocia totale non è esistita. C'era un'ampia zona grigia. Anzi era quasi integrale. Allora eravamo tutti grigi.
>
> ("Capire" 251)

> I confess that I disliked this motion picture a lot. It seemed to me regurgitation, the work of a desperate man. Truly, Pasolini was desperate. And I don't like desperation. I believe desperation paralyzes. This movie, . . . I don't even remember the title exactly, has produced damages. . . . Such totally ferocious behavior did not exist. There was a large gray zone that was almost everywhere. At that time, all of us were gray.
>
> (my trans.)

Despite the fact that he declared himself extraneous to psychoanalysis, even though he read and appreciated Sigmund Freud, Levi says he has removed Pasolini's last cinematographic work from his mind. Nevertheless, he remembers it well enough to criticize it for its bad impact on the youth and for its being historically incorrect, false, and exaggerated. As in the *Lager*, even during fascism, the gray prevailed as opposed to a clear-cut contrast of black and white. This vagueness was an uncomfortable truth, especially during the sixties and seventies, when the concept of postmodernism was still in its infancy.

The last example of Levi's sharpness of judgment is connected to the theme of work, a recurrent topic in his books and the subject of his novel *La chiave a stella* (*The Monkey's Wrench*), written in praise of manual labor. After the book's publication, Levi gave many interviews that addressed the problems of specialized labor, manual work as a trade or profession.[3] In the interview with Grassano, Levi describes the "potere . . . salvatorio del lavoro" 'redeeming power of work' ("Conversazione con Primo Levi" 169; "Conversation with Primo Levi" 123). *Sic et sempliciter*. The adjective *salvatorio* does not exist in Italian. Levi, who had a passion for philology, uses the term intentionally. *Salvatorio* is to *salvazione* as *salvifico* is to *salvezza*, and salvation in the sense of Primo's *salvatorio* describes a fully human virtue, an effort to use all human capacities, starting from reason, to help human beings survive in an environment difficult to understand and control. Salvation in the sense of *salvezza* (*salvifico*), on the other hand, is spiritual and hints at a divine intervention, outside human control, *ex machina*.[4] Labor is *salvatorio* exactly because it is within the realm of human control, serving human beings and humanity through the transformation of matter into economic and productive use. Labor, be it manual or intellectual, is essential in the practice of human creativity. Understood in these terms, to Levi labor is not a punishment but a lofty expression of human dignity and pride, an exercise that allows human beings to feel that they have mastered matter, to feel spiritual in the most humanistic sense of the word.

Levi has always maintained that his views on labor have their roots in Joseph Conrad's stories.

In the light of these reflections, students appreciate the perspicacity of Levi's answer to what Grassano describes as, referring to Auschwitz, "[il] riscatto del lavoro che da punitive e distruttivo (l'Arbeit Macht Frei del Lager), alienato e odiato nella realtà della fabbrica, s'impone invece quale vocazione, segno di competenza e amore" 'the redemption of work, from the punitive and destructive work of the camps ("Arbeit Macht Frei") to the alienating and despised work of the factory to the vocation of work . . . as a sign of ability and love' (168; 122). Here Levi begs to differ, offering the following clarification:

> Io taglieri fuori l'*Arbeit Macht Frei*, perché veramente quello non era un lavoro. Era una pura pena. Neppure una pena biblica: "Ti guadagnerai il pane con il sudore della tua fronte." Lì era un pane guadagnato per altri; mancava totalmente il rapporto tra causa ed effetto, cioè il lavoro che ti dà il sostentamento. Quello non era un lavoro, era come prendere frustrate.

> I would cut the reference you make to *Arbeit Macht Frei*, since that really was not work. It was pure suffering. And not even the biblical suffering of "by the sweat of your brow you will eat bread." There it was bread earned for others. The link between cause and effect was completely absent, as was the idea that work sustains you. It was not work, it was like being whipped.

Levi's exaltation of work calls to mind the just middle ground of the rabbinical-talmudic ethics, which always invites avoiding extremes.

Professionalism and Method

Through interviews it is also possible to explore Levi's reflection on his *mestiere* ("trade work") as a writer, on his literary calling, and on his method of intellectual work. His proficiency in the field of artistic creation is connected to his professionalism in the field of chemistry and management of a paint factory. Having as its goal to usefully serve somebody's needs, it carries the same sense of integrity and rectitude applied to and requested for paid work.

Levi acknowledges to Tesio, "La mia disposizione d'animo, anche adesso che non faccio più il tecnico, è quella dell'addetto all manutenzione; la rete telefonica, o del gas, funzionerà bene se (condizione non suffciente ma necessaria) lui sarà diligente, attento ed esparto" 'My internal attitude, even now that I am no longer working as a chemist, is the same as the technician assigned to maintenance; the telephone network or the gas lines will work well if (a necessary albeit insufficient condition) that technician will be diligent, careful, and experienced' ("Credo" 185; my trans.). Another interviewer, Roberto Di Caro, prods Levi on this point in a very direct way, to which Levi replies:

> Levi: Non c'è molta differenza tra costruire un apparecchio per il laboratorio e costruire un bel discorso. Ci vuole simmetria. Ci vuole idoneità allo scopo. Bisogna togliere il superfluo. Bisogna che non manchi l'indispensabile. E che alla fine tutto funzioni.
> Di Caro: Anche la scrittura è un problema tecnico?
> Levi: Per me sì. Mi sono sempre occupato di problemi tecnici: di progettazione, produzione, vendita. Per vent'anni, anche quando ero già direttore di impresa, passavo il tempo in laboratorio, il cervello della fabbrica . . .
> Di Caro: Scrivere è un lavoro meno preciso?
> Levi: Al contrario, per me è un lavoro molto preciso.
> Di Caro: . . . Anche nella scrittura funziona "il martello"?
> Levi: . . . un po' di martello funziona. Meglio ancora funzionano le tronchesine. Per questo il Macintosh è uno strumento meraviglioso: perché taglia via tutto senza pietà, non rimane traccia di una sola cancellatura. ("Necessario" 195–96)

> Levi: There isn't a great deal of difference between putting together a lab apparatus and putting together a good story. It needs symmetry, it has to fit the purpose, it has to have nothing superfluous, but not to miss out anything essential. And it has to work.
> Di Caro: Is writing, too, a technical problem?
> Levi: For me, yes. Anyway I have always dealt with technical problems: planning, production, sales. For twenty years, even when I was already in management, I spent time in the laboratory, the brains of the factory. . . .
> Di Caro: Is writing less to do with precision?
> Levi: On the contrary, for me it is high precision work.
> Di Caro: . . . Does "the hammer" work in writing also?
> Levi: . . . a bit of hammering works fine. Or better, the clippers. The Macintosh is a wonderful tool for this, for pitiless cutting that doesn't leave a trace. ("Essential" 167–68)

In the same interview the connection between the literary text and manual labor is underlined even more explicitly:

> Il fatto è che, mentre il ritmo della poesia la imparenta strettamente alla musica, il testo letterario [in prosa] è in un certo modo imparentato con il lavoro manuale. Si fa, almeno mentalmente, un progetto, una scaletta, un disegno, e poi si cerca di realizzare il manufatto nel modo più conforme al progetto. Naturalmente l'ho fatto dire a Faussone [il protagonista de *La chiave a stella*], è molto meno pericoloso scrivere un libro che costruire un ponte: se il ponte crolla può provocare molti danni, anche alle persone. Se crolla un libro fa danni solo al suo autore. (200)

> The fact is that, whereas the rhythm of poetry makes it closely related to music, the literary text is in a sense closer to manual labour. You make a plan, at least mentally, an outline, a design, and then you try to make the product as close as possible to the plan. Naturally, as I have Faussone [the protagonist of *The Monkey's Wrench*] say, it is much less dangerous to write a book than to build a bridge: if a bridge collapses it can do a lot of harm, to people also. If a book collapses, the only damage done is to the author. (172)

And to Enrico Boeri, Levi gives another response in lightning self-portrait: "Il mio pregio sta nell'attenermi alla realtà: un debito che il Primo Levi scrittore ha verso Primo Levi chimico" 'My virtue is that I stick to reality: a debt that Primo Levi the writer owes to Primo Levi chemist' ("Chimico" 23; "Chemistry" 69). The professionalism of the chemist—that is, the scrupulous observation and respect of the facts, the attitude toward precision and preciseness (which Italo Calvino describes as a characteristic of the literature of the future in *Lezioni americane* [translated as *Six Memos for the Next Millennium*]), and the ability to ponder, etymologically speaking, on what is necessary—is immediately transferred to and poured into the trade work of the writer, who has to narrate and sometimes invent with fantasy according to a style that has respect for the facts, real people, and fictional characters. Had Levi lived longer, he could have built on his work on the world of specialized manual laborers and written on immigration, a concern that Italy began to face in the 1990s, applying to it the same attention to the spoken language, the same detailed study of the sociological dynamics, the same ethical rigor.

Typical of Levi's reasoning and his structure are the calm analysis of the processes, the search for connections, the tests of the bonds—of molecules and social groups, of ideas and political parties, of historical roots and their consequent phenomena. As a chemist and a laboratory mouse, Levi uses a method of experimentation to correct and recorrect hypotheses and, if necessary, to recognize his errors or failures. With detachment and irony, Levi the chemist influences Levi the writer and translator and even Levi the poet on how to clean and polish the text. His becoming a literary classic, therefore, is the result of a complex process and an intense elaboration. He admits that poetry, as a product of a rhapsodic inspiration, is not part of his world; on the contrary, his "[il suo] mondo è quello di pensare una cosa, di svilupparla in modo quasi . . . da montatore, ecco, di costruirla poco alla volta" 'world is one of thinking about something, developing it almost . . . like a rigger, yes, building it up bit by bit' ("Conversazione con Primo Levi" 182; "Conversation with Primo Levi" 133). Clearly such a method—as evidenced in the protagonist Faussone—is not incompatible with a certain ease of writing and with inspiration. In fact it may be the best way to cultivate and encourage both easiness and inspiration.

The Ethic of Relative Optimism

Levi displayed the same realism in the field of ethics, when questioned about the possibility of forgiving the Germans. Without denying the desire for vengeance, he questioned the legitimacy of the "returning the blow" approach endorsed by Jean Améry, the German-Jewish intellectual about whom Levi writes extensively in the chapter "The Intellectual in Auschwitz" in *The Drowned and the Saved*. In an interview with Risa Sodi, Levi notes that Améry wrote a letter in which he "[m]i considerava una persona sempre disposta a perdonare, un *Verzeihende*" 'considered me as a person who is always ready to forgive, a *Verzeihende*' ("Un'intervista con Primo Levi" 236; my trans.). Even many years after Améry's suicide, Levi responds to this accusation with his insistence that "[n]on è una cosa vera. . . . Io credo che se qualcuno ha commesso un crimine, deve pagare. Non spetta a me dire: ti assolvo dalla punizione" 'this is not true. . . . I believe that, if somebody has committed a crime, he must pay. It is not up to me to say: I absolve you from the punishment.' Forgiveness does not concern him; what matters to him are justice and the idea of education or *salvazione* through understanding. He is concerned with identifying the causes of such inhuman acts so that they may be foreseen and prevented in the future.

Forgiveness presupposes a good and an evil that are clear-cut and evident, but often the complexity of the world is gray and more difficult to diagnose. In a conversation with Giorgio Segrè on Jewish themes, Levi expands his reflection on the "Gray Zone" as a key to demythologize every black-and-white representation of the world:

> Noi tutti esseri umani siamo degli animali che preferiscono le cose semplici. Ma le cose non sono semplici, sono sempre complesse . . . Per cui questo binomio, vittima e aguzzino, va studiato. . . . È molto triste. È la tesi di Hannah Arendt, questa della banalità del male. Questa tesi assomiglia a quanto sto dicendo: cioè era molto più importante l'ambiente che non la natura umana interna. Non si parla di mostri. Io di mostri non ne ho visto neanche uno. ("Intervista a Primo Levi" 278–79)

> We human beings are animals who prefer things kept simple. But here nothing is simple. Things are complex at every stage. . . . [Therefore] the victim-torturer pair needs examining. . . . It could not be more significant or sadder. It is Hannah Arendt's thesis on the "banality of evil." Her idea is very close to what I am saying, that the environment was much more important than intrinsic human nature. There were no monsters. I didn't see a single monster in my time in the camp. (my trans.)

Echoing the well-known notions of Hannah Arendt on the Eichmann trial in Jerusalem in 1961, there are times, then, when the optimism of the will, tempered by the pessimism of intelligence, calls for attention to certain nuances, to the hidden bends of reality in virtue of which even something that is not a totally legal trial, such as the Nuremberg trials, is just and necessary.

In the final analysis with students, the stress is placed on the problem of education, the bad education of fascism and Nazism, and on the complexity of the human heart. Levi was a centaur, and being centauric, so to speak, is the *humana conditio*: every human being is a centaur insofar as he or she is a hybrid of good and bad instincts, of reason and sentiments, of autonomy and dependence, of social altruism and biological egotism.

NOTES

[1]All the material published in these two anthologies was previously collected in the two-volume *Opere*, also edited by Belpoliti and published by Einaudi (1997). The first and best collection of interviews to be published was Poli and Calcagno's *Echi di una voce perduta* (1992).

[2]Examples of extended conversations and dialogues include Levi, *Conversazione* (*Conversations*); Levi and Regge; and the interviews with Greer, Roth, Grassano, and Sodi in Levi, *Conversazioni* and *Voice*.

[3]Levi's strong belief that labor is, or at least may become, a form of redemption is well known. The bricklayer Lorenzo, who had a major role in saving Levi's life in Auschwitz (as recalled in *Se questo è un uomo*), unhappy as he was to work for the Germans, did his work in earnest because, regardless of circumstances, he believed in work well done.

[4]In *A Centaur in Auschwitz*, I coined the neologism "salvaction" to capture and translate the Italian word *salvazione* and distinguish it from *salvezza* or from *redenzione* ("redemption"), to mark a difference that is present in the Italian language but absent in English (Giuliani 27–33).

At Loggerheads with *Lager* Jargon: The Untranslatable in Levi

Pietro Frassica

Prominent among Primo Levi's literary experiences are his reflections on the problem of translation. His ability to identify faults in translations and intervene with precision is a constant in his works and in the opinions expressed in the many interviews he granted (see, e.g., Beccaria; Mengaldo). His evaluation of translation problems can be applied to any type of text, beginning with the Bible. It is precisely on the translation of this fundamental text that Levi expresses some reservations in the *Dialogo* with Tullio Regge: "Not to mention the fact that if you manage to read it in the original, you can notice all the tampering it has been subjected to: the translations are in fact reworked" (3). Furthermore, for Levi, the thrill of writing is in the search for and the creation of "the right word, that is, commensurate, concise, and strong," to describe the events "with the greatest rigor and the least clutter" (*Periodic Table* 153). This need to explore various linguistic aspects of a text has generated in Levi a special attraction to writers such as Stefano D'Arrigo, Thomas Mann, Giuseppe Gioacchino Belli, Herman Melville, Carlo Porta, Isaac Babel, and François Rabelais, who, to paraphrase Levi's words in *The Search for Roots*, invented an inimitable language, making of it a new and versatile tool (178). This invention is significant as well in situations such as the concentration camps, where different languages and single words become more like animal sounds than human utterances, thus reducing, if not eliminating altogether, the possibility of real communication. The problem stems from the plurality of languages in Auschwitz, which gives rise to an inimitable language whose sounds communicate the violence of a system and contempt for man. In describing such a degrading regimen of shame, Levi asks himself, "To what degree is it legitimate to exploit violence in literature?" (*Search* 145). Certainly, the writer knows the limits, since he adds, "as soon as you cross it you fall into mortal sins, aestheticism, sadism, prostitution for the cannibalistic consumption of a certain public." These concerns make Levi a very cautious writer. At the same time, he uses his personal experience and the language born in the concentration camps to make more comprehensible the harshness and violence of the Holocaust for younger generations, who would like to better understand this tragic event (Young).

From the opening pages of Levi's *Survival in Auschwitz*, the reader is confronted with the importance of language through the emphasis the author places on the prisoners' difficulty of understanding, instead of being understood, and on the incommunicable nature of the atrocities they experience. Only by considering the language spoken in Auschwitz as a unique phenomenon can readers begin to appreciate the unimaginable horror and inhumanity in the concentration camp. Already in the first chapter, which concerns the train journey to Auschwitz, there is a marked transition toward otherness, the state that Levi feels is reserved for prisoners in the camps, a world apart from humanity. At the end of the journey Levi comments ominously, "We felt ourselves by now 'on the other side'" (14).[1] The motif of "the other side" returns throughout the book, along with the image of the barbed wire, the dividing line between the world of men and nonmen.

After a long, exhausting journey, the prisoners' most immediate need is to understand where they are and what is happening around them:

> The door opened with a crash, and the dark echoed with outlandish orders in that curt, barbaric barking of Germans in command which seems to give vent to an ancient anger. A vast platform appeared before us, lit up by reflectors. A little beyond it, a row of lorries. Then everything was silent again. Someone translated: we had to climb down with our luggage and deposit it alongside the train. (15)

But in seeing their first contacts at the camp, one has the impression that the nightmare of not understanding the orders given by the Germans and the linguistic confusion among prisoners corresponds to the nightmare of confinement and harsh regulations imposed on them. Some prisoners serve as translators in the camps. They clarify and formulate answers to the new prisoners' many questions. But in the camps, one cannot ask why. Levi knows this lesson well, having been forced to learn it a few days after his arrival, while nervously pacing the barracks to which he had been assigned. He writes, "Driven by thirst, I eyed a fine icicle outside the window, within hand's reach. I opened the window and broke off the icicle but at once a large, heavy guard prowling outside brutally snatched it away from me. 'Warum?' I asked him in my poor German. 'Hier ist kein warum' (there is no why here), he replied, pushing me inside with a shove" (24–25).

Understanding, in some ways, also means experiencing a sense of familiarity. If the Nazis allow for understanding among the prisoners, they risk reinserting them into the human world; the prisoners must constantly be reminded that they are not at home. The nagging refrain, heard over and over again by the new prisoners, incredulous at the spectacle of the events unfolding before their eyes, is, "you are not at home, this is not a sanatorium, the only exit is by way of the chimney. (What did it mean? Soon we were all to learn what it meant.)" (24).

The unanswered questions and the incomprehensible language are the emblems of a situation with no escape. Sometimes, improvised interpreters appear on the scene, but their assistance clarifies the situation only superficially. They often translate only partially, creating tension and bewilderment among the prisoners; others are of no help at all: "This Flesch, who is most unwilling to translate into Italian the hard cold German phrases and refuses to turn into German our questions because he knows that it is useless, is a German Jew of about fifty" (20). Thus there are numerous examples of nonunderstanding, of untranslatability, in the pages of Levi's book. These examples create a state of tension in the reader that reflects that of the prisoners, who wander like specters in a fog of incomprehension. They are unable to sleep, traumatized by their inability to understand the orders given to them: "One wakes up at every moment, frozen with terror, shaking in every limb, under the impression of an order shouted out by a voice full of anger in a language not understood" (56). The absurdity of the events, which are rapidly transforming the prisoners who have just arrived in the camps, is reflected in an unfamiliar language. Suddenly four men burst in with razors, soap brushes, and clippers, and the prisoners are seized and in a moment find themselves shaved and sheared without receiving any intelligible response to their many questions: "The four speak a language which does not seem of this world. It is certainly not German, for I understand a little German" (19).

At times it is not easy for the prisoners to find expressions, even in their own language, to convey their feelings of humiliation and frustration: "Then for the first time we became aware that our language lacks words to express this offense, the demolition of a man" (22). The author is very frustrated, because lack of understanding forces him to keep silent: "The confusion of languages is a fundamental component of the manner of living here: one is surrounded by a perpetual Babel, in which everyone shouts orders and threats in languages never heard before, and woe betide whoever fails to grasp the meaning" (33). Lack of understanding means lack of communication, a punishment that makes human coexistence very difficult, as witnessed by the biblical tale of Babel. Levi establishes this metaphor with the description of the tower built in the middle of Buna, the industrial factory connected with Auschwitz. As the Tower of Babel was built by deported slaves, the Carbide Tower in Auschwitz is built by the inmates: Levi brings out the variety of languages spoken there through the many names by which the prisoners refer to the bricks of the tower: "The Carbide Tower, which arises in the middle of Buna and whose top is rarely visible in the fog, was built by us. Its bricks were called: *Ziegel*, *briques*, *tegula*, *cegli*, *kamenny*, *mattoni*, *téglak*, and they were cemented by hate; hate and discord, like the Tower of Babel, and it is this that we call it: —*Babelturm*, *Bobelturm*; and in it we hate the insane dream of grandeur of our masters, their contempt for God and man, for us men" (66). Therefore, as Cesare Segre writes, the Carbide Tower is "una bestemmia di pietra" 'a stone curse' ("Primo Levi" 86; my trans.). Levi analyzes the implications of the promiscuity of languages as a linguistic barrier in "On Obscure Writing" (in *Other People's Trades*) and in *The Drowned and the Saved*. These implications are connected to the problem of translation, as Levi describes in the article "Lascipassare per Babele" (literally, "a type of passport to Babel"), later included in *L'altrui mestiere* under the title "Tradurre ed essere tradotti" ("To Translate and to Be Translated").[2] It is not by chance that this article begins with a quotation from Genesis and with the myth-curse of Babel. This theme is present throughout Levi's work, because the linguistic conflict arising from a plurality of languages tends to become political and racial. Therefore, the work of the translator is to reduce the damage of the curse of Babel. Out of context, a word can become a howl or an animalistic cry. Faced with this linguistic complexity, Levi recounts what he did to restore communication. *Survival in Auschwitz* goes therefore from a need to tell "without a real plan" to a precise construction that the chemist weighs and measures carefully, opposing the order of his literary tale to the linguistic confusion. It is perhaps this construction that gives Levi's text a kind of classical solemnity.

Though it is a long poem of a vision, consisting of fragmented episodes with scenes of violence and personal human experiences, *Survival in Auschwitz* is nevertheless structured in such a way that every element fits together. In this respect readers may recall the visit of Aeneas to Avernus and, of course, the journey of Dante and the confusion of idioms among the souls he met. Readers may also trace connections to more recent authors, such as Luigi Pirandello, for whom the same word, uttered by different persons, does not express the same feelings, as in *Six Characters*, in which the characters are distressed to realize that their words lose their meaning when spoken by the actors.[3] The characters feel trapped in a manner similar to Levi and the prisoners. In all these cases, lack of understanding and of being understood is tantamount to a lack of freedom. Given the extreme importance attached to the communicative value of language and given the fundamental impossibility of full communication, there is an enormous pressure on language. This pressure surfaces only rarely, and when it does become explicit, it betrays the immense frustration Levi obviously feels in trying to represent the conditions of atrocity. We see Levi lapsing into a deep sense of the unrepresentability of camp life after he describes the perils of beginning to write. He makes the distinction between free and enslaved language: "We say 'hunger,' we say 'tiredness,' 'fear,' 'pain,' we say 'winter' and they are different things. They are free words, created and used by free men who lived in comfort and suffering in their homes" (*Survival* 112–13).

It must have been very painful for Levi to try to express his views on these common and yet highly emotionally charged experiences. When trying to convey the nature of language in the camps, Levi makes literary references to delineate the problems he encountered. In a chapter in *The Drowned and the Saved*, ironically titled "Communicating," Levi cites Michelangelo Antonioni's film *Red Desert* to characterize the concept of "total linguistic barrier":

> I never liked the term *incommunicability*, so fashionable in the 1970s, first of all because it is a linguistic horror, and secondly for more personal reasons.
>
> In today's normal world, which by convention and contrast we call from time to time "civilized" or "free," one almost never encounters a total linguistic barrier, that is, finds oneself facing a human being with whom one must absolutely establish communication or die, and then is unable to do so.
>
> A famous but incomplete example of this is in Antonioni's film *Red Desert*, when one night the protagonist meets a Turkish sailor who knows not a word of any language but his own and tries in vain to make himself understood. Incomplete because on both sides, the sailor's as well, the will to communicate exists, or, at least, the will to reject contact is lacking.
>
> According to a theory fashionable during those years, which to me seems frivolous and irritating, "incommunicability" supposedly was an inevitable ingredient, a life sentence inherent to the human condition, particularly the life style of industrial society: we are monads, incapable of reciprocal messages, or capable only of truncated messages, false at their departure, misunderstood on their arrival. Discourse is fictitious. . . . Except for cases of pathological incapacity, one can and must communicate, and thereby contribute in a useful and easy way to the peace of others and oneself, because silence, the absence of signals, is itself a signal, but an ambiguous one, and ambiguity generates anxiety and suspicion. . . .
>
> From the standpoint of communication—indeed, of failed communication—we survivors have known a peculiar experience. It is an irksome habit of ours to intervene when someone (our children!) speaks about cold, hunger, or fatigue. What do you know about it? You should have gone through what we did. (88–89)[4]

Elsewhere Levi talks of how a new language would have been born if the camps had lasted longer. All Levi has at his disposal is the language of free men, which he cannot invest fully with a new enslaved significance. Moreover, for Levi and his unfortunate companions, to understand is not only to feel freer but to survive; therefore, they are sometimes obliged to play a perverse game. They cannot understand, though they would like to, yet they must pretend to do so.

The untranslatability of the language of the concentration camp corresponds to Levi's "disastrous" attempt to translate some verses of the *Divine Comedy* into French for Jean, a young Frenchman who wants to learn Italian. Having spoken some verses from canto 26 of the *Inferno*, known as the canto of Ulysses, Levi says: "Here I stop and try to translate. Disastrous—poor Dante and poor French! All the same, the experience seems to promise well: Jean admires the bizarre simile of the tongue and suggests the appropriate word to translate 'age-old'" (*Survival* 102). His translation is also made more difficult by the fact that he can only recall fragments of Dante's verses: "and I try, but in vain, to explain. . . . [T]here is another lacuna here, this time irreparable." He continues: "I would give today's soup to know how to connect 'the like on any day' [verses he had garbled] to the last lines. I try to reconstruct it through the rhymes, I close my eyes, I bite my fingers—but it is no use, the rest is silence" (104). The absence of communication caused by the multilingualism of the camp is compounded by Levi's mortification at his inability to recall anything other than fragments of Dante's verses. Even literature, which could have allowed him a few moments of freedom, is destined to fall miserably into the horror of the camp.

An extreme example—often quoted—of the human and linguistic drama, experienced by Levi and described in *The Reawakening* (*The Truce*), is the three-year-old Hurbinek, born clandestinely in the camp and about whom no one seemed to know anything. A child of nothingness—of death, of Auschwitz—and paralyzed from the waist down, he had not been taught how to speak. The unusual name of Hurbinek was given him by a woman prisoner who had tried to interpret, to translate the few inarticulate sounds occasionally emitted by the child. Mute before the many languages sounding through the camps, he expresses through his profound and imploring glances his intense need to speak, to shatter the tomb of his muteness. Shortly before his death he succeeds in enunciating an enigmatic message, something like "mass-klo" or "matis-klo," a sound probably belonging to one of the many languages spoken in the inferno of the camps but that no one could understand (191). Or perhaps it was simply a sound, somewhere between savage and human, and in any case relating to the primal necessities he had been denied.

At the other extreme of the narrative chiaroscuro, the clear shadows, in *The Reawakening*, yet still tied to the language barrier, we find a comic episode, which could not have happened in the camp. Levi and his companions, having been liberated, return at a snail's pace to Italy through war-devastated Eastern Europe. The train stops constantly, sometimes for days. At one such stop Levi and his friend Cesare attempt to barter six ordinary earthenware plates for a chicken. Cesare, far less inhibited than Levi, calls on mime and onomatopoeia, without realizing that these tactics also depend on cultural convention. Cesare produces a terrible imitation of chicken behavior, crouching, scratching with one foot and then the other, pecking here and there with his hand. Between one imprecation and the next, Cesare also cackles, "Coccodè, coccodè," as Italian chickens do, but this interpretation of chicken speech is highly conventional;

it is current only in Italy and is not found elsewhere. Only when the narrator draws a chicken complete with an egg is an old lady enlightened, and, radiant, she translates, "Kura! Kuritsa!" ([Summit, 1986] 300).

It is also appropriate to recall that Levi's sense of humor emerges even at those terrible moments in which the Italian language was most debased by fascist laws and repressions. Under Mussolini, for example, foreign words and phrases were not permitted. In 1942, Levi had just graduated from the University of Turin and was looking for work, although the racial laws against Jews frustrated his attempts. But one day he received a telephone call from a manager offering him a job:

> I was futilely looking when one morning, a very rare event, I was called to the mine's telephone: from the other end of the line a Milanese voice, which seemed to me crude and energetic, and which said that it belonged to a Dr. Martini, summoned me to an appointment on the following Sunday at the Hotel Suisse in Turin, without vouchsafing me the luxury of any details. But he had said "Hotel Suisse" and not "Albergo Svizzera" as a loyal citizen would be obliged to say: at that time, which was the time of Starace, one was very attentive to such piddling details, and one's ears were expert at intercepting certain nuances.
>
> In the foyer (oh, pardon me, in the lobby, which isn't a French word) of the Hotel Suisse, an anachronistic oasis of plush upholstery, velvets, shadows, and draperies, Dr. Martini, who was prevalently a *commendatore*, as I had learned just before from the doorman, was waiting for me. (*Periodic Table* 109–10)[5]

The writer in all his work shows a special interest in the correspondence between language and historical and cultural identity. The linguistic complexity of the camps, which puts Levi in contact with a variety of Jewish languages and dialects, generates some very interesting observations. He is particularly attracted to Yiddish and its variations, as demonstrated in the novel *If Not Now, When?* and in his profound analysis of Judeo-Piedmontese in *The Periodic Table*. In the chapter referring to the conversation of the old cobbler ("Arsenic"), Levi apologizes for its being "a trifle faded due to the translation from Piedmontese, an essentially spoken language" (172). Beyond the fact that translation cannot always adequately represent the original, it is evident for the reader that though Levi writes in but one language, his associative and auditory experience is certainly that of many different peoples and is reflected in the many languages spoken in the camps.

The point of departure for Levi's linguistic investigation always remains the *Lager*. Even in *The Periodic Table*, written thirty years after his experience in the concentration camp, Levi still seems to be influenced by the complex linguistic experience of Auschwitz. He reminisces in the chapter "Potassium":

> In substance it was a radio-receiving apparatus, built to reveal the slightest differences in frequency; and in fact, it went howlingly out of tune and barked like a watchdog simply if the operator shifted in his chair or moved a hand, or if someone just came into the room. Besides, at certain hours of the day, it revealed a whole intricate universe of mysterious messages, Morse tickings, modulated hisses, and deformed, mangled human voices, which pronounced sentences in incomprehensible languages, or others in Italian, but they were senseless sentences, in code. It was the radiophonic Babel of the war, messages of death transmitted by ships or planes from God knows whom, beyond the mountains and the sea. (55)

It is in the concentration camps that the linguistic barrier, which the prisoners associate with their sentence and the silence of death, is made concrete, and its enormity pervades the chapter "The Drowned and the Saved," in *Survival in Auschwitz*. The subject is analyzed even more profoundly by Levi in the chapter "Communicating," in *The Drowned and the Saved*, where he shows how the linguistic barrier of the camps was already a veritable death sentence for most of the prisoners:

> The greater part of the prisoners who did not understand German—that is, almost all the Italians—died during the first ten to fifteen days after their arrival: at first glance, from hunger, cold, fatigue, and disease; but after a more attentive examination, due to insufficient information. If they had been able to communicate with their more experienced companions, they would have been able to orient themselves better: to learn, first of all, how to procure clothing, shoes, illegal food, how to avoid the harsher labor and the often lethal encounters with the SS, how to handle the inevitable illnesses without making fatal mistakes. (93)

To know German may have meant life, or at least an extension of it. Levi continues:

> My Italian companions did not understand it, that is, almost all with exception of a few from Trieste were drowning one by one in the stormy sea of not-understanding: they did not know what the orders meant, they received slaps and kicks without comprehending why. The camp's rudimentary ethic stipulated that a blow must in some way be justified, so as to facilitate the establishment of the transgression-punishment-repentance parabola; therefore, often the *Kapo* or his substitutes accompanied the blow with a grunt: "You know why?" which was followed by a summary "communication of the crime." But for the newly deaf and dumb the ceremony was useless. They instinctively sought refuge in corners to protect their backs; aggression could come from any direction. They looked

> around them with bewildered eyes, like trapped animals, and that is what they had in fact become. (96)

"Communication," as Levi writes, "generates information and . . . without information you cannot live" (93).

According to Levi, there was a sense that for the German-speaking prisoners the violence committed against language in the camps was a greater desecration than the physical violence committed against the prisoners. And perhaps it was even worse for those prisoners, like the philosopher Jean Améry, who were intellectuals and thus more dependent on language as a means of thinking and expression. In *The Drowned and the Saved* Levi writes:

> Améry-Mayer also affirms that he suffered from the mutilation of the language that I described in Chapter 4: and yet his language was German. He suffered from it in a different way than we who, not knowing German, were reduced to the condition of deaf mutes: in a way, if I may put it like this, that was spiritual rather than material. He suffered from it *because* German was his language, because he *was* a philologist who loved his language, just as a sculptor would suffer at seeing one of his statues befouled or mutilated. Therefore the suffering of the intellectuals was different in this case from that of the uncultivated foreigner: for the former the fact that the German of the Lager was a language he did not understand endangered his life; for the latter, it was a barbaric jargon that he did understand but that scorched his mouth when he tried to speak it. One was a deportee, the other a stranger in his own country. (97)

The prisoners' inability to understand orders only reinforced the hatred of the jailers, who saw it as a mixture of disobedience and—what for them was unpardonable—stupidity. For the ignorant man it is impossible to conceive of a language that is different from his own. Besides this, as encouraged by Nazi propaganda, the Germans were under the illusion that their language was culturally superior.

The only universal language is that of violence: not by chance the *trunchen* was known as *der Dolmetscher*, the translator or interpreter. Levi realized that it was imperative for him to learn the kind of German that was spoken in the camps. As a student a few years before his imprisonment, he had learned some German words, "[f]or the sole purpose of understanding textbooks of chemistry and physics: certainly not to actively transmit my thought or understand the spoken language" (95). It was not enough. Levi writes:

> I implored . . . an Alsatian to give me a private and accelerated course, spread over brief lessons administered in a whisper, between the moment of curfew and the moment when we went to sleep, lessons to be recom-

> pensed with bread, since there was no other currency. He accepted, and I believe that never was bread better spent. He explained to me what the roars of the *Kapos* or SS meant, the foolish or ironic mottoes written in Gothic letters on the hut's roof trusses, the meaning of the colors of the triangles we wore on our chests above the registration number. So I realized that the German of the camps—skeletal, howled, studded with obscenities and imprecations—was only vaguely related to the precise, austere language of my chemistry books, or to the melodious, refined German of Heine's poetry that Clara, a classmate of mine, used to recite to me. (97)

In "The Gypsy," included in the collection of short stories *Moments of Reprieve*, written between 1975 and 1981, we find the results of the German class Levi took in the *Lager*:

> I had gotten my German in the Camp, and, without my realizing it, it reproduced the drab, vulgar barracks jargon. I did not know many terms, exactly those needed to express feelings. I felt inept, as if I had to carve the letter in stone. My bunkmate patiently waited until I was finished, then he said something in a language I did not understand. I asked him in German what he wanted, and he showed me his form, which was blank, and pointed to mine, which was covered with writing. In short, he was asking me to write for him. Not only did he not know how to write in German; he didn't know how to write at all. He was a gypsy, had been born in Spain, and had wandered about in Germany, Austria, and the Balkans, only to end up in the Nazis' dragnets in Hungary. He introduced himself formally: Grigo, his name was Grigo, he was nineteen, and he begged me to write to his fiancée. (68–69)

Only years later did Levi realize that the camp's German was a language apart, a language tied to a specific place and time, and that, as a language that wrought destruction, it must also disappear. The attempt by the Nazis to destroy the evidence of the words that might be brought against them is a final outrage to Levi.

Where violence is inflicted on man, it is also inflicted on language. In this sense, Levi, in the chapter "Communicating," in *The Drowned and the Saved*, gives several examples that indicate how different the German language spoken in the camps was from ordinary German. For instance, *to eat* was rendered by *fressen*, a verb that in proper German is applied only to animals. In "Letters from Germans," the last chapter of *The Drowned and the Saved*, Levi talks about the German translation of *Survival in Auschwitz* and his long epistolary discussion with the translator, Heinz Riedt. He was a man of letters and refined education and did in fact know the German of the barracks (he had a few months of military service), but "he did not know the degraded, often satanically ironic jargon of the concentration camps" (172). The translator found Nazism repugnant; during the war, after feigning illness, he had managed to spend his convalescence studying Italian at the University of Padua and eventually joined the Italian resistance. Each letter contains a list of proposals and counterproposals, which are an invaluable resource and a philological model for students of the Holocaust. As Levi writes:

> I indicated a thesis to him, one suggested to me by the acoustic memory; . . . he presented me with an antithesis: "this is not good German, today's readers would not understand it"; . . . finally we arrived at the synthesis, that is, a compromise. . . . I wanted that in the book, particularly in its German guise, nothing should be lost of its harshness and the violence inflicted on the language. (172)

Levi had made an effort to reproduce the language as best as he could in his original Italian. What he was asking for was not a translation but rather a restoration: "a retroversion to the language in which events had taken place and to which they belonged" (173). Finally the translator understood Levi's feelings, and the author accepted that his acoustic memories of the camps represented a language that was not completely translatable. Author and translator realized that the language created within the German language was generated by an unprecedented extreme situation; the language therefore had to vanish along with the camps. Author and translator compromise: very often translation and compromise are synonymous, and so Levi's description of the camps comes to represent the struggle for faithful language. In one sense, this language must be important to Levi merely because it exists. The words on the page are a concrete defiance of the Nazi attempt to destroy every type of evidence. They provide testimony of a period the Nazis intended to shroud in silence.

Levi, as a man of science, had his own particular view of literature, which makes it difficult to place Levi the writer in any school or literary tendency: his singular and unmistakable characteristics make him unique in the panorama of twentieth-century Italian literature. Levi brings to his writing, particularly in his first two books, a scientific training and understanding from which other Italian writers cannot draw (Mengaldo). In this light the special language of scientific inquiry becomes parallel to the special language of the camps.

Levi saw translation as a transparent reading, in the sense given by Walter Benjamin, who considers true translation to be that which must never hide the original, just as scientific language must never hide a scientific truth. Only in this way can the "pure language," that is, its incommunicable nucleus, be preserved and transmitted. What Levi involuntarily wishes for, however, is an act of translation that is also an act of transgression because it attempts the impossible: a translation into a language that is synonymous with death, heard only by the inmates of the camps, and that has been reduced to ashes along with them.

NOTES

[1]This and all quotations from *Survival in Auschwitz* are taken from the 1987 Macmillan translation.

[2]This article, like many others from *L'altrui mestiere*, was not included in the English translation (*Other People's Trades*).

[3]In Pirandello's *Six Characters in Search of an Author*, the Father argues that the different meanings each person assigns to words makes communication difficult, if not impossible: "But can't you see that all the trouble lies here! In the words! All of us have a world full of things! And how can we understand one another, sir, if in the words I speak I put the meaning and the value of things as I myself see them, while the one who listens inevitably takes them according to the meaning and the value which he has in himself of the world he has inside of *himself*. We think we understand each other, we never understand one another" (224).

[4]This and all quotations from *The Drowned and the Saved* are taken from the 1988 Summit translation.

[5]Levi adds a footnote to this passage: "A[chille] Starace was for many years secretary of the Fascist National Party. He distinguished himself by the stupid zeal with which he strove to 'purify' the customs of the Italians, combating the use of foreign words (in fact, such words as 'hotel' or 'foyer')" (110).

Teaching Levi in an Advanced Language Course

Letizia Modena

In *Remapping the Foreign Language Curriculum: An Approach through Multiple Literacies*, Janet Swaffar and Katherine Arens press for a rethinking of the curricular imperatives and methodologies of foreign language teaching at the college level. In particular, they advocate a remapping of the foreign language curriculum that does not isolate language courses from content courses but instead integrates the two in a holistic project (8). In my advanced Italian language course, Conversation and Composition, I use selected works by Primo Levi to help bridge the gap between language and content.

Levi serves as an exemplary introduction to Italian literature in general, because of his international renown and because of the fundamental human issues that his works raise. Moreover, because his prose is elegant and subtle, yet clear and concise, it both enhances reading and oral comprehension and allows students to develop their writing and speaking proficiency. Why do I choose a single author to integrate language and content? Anthologies or readers are by definition a collection of literary and cultural readings. Yet even when the selection is remarkable in scope, it is not ideally suited to my advanced conversation and composition course, which is not a literature or culture course: students have had only five semesters of Italian (two semesters of both elementary and intermediate Italian and one semester of advanced). The goals of an advanced conversation and composition course do not allow most of us to properly contextualize the materials and their authors, much less to give students the background necessary to appreciate Italian literature and culture. Teaching from a reader implies switching from one short story to the next, from one author to the next, from one time frame and topic to the next. The result is that students and instructors often get a sense of fragmentation. By moving away from the traditional division between language and literature courses, however, and organizing readings, compositions, and oral comprehension and conversation activities primarily around a single author, we can avoid that loss of continuity and balance in an advanced language course.

My class focuses primarily on Levi's *Se questo è un uomo*. Though this text is challenging even for native speakers of Italian, my students' familiarity with the Holocaust can mitigate some of their linguistic difficulties. As Swaffar and Arens note, "From the reader's standpoint, interest, familiarity with the topic or with the context of the text, prior knowledge and ability to activate a schema that helps organize incoming information and fix it in memory all make a text more readable" (57–58). Having college-level students read a text about a topic they know, even if it appears to exceed their linguistic competence, is one way of integrating language and content. In such instances, as Swaffar and Arens observe, students fall back on their cognitive knowledge to compensate for their linguistic limitations in the target language (16). The readings for my course also include three stories from Levi's *Storie naturali*: *La bella addormentata nel frigo*, "Trattamento di quiescenza," and "Versamina." In what follows I address several language-teaching applications of these works and detail various activities tailored to the language-class instructor.

To expose my students to literature, I use a prereading, or introduction, that creates "a framework of expectation of general and prior knowledge that will guide the readers' first work with the text" (Swaffar and Arens 72). Thereafter, to enhance reading comprehension as well as writing and oral skills, I have students participate in various activities, such as writing brief summaries of the assigned section that are subsequently presented orally in class, reporting ten key phrases that faithfully represent the section read, or answering comprehension questions. In the final phase, students work on some of the main conceptual focuses of the selection to generate their own writings. At this point, I ask students to rework and paraphrase specific passages; reflect on the author's ideological or philosophical outlook in relation to their own life experiences; and, whenever possible, come up with new scenes or scenarios, writing as one of the characters or role-playing in class.

Se questo è un uomo

One aim of my advanced conversation and composition course is to introduce students to a broad range of writing, and *Se questo è un uomo* allows them to analyze a writer's techniques in different registers and genres (descriptive, narrative, argumentative, expository). I select excerpts that I consider readable at their level and provide them with a glossary. By translating into English the opening poem, "Shemà" (7),[1] students simultaneously reflect on the contents of the book, Levi's determination to preserve the Holocaust in the collective memory, and the poem as a language unit. The use of the imperative ("considerate," "meditate") is a clear example of how a verb's mood or tense embodies content: in this case, Levi's command to reflect on the words of the poem and decide if the desperate state there portrayed can still be considered human—ultimately to decide "se questo è un uomo" 'if this is a man.' Alongside the poem, students may download Alberto Gozzi's 1985 interview with Levi, which is readily available online ("Primo Levi si racconta"). The audio file of this interview can be used as an oral comprehension exercise; it also serves to familiarize students with Levi's literary work. In the interview, Levi reflects on what constitutes a public intellectual, the value of testimonial literature, his lack of hatred in *Se questo è un uomo*, and even his "naturalistica" 'naturalistic' curiosity about human nature.

From the preface of *Se questo è un uomo*, I invite students to think about Levi's claim that the concentration camp is nothing other than the idea that "ogni straniero è nemico" 'every stranger is an enemy' realized in all its consequences (9; 9). This leads to class discussions that go beyond the tortured and murdered Jews of World War II to embrace other ethnic groups in contemporary Italy: specifically, the debates on immigration and how Italy's development into a multiethnic and multiracial society is reviving prejudice and bigotry buried beneath the surface of national unity. I have students read newspaper articles on acts of intolerance and violence committed against recent immigrants—recent "strangers"—then bring written summaries to class.

As a prereading activity, I give students an excerpt from the first chapter, "Il viaggio" ("The Journey"), along with a glossary, and have them reconstruct the train's itinerary on a map, starting from Fossoli, Modena, and heading north, crossing the border via Trento-Bolzano-Brennero, to reach Austria, the Czech Republic, and Poland, en route to Auschwitz. Comprehension questions lead to an understanding of the text that should be neither too general nor too detailed: it is enough for students to be able to index the main outlines of the text. After the comprehension questions, students work on the main conceptual focus of the selection to produce their own text. Within the excerpt, I have students concentrate on the passage in which Levi asserts that perfect happiness is unrealizable and, likewise, that perfect unhappiness is equally unattainable (14–15). I ask them, What things, according to Levi, make these opposites impossible to achieve? Do you agree with Levi's assertion? Do you think it's possible to be perfectly happy or perfectly unhappy? I then prompt them to describe a concrete situation that supports their own opinion on the topic.

In the second chapter, "Sul fondo" ("On the Bottom"), Levi describes how all personal items were taken away upon his arrival at Auschwitz, and he compels us again in the imperative:

> Ma consideri ognuno, quanto valore, quanto significato è racchiuso anche nelle piú piccole nostre abitudini quotidiane, nei cento oggetti nostri che il piú umile mendicante possiede: un fazzoletto, una vecchia lettera, la fotografia di una persona cara. Queste cose sono parte di noi, quasi come membra del nostro corpo. (23)
>
> But consider what value, what meaning is enclosed even in the smallest of our daily habits, in the hundred possessions which even the poorest beggar owns: a handkerchief, an old letter, the photo of a cherished person. These things are part of us, almost like limbs of our body. (27)

The concentration camp transforms people into hollow men, for being deprived of everything they possess (home, daily routine, clothes—everything they hold dear) deprives them of their very selves. Whenever I teach this chapter, students have actively responded to Levi's command, reflecting both in class (orally, in pairs) and subsequently at home (in writing) on their most cherished daily habits, possessions, and memories; why they are important; and in what measure they make up who they are and distinguish them from others.

Before tackling the chapter "Il canto di Ulisse" ("The Canto of Ulysses"), I prepare a multisectional summary that clarifies what students are going to read, to avoid cognitive overload. In the first section, students get to know Levi and Pikolo, the task that they have been assigned (the walk to get soup for the group), and the means by which they transform the occasion into a special unforgettable experience (their conversation about Dante's *Inferno* 26, known as the canto of Ulysses). Students come to identify personally with how the two men create a meaningful, unexpected, and sanity-saving friendship and intellectual exchange even under the most improbable of circumstances. I ask students, working in pairs, to discuss what they do when they are surrounded on all sides by sadness, fear, or other emotions. What do they think they would do in Pikolo and Levi's shoes? How would they spend one hour, if they had only one hour of relative freedom every day, like Levi and Pikolo had? In the second section of my summary, students read about the canto at the center of Levi and Pikolo's conversations. I underline the fact that Pikolo has been to Italy, likes it, and wants to learn Italian, just like they do. Pikolo is a young, passionate, and inquisitive traveler, and it is not a coincidence that Levi chooses to start Pikolo's language lessons with the words of Dante's Ulysses, one of the most curious and daring navigators of all times. This second section paraphrases and summarizes Ulysses's speech to Dante and emphasizes that Dante's Ulysses is a person eager to explore the unknown, a symbol that is still pervasive today. Indeed, on the launchpad at the Kennedy Space Station, there are inscribed the verses from Dante's *Inferno* that Levi recites to Pikolo:

> Considerate la vostra semenza:
> Fatti non foste per viver come bruti,
> Ma per seguir virtute e conoscenza. (102)
>
> Think of your breed; for brutish ignorance
> Your mettle was not made; you were made men,
> To follow after knowledge and excellence. (113)

As part of their homework, I expect students to paraphrase and explain what the verses mean to them. In addition, I ask them to identify the Ulysses figure in books, films, video games, or television shows they know and to explain what qualities it takes to be an explorer or some other figure who pushes the limits and survives.

When students actually read Levi's chapter on canto 26, they focus on the last half and meet outside class in discussion groups. At this point, they are already familiar with the content of the excerpt and its main vocabulary. I help my students understand that comprehension is about getting the main idea:

they do not need to understand every word; they need only to be able to locate clusters of meaning by identifying the words (cognates or others) they readily understand. The words "splendore," "tiepido," "estiva," and "chiaro," for example, can help students determine what the weather was like that day; the seemingly contradictory "lavoro abbastanza faticoso" and "gradevole marcia" point to whether the task was unbearable; "camminando" and "parlavamo" indicate what Levi and Pikolo are doing (100). I ask students to synthetically annotate the key points of each paragraph and to summarize the episode while making use of the new words they have learned. In another discussion-group meeting, students are asked to prepare a brief report on Dante, the *Divine Comedy*, and the *Inferno*'s place within it. By reading Levi's "Il canto di Ulisse," students experience the rewarding feeling of having dealt, although still in a language class, with two of the most hallowed and resonating exemplars of Italian literature and culture.

An in-class activity draws out the parallel I have already established between Pikolo and the American student of Italian. Working in groups, students compare Levi's quotations from Dante to an English translation of the same verses, *Inferno* 26.85–142. Levi and Pikolo exemplify a communicative situation between foreigners. This activity requires that students tackle Dante's verses in search of recognizable words ("fiamma," "vento," "mare") and locate the English translation. Once they have accomplished this first step, they can derive from the translation the meaning of other words in Ulysses's speech. I make it clear that they are working on language and translation just as Levi is doing with Pikolo and that, like Pikolo, they are making an effort to comprehend and learn Italian. The enterprise can at times be "[d]isastroso" or "promett[ere] bene" (101). It can be necessary to slow down and start again—"Pikolo mi prega di ripetere," Levi writes (102). But, in the end, the message gets across and human communication is worth the effort: Pikolo "ha ricevuto il messaggio, ha sentito che lo riguarda."

To expand their vocabulary and reflect on linguistic nuances, students engage in translation workshops, in which they compare the Italian text and Stuart Woolf's translation in *Survival in Auschwitz*. With the use of a dictionary, students understand and discuss the translator's lexical choices as well as stylistic issues such as the flexible positioning of adjectives in Italian and their effect. Pier Vincenzo Mengaldo's "La lingua e la scrittura" ("Language and Writing") is a good source of ideas for the professor who intends to create translation workshop activities. Since Levi was a translator, I think it is important to make the students acquainted with the intrinsic difficulties of translation through a brief selection of Levi's thoughts in "Tradurre ed essere tradotti" ("Translating and Being Translated"), in *L'altrui mestiere*. I suggest using the opening passages of "Il canto di Ulisse" as an excerpt for comparison. I invite students to begin by reflecting on the word order, use of tenses, and lexical accuracy of Woolf's translation. Next, they work in groups to compare the original Italian text, their own translations, and the choices made by the translator. Looking at the sentence "Oscillò la scaletta di corda che pendeva dal portello: qualcuno veniva" (98), for example, which Woolf translates as "The rope-ladder hanging from the manhole began to sway: someone was coming" (109), stimulates observations on word order, the use of the gerund "hanging," and the rendering of the preterite "oscillò" with "began to sway" and the imperfect "veniva" with the past continuous "was coming." When we read that Pikolo is "scaltro e fisicamente robusto" (99) and compare this with the English "shrewd and physically robust" (110), we go over the possible English translations of "scaltro" and their connotations and discuss whether "robust" in English is used as frequently as "robusto" in Italian. Throughout these in-class translation workshops, I strive to make my students become conscious of the fact that a book represents, through words alone, an entire world, and oftentimes the more precise the terminology, the more precise the corresponding material reality depicted in a book. Such is the case with Levi's writing, which I consider to be among the most lexically rich and precise in all of Italian literature. Thus I ask students, Does Woolf's choice of "bowl" to translate "gamella" do justice to Levi's connotative option (109; 98)?

Lexical enrichment can be achieved through other activities in addition to the translation workshops. I frequently ask students to explain selected words in *Se questo è un uomo* through paraphrase and have them prepare oral presentations on the book based on target vocabulary. Numerous lexical exercises can be built up from readily available electronic materials. I recommend the Web site *Minerva* (www.minerva.unito.it), which offers a detailed yet accessible biography of Levi and excerpts from *Se questo è un uomo*, *La tregua*, *Il sistema periodico*, and *La ricerca delle radici* (all under the heading "Omaggio a Primo Levi"). Instructors may ask students to use these sources to do lexical searches aimed at verifying grammatical functions. I might ask students to search for "uno" in the chapter "Il viaggio" and then reflect on the findings and explain their raison d'être, whether as an indefinite article; as part of the indefinite pronouns or adjectives "ognuno," "nessuno," "qualcuno," "ciascuno"; or in expressions such as "poco sapevamo l'uno dell'altro," "uno per uno," "ad uno ad uno."

Storie naturali

Instructors who wish to spread shorter readings across the semester, without losing the coherence and balance mentioned earlier, may wish to integrate selections from Levi's *Storie naturali* into their upper-level language courses. I begin by telling my students that in many of the stories, Levi explores the human reaction to an imaginary device and the human moral choice regarding its use. In *La bella addormentata nel frigo* ("Sleeping Beauty in the Fridge"; 89–107), for example, Levi imagines what people might do with a machine that allows human beings to enter into a state of hibernation. A group of friends gathers to witness the defrosting of Patricia, a young woman who went into hibernation

163 years earlier and who proves to be an invaluable source of historical information when she occasionally awakens. The friends, captivated by her unchanging beauty, respond to her presence in different, and all too human, ways.

I begin by guiding students to a basic understanding of the plot. Next, I have them work in groups with specific sections, to shorten and simplify some of the interlocutors' utterances. Finally, they perform in class their own sketch of *La bella addormentata nel frigo*, engaging in a multiple-ending activity whereby they imagine different outcomes for the characters and speculate about Patricia's destiny. A thirty-minute audiovisual recording of a performance of the play is available on the *Rai Teche* Web site and can be used as a pedagogical resource for listening and comprehension exercises and, even more usefully, as a model for students' performances.

Another selection from *Storie naturali*, "Trattamento di quiescenza" ("Retirement Benefits"; 163–83), is an excellent source of language-acquisition activities and represents what Ernesto Ferrero characterizes as a summoning of virtual reality and its perils (Introduzione xiii). I have students read Levi's description of the total recorder (166–67), the virtual-reality device that he imagined in the 1960s and that we have enjoyed since the 1990s. Levi's total recorder allows users to relive the lives of others, experiencing other people's sensorial experiences in given situations. The science-fiction angle provided by this short story may be creatively exploited through a wide range of activities. Students may read brief passages, such as the one where the protagonist uses the total recorder to experience firsthand the joyous energy of a soccer player about to score. Another virtual-reality film surveys the physical and emotional experience of a first-generation Italian American who gets into a fight with people who harass him because of his origins. This excerpt opens up to an in-class conversation on ethnic and racial strife in the United States, Italian immigrants and their hardships, and the theme mentioned earlier, "every stranger is an enemy." Afterward, students can produce their own virtual-reality descriptions, focusing, like Levi, on sensorial and emotional perceptions, or follow the titles that Levi suggests for the virtual-reality experiences.

In "Versamina" (78–88), the third and final selection from the *Storie naturali* that I teach in my advanced conversation and composition course, Levi tells the story of Kleber, a scientist who invented a chemical derivative to turn pain into pleasure. Kleber tests this chemical on animals, which begin to seek pleasure from activities that before had caused them pain, and the animals kill themselves in the process. I give my students a synopsis of the short story that contextualizes the excerpts they will read. The comprehension of the synopsis is followed by a reading of the sections on the animals' reactions to the substance (83–84). As dogs refuse meat in favor of lettuce, flirt with chickens and cats, and growl at the trees, the story turns upside-down all common expectations, in a Shakespearean reversal: "fair is foul, and foul is fair," concludes Levi (88), quoting *Macbeth*. Such a reversal can be exploited for grammar lessons; for example,

I might ask students to conjure up other topsy-turvy situations, using "piacere" in structures such as "al cane non piace più litigare con i gatti; gli piace di più corteggiarli." In addition, the situation lends itself easily to a review of conditional clauses: "se un bambino prendesse quella sostanza chimica, riderebbe quando cade e si fa male e piangerebbe quando riceve un gioco in regalo"; "se noi studenti prendessimo quella sostanza chimica, cosa ci piacerebbe e cosa ci dispiacerebbe?" (85). Another interesting and readable section in "Versamina" is on the fate of the scientist, who cannot resist the temptation of turning pain into pleasure and becomes addicted to the drug (86–87). The selections also constitute a useful review of imperfect and past-perfect verb tenses.

Altogether the passages from "Versamina" create a space for debate on scientific progress and its dark side, on such issues as bioethics or animal rights versus medical benefits from experimenting on animals. Equally stimulating as a basis for class conversation and written work are Levi's concluding remarks on the necessity of pain: "il dolore non si può togliere, non si deve, perché è il nostro guardiano" (87); "Non si può sopprimerlo, farlo tacere, perché è tutt'uno con la vita, ne é il custode" (88). As oral or written practice, students may be invited to justify or to dispute Levi's affirmations. If this short story and *Se questo è un uomo* are taught during the same semester, as I have done, instructors may ask students to link "Versamina" to Levi's earlier reflections on the impossibility of complete happiness or complete unhappiness.

An advanced Italian language course organized around the works of Levi lessens the gap between language courses and upper-division work in literature or cultural studies. "[A] pedagogy that integrates language and content issues," as Swaffar and Arens put it, "ease[s] students' transition from lower-division work with tasks and tests tailored to meet their learning level" (18, 14). At the same time, I am convinced that my presenting intellectually challenging materials to students while I am teaching them the Italian language decreases the likelihood that later courses for advanced students or majors will "scare students away" (14). In other words, students in my advanced conversation and composition course are less afraid to face the demanding texts that characterize upper-level curricula in most Italian programs. Ultimately, the integration of content and language in advanced language courses should also help increase the number of minors or majors in Italian.

Through comments made in class and in their written evaluations, my students have expressed their pride and joy at realizing they could read in Italian an author like Levi, whose works enjoy universal acclaim. They also acknowledged that the course had greatly expanded their lexical ability and that they were highly motivated to continue their Italian studies. There is one fundamental aspect of Levi's writings that students grasped, and that fits well within the focus of this course: his ability to logically argue his points, his linguistic and structural precision and clarity. Students enjoyed and identified with Levi's love for life, his insistence on the value of remembering, his relentless exploration of human nature, and his imagination. Such intimate, active empathy made them more engaged than they would normally be when expressing their ideas, especially in writing at home. Integrating Levi's works into my advanced Italian language course has taught me that the greater the students' respect for the subject of the course, the greater their sense of responsibility and dedication to it.

NOTE

[1] All references to *Se questo è un uomo* are to the 2005 Einaudi edition; all references to *Survival in Auschwitz* are to the 1996 Touchstone translation.

Translation Matters: Levi, Translation, and Holocaust Testimony

Lina Insana

The emerging and fertile field of translation studies can illuminate our understanding of Primo Levi's testimonial and literary project by recasting the survivor's transmission of testimony as a complex process of textual and experiential translation.[1] Whether we define the source text as the historical event of Auschwitz (as Shoshana Felman writes, "History is the 'original,' the writings—its translations" [40]); as a pivotal canto of Dante's *Inferno*; as a repeated fragment of Samuel Taylor Coleridge's *Rime of the Ancient Mariner*; or as Franz Kafka's *Der Prozeß* (*The Trial*—on which Levi came to project a constellation of Holocaust problematics), Levi's testimonial project is consistently and closely bound up with practices of, the figuration of, and meditations on *translatio*: the "carrying over" from one spatial, temporal, conceptual, linguistic zone to another. Levi's transmissions of these source texts, variously defined, represent moments of profound meditation on the condition of the survivor, sites of reflection on the most traumatic aspects of persecution, survival, and witnessing. It is within frameworks of translation, for example, that Levi explores the narrative model and cultural touchstone of Dante, the figure of Ulysses as a figure of the persecuted European Jew, the traumatic reoccurrence of survivor guilt, and the ultimate contagion of Auschwitz. That Levi's renderings are often marked by underminings, omissions, and even outright inversions of the original text should not surprise us; indeed, it is Levi's attempt to reverse the corrupt source text of Auschwitz that restores to him the subjecthood and psychological agency necessary to bear witness in the first place.

Roberto Benigni's now famous staging of Guido's simultaneous (mis)interpretation for his son, Giosué, in the film *La vita è bella* (*Life Is Beautiful*) is emblematic of this process and its implications, for better and for worse, and can powerfully illustrate the intersecting territories of Holocaust and translation studies. Reflecting the polarization of this film's viewing public, university students typically either love this scene, in which Guido misinterprets a German official's orders to the newly arrived group of prisoners, or hate it. A structured discussion of the scene, guided by the ethical implications of translation rather than a thematic or historical approach, can help a class plot out the parameters of Holocaust representation and testimonial transmission and establish contexts for fruitful comparison of texts. What is at stake in Guido's mistranslation of the Nazi official's barking orders? What should be translated and what should not? According to what moral system are these decisions made or interrogated? How does Guido shape his son's understanding of the Holocaust through his mistranslation? How might Giosué figure the viewer's tabula rasa naïveté regarding the brutality of camp realities, and how does this bear on the version of events that is filtered down to us by Giosué's point of view? Is Giosué's (and, by extension, the viewer's) understanding of the Nazi Final Solution unduly simplified by this approach? In this context, Guido's transgressive translation performance might be seen as indicative of a certain strategy of accommodation,[2] directed both at Giosué and at the uninitiated viewer-witness that he figures within the story; it might be seen as an indictment of the absurdity of the Nazi order (Marcus, "'Me lo dici'"); and it might also represent a different key to the film's general interpretation, in which *La vita è bella* renders a faithful cinematic "translation" of the key texts of the Holocaust memoir tradition: Elie Wiesel's *Night* and Levi's *Se questo è un uomo* (*Survival in Auschwitz*).[3]

The translation studies approach to Holocaust representation, which understands translation to be a metaphor for the transmission of the Holocaust source text, offers a pedagogically rich framework that encourages students of Levi and Holocaust testimony to reflect not only on the complexity of processes of survivor witnessing but also on the mechanisms by which first-person narratives are disseminated both across languages (interlingual translation, or translation proper in Jakobson's terms) and across systems of signification (intersemiotic translation). For the student of Levi, translation also offers a schema within which to understand the importance of intertextuality and citation in his Holocaust narrative (Belpoliti, "Se questo"; Cavaglion; Usher), especially in developing a stable of viable literary and cultural model in the face of unexampled atrocities and as a practice that figures the survivor's struggle to overcome challenges of expression, representation, and transmission. Finally, as we move farther and farther away from Levi's 1987 death, translation studies positions us to confront a constellation of contemporary issues in Holocaust representation, from theatrical and cinematic refractions of survivor narratives (e.g., Sher's portrayal in Wilson's *Primo* and Rosi's *La tregua*) to the entire field of Holocaust postmemory (e.g., Ferrario and Belpoliti's documentary *La strada di Levi*).[4]

Translation's force as both a metaphor for the transmissive impulse of the survivor and a theoretical paradigm for the challenges of testimony is equaled by its undeniable practicality, making it a broad and malleable pedagogical tool in classes of all levels. My graduate students have benefited from exploring translation studies' implications for the analysis of Holocaust literature. In particular, Walter Benjamin's canonical essay "The Task of the Translator" is a point of entry into the idea that multiple linguistic renderings of the same referent collectively move toward a kind of pure, sacred language and thus work together to counteract the fragmentation of Babel. This notion echoes, at the linguistic level, the analysis of Holocaust literature scholars such as Alvin Rosenfeld, for whom the study of Holocaust literature must seek to collect

> the shards and fragments that reveal, in their separateness and brokenness, the uncountable small tragedies that together add up to something

> larger than the tragic sense implies. If every broken head is a fragment of divinity . . . then the most we can do as readers intent on glimpsing something close to wholeness is to assemble some of the shattered pieces. (33–34)

It also resonates strongly with a recurrent imagistic trope in Levi's Holocaust writings, that of Auschwitz as Babel, a site of human arrogance, linguistic alienation, and the death of communication.

Just as one survivor's testimony calls out for the testimony of the aggregate survivor community, so does the fragmented language of Auschwitz—what Levi calls *Lagerjargon*—seek completion and complementarity through the multiplicity of interlingual translation. This is a movement that Levi performatively stages twice within the pages of *Se questo è un uomo*, first with the bread (Benjamin also uses the example of bread in "Task") that acts as the camp's principal currency: "entro cinque minuti inizia la distribuzione del pane, del pane-Brot-Broit-chleb-pain-lechem-kenyér, del sacro blocchetto grigio che sembra gigantesco in mano del tuo vicino, e piccolo da piangere in mano tua" 'within five minutes begins the distribution of bread, of bread-Brot-Broid-chleb-pain-lechem-keynér, of the holy grey slab which seems gigantic in your neighbour's hand, and in your own hand so small as to make you cry' (33; 34).[5] Reading Levi's babelic repetition within the context of Benjamin's theories of translation and pure language opens up a dialogue about Levi's linguistic theories that emerge from the pages of his first memoir. It also points up Levi's extraordinary integration, in this list of differing "modes of intention" (as Benjamin refers to the differences between linguistic expressions of the same object) of the camp's languages of oppression and victimization, oscillating between the *Lagerjargon*'s superstrates (German and Polish) and its substrates (Yiddish, Hebrew, and Hungarian), in addition to more peripheral linguistic elements such as French and Levi's Italian, which begins the sequence. In this passage's staging of the Babel of the Shoah, Levi simultaneously stages the beginnings of its reversal, the assemblage and then transmission of this collection of fragments.

It is not by chance that in Levi's explicit characterization of the *univers concentrationnaire* as Babel (in the chapter "Una buona giornata" ["A Good Day"]), he repeats the trope of reassembling the fragmentary languages of man, this time with the bricks that make up Buna's Carbide Tower, Auschwitz's Tower of Babel:

> La Torre del Carburo, che sorge in mezzo alla Buna e la cui sommità è raramente visibile in mezzo alla nebbia, siamo noi che l'abbiamo costruita. I suoi mattoni sono stati chiamati Ziegel, briques, tegula, cegli, kamenny, bricks, téglak, e l'odio li ha cementati; l'odio e la discordia, come la Torre di Babele, e cosí noi la chiamiamo: Babelturm, Bobelturm; e odiamo in essa il sogno demente di grandezza dei nostri padroni, il loro disprezzo di Dio e degli uomini, di noi uomini.

> E oggi ancora, cosí come nella favola antica, noi tutti sentiamo, e i tedeschi stessi sentono, che una maledizione, non trascendente e divina, ma immanente e storica, pende sulla insolente compagine, fondata sulla confusione dei linguaggi ed eretta a sfida del cielo come una bestemmia di pietra. (68)[6]

> The Carbide Tower, which rises in the middle of Buna and whose top is rarely visible in the fog, was built by us. Its bricks were called *Ziegel*, *briques*, *tegula*, *cegli*, *kamenny*, *mattoni*, *téglak*, and they were cemented by hate; hate and discord, like the Tower of Babel, and it is this that we call it:—*Babelturm*, *Bobelturm*; and in it we hate the insane dream of grandeur of our masters, their contempt for God and men, for us men.
>
> And today just as in the old fable, we all feel, and the Germans themselves feel, that a curse—not transcendent and divine, but inherent and historical—hangs over the insolent building based on the confusion of languages and erected in defiance of heaven like a stone oath. (66)

Like bricks, Levi stacks the signifiers in a textual column that strives, however imperfectly, to represent language during and after Auschwitz. Through the image of the tower, Levi stages the human and linguistic disintegration brought about by the arrogance of the Final Solution, but he also moves toward the promise that the building blocks of human communication might possibly be salvaged. If the German term for "brick" can claim pride of place at or near the beginning of the sequence, here the language of oppression and murder is followed, after French, by Latin and then by Polish and Hungarian words of related etymology, in addition to the Russian and English words.[7]

Translation, then, speaks metaphorically to Levi's impulse to transmission but also invokes a paradigm by which we may understand the imperfection that defines and so constrains that impulse, pulling against it almost as counterweight; in the end, the translation of the Holocaust is just as impossible as it is necessary. Levi often employs a rhetoric of ineffability to address precisely this problem, telling the reader that human language is inadequate to represent the camp reality, as he does, for example, at the end of the chapter "Al di qua del bene e del male" ("This Side of Good and Evil"), in *Se questo è un uomo*: "Vorremmo ora invitare il lettore a riflettere, che cosa potessero significare in Lager le nostre parole 'bene' e 'male,' 'giusto' e 'ingiusto'" 'We now invite the reader to contemplate the possible meaning in the Lager of the words "good" and "evil," "just" and "unjust"' (82; 78). He is certainly not alone among Holocaust survivor-memoirists in this recourse, but his characteristic reserve applies even to his (quasi) declarations of the need for a new language. As he states in the beginning of the chapter "Ottobre 1944," "Se i Lager fossero durati piú a lungo, un nuovo aspro linguaggio sarebbe nato; e di questo si sente il bisogno per spiegare cosa è faticare l'intera giornata nel vento, sotto zero, con solo indosso camicia, mutande, giacca e brache di tela, e in corpo debolezza e fame e consapevolezza della fine che viene" 'If the Lagers had lasted longer a new, harsh language would have been born; and one needs this language to express what it means to toil the whole day in the wind, with the temperature below freezing, wearing only a shirt, underpants, cloth jacket and trousers, and in one's body nothing but weakness, hunger and knowledge of the end drawing nearer' (119–20; 112–13 [my adapt.]). Stopping just short of a claim that would in effect undermine his representation of the *univers concentrationnaire*, Levi recuperates not only Italian but human language in general from the abyss of Holocaust signification. In the process, he salvages the prospect that translation—from the *univers* to the space of postwar Italy, from the *Lagerjargon* to Italian, from Auschwitz to after—might be a viable enterprise.

But translation, however viable, is not a transparent process (Venuti), and any reflection on the survivor as translator must take into account the myriad levels of mediation and filtering that separate the atrocities waged against the Jews of Europe (and all the other "undesirables" that the Final Solution caught up in its machinery) from our reception of them as secondary witnesses,[8] the event from its reading or interpretation. Even as we are struck by the inexorability of the testimonial impulse in survivors like Levi, we must take into account certain matters when considering the complicated task of the Holocaust witness as translator. Instructors, in emphasizing matters of transmission, can direct the student of Holocaust literature to consider that all written accounts of the Holocaust are textual artifacts both mediated—by time, language, literary conventions, editorial demands, and even political exigencies[9]—and mediating, no matter how transparent a document a work of testimony claims to be.

I have found this approach to be both sufficiently general to link Levi to the broader issues of Holocaust literature and resonant with Levi's unique issues and preoccupations, particularly when applied to the celebrated eleventh chapter of Levi's *Se questo è un uomo*, "Il canto di Ulisse" ("The Canto of Ulysses"). My look at Levi's infamous translation of Dante's twenty-sixth canto into French takes translation and transmission as its principal optic and actually begins long before Jean, the Pikolo, invites Primo to get the soup with him, setting up perhaps the most well-known language lesson in Holocaust literature. Specifically, Levi's encounter with Sergeant Steinlauf in the third chapter, "Iniziazione" ("Initiation"), alerts the reader in subtle ways to many of the themes fundamental to the canto chapter: the importance of translating and mediating figures like Levi; the use of tropes of translation to represent testimonial processes, especially in moments of heightened affective human interaction; and the centrality of Dantean models, appropriated, translated, and woven by Levi into a complex and very self-conscious intertextuality. I reproduce the greater part of the passage here:

> Ho scordato ormai, e *me ne duole*, le sue parole diritte e chiare, le parole del già sergente Steinlauf dell'esercito austro-ungarico, croce di ferro

> della guerra '14–18. Me ne duole, *perché dovrò tradurre il suo italiano incerto e il suo discorso piano di buon soldato nel mio linguaggio di uomo incredulo*. Ma *questo ne era il senso*, non dimenticato allora né poi: che appunto perché il Lager è una gran macchina per ridurci a bestie, noi bestie non dobbiamo diventare; che anche in questo luogo si può sopravvivere, e perciò si deve voler sopravvivere, *per raccontare, per portare testimonianza*. . . . Dobbiamo quindi, certamente, lavarci la faccia senza sapone, nell'acqua sporca, e asciugarci nella giacca. Dobbiamo dare il nero alle scarpe, non perché cosí prescrive il regolamento, ma per dignità e per proprietà. (35; emphasis added)

> *It grieves me* now that I have forgotten his plain, outspoken words, the words of ex-sergeant Steinlauf of the Austro-Hungarian army, Iron Cross of the '14–'18 war. It grieves me *because I have to translate his uncertain Italian and his quiet manner of speaking of a good soldier into my language of an incredulous man*. But *this was the sense*, not forgotten either then or later: that precisely because the Lager was a great machine to reduce us to beasts, we must not become beasts; that even in this place one can survive, and therefore one must want to survive, to *tell the story, to bear witness*. . . . So we must certainly wash our faces without soap in dirty water and dry ourselves on our jackets. We must polish our shoes, not because the regulation states it, but for dignity and propriety.
> (36; emphasis added)

Levi's "translation" from the straightforward and clear yet "uncertain" Italian of his camp mate into his own language, that of the "incredulous man" that Levi was at the time of the episode, is a telling moment. It shows the multilayered process of narrating and witnessing that has its fragile beginnings in the camp: the essence of Steinlauf's message is nothing less than the victim's imperative to witness, self-translated into the soldier's nonnative Italian for Levi's consumption and understanding. This puts Levi first in the position of narratee, who must validate another victim's subjecthood and witness position, in this case in response to Steinlauf's experiential "text." Levi must then take over as mediator for the reader, translating the sergeant's uncertain yet clear Italian into the powerful literary Italian that is linguistically familiar to his readers but that carries a conceptual message that is radically difficult and obscure. Levi is shown in this episode to be the ideal translator. Not only does he know firsthand the experience of the referent, but he also speaks the language of the recipient: he, too, was once that "incredulous man" and can empathize with the communicative barrier of disbelief that he now—just as Steinlauf did—must overcome.

Levi's frustration at his inability to maintain some sort of formal equivalency in his various translation acts is evident both in this episode and in his translation of the twenty-sixth canto of the *Inferno* to Jean; each causes Levi the same kind of sorrow that afflicted Dante as he struggled to transmit his encounter with the noble figure of Ulysses. Levi's affective stance toward Steinlauf is lexically linked to Dante's encounter with Ulysses by the verb *dolere*, which for Dante reflects his conflicted anxiety toward Ulysses's potentially dangerous rhetorical model: "Allor mi dolsi, e ora mi ridoglio / quando drizzo la mente a ciò ch'io vidi" 'I sorrowed then, and sorrow now again, when I turn my mind to what I saw' (*Inferno* [1977] 26.19–20). Levi, instead, uses the verb to express his grief at the imperfection of the translating cum testimonial process. While Dante's elegant temporal *chiasmos* neatly encapsulates the poet's claims to authoritative representation of the pilgrim's experiences, Levi's "Ho scordato ormai, e *me ne duole*, le sue parole diritte e chiare," borrowing Dante's key word *dolore* in the present tense but not in the past, reveals an anxiety that is unique to the present temporal frame of writing and survival, to the survivor's transmission of the *univers concentrationnaire*.

Ultimately, however, at issue are not Steinlauf's words but his sense, which Levi has decidedly never forgotten ("non dimenticato allora né poi"), and Levi's ability to both absorb Steinlauf's "discorso" and draw it into an implicit comparison with the stages of his own language through which the translation must pass—incredulous then, knowing now. Nowhere is the complex play between experience and testimony clearer than in the interaction between Steinlauf and Levi, which is heightened by Levi's characterization of his former language as incredulous; in this one subtle gesture, Levi the writer distances himself from his naive textual alter ego and performs the passage from figure of the uninitiated reader to knowing survivor, right before our eyes.

Levi's encounter with Sergeant Steinlauf in chapter 3 is a prologue to the emotional apex of *Se questo è un uomo*, "Il canto di Ulisse." Here, the translating figures are doubled, as Levi's bilingual recitation of the twenty-sixth canto of Dante's *Inferno* finds the perfect audience in Jean: part Dantean guide, part ideal interlocutor, and ultimately cotranslator of Levi's various source texts. Jean is immediately marked as Levi's guide through (and eventually out of) this particular hell, when he literally lifts Levi out of the underground tank in which he toils at the beginning of the chapter; Jean's engagement with Levi's twin projects of translation and testimony also enables Levi's tentative reemergence as a sentient man at the end of the chapter. Much like Dante's Vergil in the original canto, Jean is a translator whose knowledge of the language of privilege (here, German) grants him the power to mediate between an infernal reality and a linguistically marginalized narrating voice. Jean's construction under the sign of guide does not exclude him, however, from an explicit alignment with such "sinful" Ulyssean traits as intellectual curiosity—Jean's desire to learn Italian is motivated by pleasure and the experience of travel—and the transgressive audacity that such curiosity implies for a prisoner in the Nazi *Lager*.

Jean's bilingualism, his curiosity, and his willingness to engage in intellectually risky activities converge to make him a guide for Levi's transgression through translation and the pursuit of intellectual goals. Indeed, by the time Levi's recitation and simultaneous translation is under way, Jean's importance as a translator figure has given way to his role as the ideal audience for Levi's challenging source text. Jean's active engagement with the process of translation comes to figure the reader's dynamic and active role in the testimonial process; Jean will actually participate in the negotiation of meaning between Dante's and Levi's Italian and his own French by being "attentissimo" ("extremely attentive") to the process, by admiring the *contrappasso* logic of Dante's imagery, and by suggesting a translation when Levi's skill falters. Ultimately, out of Levi's complex translation of and textual dialogue with the Dantean source text, Jean emerges as nothing less than a salvific figure: Jean's mention of "Primo" ("Aujourd'hui c'est Primo qui viendra avec moi chercher la soupe" 'today it is Primo's turn to come with me to fetch the soup'; 107; my trans.) is an homage to the medieval signature tradition, in that it is the first mention of Levi's name in the entire text. Though this is most certainly a gesture that is corrective of the dehumanizing practice of tattooing prisoners' forearms with serial numbers, with which they were "baptized" *Häftlinge*, it also recalls the analogous (and sole) utterance of Dante's name, near the center of the *Commedia*, by the salvific figure, interpreter, and guide *per eccellenza*, Beatrice.

This episode, with its extended reflection on the ethics of translation within the *filo spinato*, or barbed-wire fence, urges us to reflect on the trope of translation *en abyme* and thus to look at once beyond the translating text and deeper into it. In the first instance, looking beyond the text gives us insight into how Levi's translation to Jean might be carried forward into a dynamic and interactive model of Holocaust witnessing. As we look deeper into the translating text, we are compelled to examine what is ultimately at stake in any use of the trope of translation: How does the source text in question demand its own translation? Does it function as a translating text in its own right? How does it inform our understanding of the translation process? Does the source text act, *en abyme*, to shed light on Levi's stance vis-à-vis his role as translator? When I teach this chapter of Levi's text, I am careful to point out the importance of Levi's choice of Dante's Ulysses as the material for his Italian lesson. As it is taken up by Levi in *Se questo è un uomo*, this particular "figure of the myth" of Ulysses is a profound meditation on mediation through translation (Boitani, *Ombra* and *Shadow*) and the ways in which the source text is transformed by and through its various afterlives.[10] Levi's Ulysses is a palimpsest that shows glimpses of Homer's noble wanderer, even as Levi views him through intervening and competing lenses: that of his own experience, on the one hand, and, on the other, a Dantean lens colored by Vergil's implicit disdain for Ulysses, the foil for an Aeneas far more in line with Christian values such as humility and submission to the collective good. Levi's strong mediation further shapes the Ulysses figure, which emerges as much from Levi's often pedestrian and even sacrilegious translation (when he is forced to translate a poetic *terzina* in prose) as from what is not translated, ostensibly because of the lacunae of displacement, exile, and oppression. But Levi's omissions as translator participate in a carefully executed reconstruction of the Ulysses figure that better reflects what Levi needs him to be. By eliding specifically the most transgressive and damning aspects of Dante's portrayal of the Greek hero—the negative connotations of his voyage past the pillars of Hercules—Levi effects a reversal of Ulysses's condemnation to Dante's hell, a condemnation that Levi saw as akin to his own. In a 1980 interview with Daniela Amsallem, he states:

> Auschwitz serait la punition des barbares, de l'Allemagne barbare, du nazisme barbare, contre la civilisation juive, c'est-à-dire la punition de l'audace, de la même manière que le naufrage d'Ulysse est la punition d'un dieu barbare contre l'audace de l'homme.
>
> Je pensais à cette veine de l'antisémitisme allemand, qui frappait principalement l'audace intellectuelle des Juifs, comme Freud, Marx, et tous les innovateurs, dans tous les domaines. C'était cela qui perturbait un certain philistinisme allemand, beaucoup plus que le fait du sang ou de la race. (qtd. in Anissimov 265)

> Auschwitz is the punishment of barbarians, of barbarous Germany, of barbarous Nazism, against the Jewish civilization, that is to say, of their audacity, in the same way that Ulysses's shipwreck is the punishment of a barbarous god against the audacity of man.
>
> I was thinking of this vein of German anti-Semitism, which principally attacked the intellectual audacity of the Jews, such as Freud, Marx, and all the innovators, in every field. It was this [audacity] that disturbed a certain German philistinism, much more than issues of blood or race. (my trans.)

In the end, we are invited to witness Levi's condemnation to almost certain death in the Nazi *Lager* through the lens of Ulysses's anachronistic damnation to Dante's *Inferno* and to understand the figure of the witnessing survivor in the key of that figure's rhetorical and intellectual transgressions. The Jewish survivor of the Nazi Holocaust, as Levi understands that figure in 1957, is a transgressor in mind and words, initially imprisoned for his intellectual acumen but also inherently and repetitively risking transgression, as a survivor, in his compulsion to tell the tale that, according to his oppressors, would never be believed—or told. In foregrounding precisely these various figures and processes of transgressive transmission—Ulysses, Jean, the narrating survivor—Levi performatively points up his mediating role in the testimonial process, conveying at once the necessity of the work of memory and testimony and its difficulty.

Over time, Levi's philosophical and authorial preoccupations with the Holocaust shifted from strictly documentary concerns to broad issues of justice, contagion, the gray zone, and survivor guilt. Though Levi's literary production between 1947 and 1987 reflects an astonishing generic flexibility—from the personal memoir to the occasional essay, from short science fiction to the historical novel, from poetry to personal anthology—the trope and practice of translation remained a constant paradigm for his position of mediation between the Holocaust and the uninitiated "others" that he wanted to make participate in it.[11] Levi eventually came to construct the intermediary figure (between Auschwitz and after) of Holocaust survivor as one fraught with its own interior fragmentation, subject to shifting positionality, and ultimately condemned to a lifetime of oscillation between death and life, between shame over having been oppressed and guilt over having oppressed another, between being the survivor who tells on his own behalf and the survivor who listens and then tells "per conto di terzi" 'by third parties' on behalf of the truly submerged (*I sommersi* 1056; my trans.). Not surprisingly, translation was an integral part of this construction: Levi's obsession with and eventual translation of a four-verse passage from Coleridge's *Rime of the Ancient Mariner* can be situated at the convergence of all these issues and in fact emblematizes Levi's engagement with a constellation of survivor issues from the mid-1960s until the end of his life.[12]

Levi first began describing himself in reference to the Ancient Mariner in the 1966 preface to the published version of the theatrical production of *Se questo è un uomo*; he took up this theme again in the pages of 1976's *Il sistema periodico* (*The Periodic Table*). In the first context, the poem was used as a model for the responsibilities of the secondary witness, who is placed in a position of judgment after hearing the survivor's tale; in the second, described in the chapter "Cromo" ("Chromium"), Levi recalls feeling much like Coleridge's traumatized protagonist upon liberation from Auschwitz, interrupting the peace of others to tell his tale and free himself—albeit momentarily—from its burden.

Levi's reflections on the Ancient Mariner's ability to figure the narrating survivor's condition culminated in his 1984 poem "Il superstite" ("The Survivor"), which slips effortlessly (and almost transparently) from direct citation of Coleridge's Romantic classic to faithful translation, to mistranslation, and then to original poetic verse. A four-line stanza from *Rime* constitutes Levi's poem's principal source text and subtext, provides the title for the collection of which "Il superstite" is a part (*Ad ora incerta*), and two years later appears in the epigraph to *I sommersi e i salvati*:

> Since then, at an uncertain hour,
> That agony returns:
> And till my ghastly tale is told
> This heart within me burns. (lines 582–85)

The focus in this particular citation from the *Rime* would seem to be the survivor's spontaneous and unexpected impulse to narrativity and, by implication, the traumatically repeating cycle of memory, narration, and exculpation to which he is unwillingly subject.[13] But just as this brief passage pretends to synecdochically represent Levi's narrative relationship to the Ancient Mariner—both poem and protagonist—Levi uses it as a springboard to explore other, broad problems of the survivor condition, to wit, survivor guilt and the challenges of survivor witnessing. In "Il superstite," then, Levi's anxieties about finding a willing interlocutor and having survived in someone else's place dovetail with his long-standing preoccupation with translation both as an act of transmitting a particular source text (precisely a text obsessed with its own transmission)[14] and a unique manipulation of that source text that unsettles and disturbs any easy claims to the survivor's subject position, the possibility for exculpation through testimony, even the very notion of what survival means. Levi's "Il superstite" uses narrative layering and distancing strategies that put the repetitive trauma of transmission, already present in the Coleridge source text, into strong relief. Specifically, Levi's skillful citation and immediate mistranslation of the Coleridge text subtly introduce a splitting of the narrative voice that is then further developed through the poem's use of quotation, both overt (quotation marks to set off the survivor's command to his "drowned" comrades) and occulted (the point of view of the "drowned" in their implicit accusations of the "saved"; the unmarked paraphrase of Dante that constitutes the poem's last verse). The result of this demarcation of the various levels of transmission is, paradoxically, the creation of a poetic space for the zone of survivor guilt and shame.

The first line of the oft-cited Coleridge passage (582) is reproduced *tale quale*, as the first verse of Levi's poem: "*Since then, at an uncertain hour*"; it is set in italics, clearly marking it as a direct citation of the Coleridge source text. The second line is Levi's almost literal translation of the first-line citation, in regular type: "Dopo di allora, ad ora incerta." This is followed in the third verse by a close translation of Coleridge's next line (583), "That agony returns" ("Quella pena ritorna"), and then a significantly altered rendering of the next two verses.

Starting with line 6, Levi's "Il superstite" makes a transition from the Coleridge source text and his interpretation of it to a more properly original segment (lines 6–13) describing the "sommersi" ("drowned") that the poem's survivor persona will soon address. By then admonishing the "gente sommersa" ("drowned people") in lines 14–20, Levi ostensibly places the survivor's voice in the diametrically opposed camp of the "salvati" ("saved"), who must defensively account for their survival to both the "sommersi" and to the poem's audience of outsiders, who, privy to both sides of the dialogue, are placed in the position of judge. As such, he sets up a seemingly neat distinction between survivors and their dead companions, complete with a dialogue within a monologue that presents both points of view:

> Indietro, via di qui, gente sommersa,
> Andate. Non ho soppiantato nessuno,
> Non ho usurpato il pane di nessuno,
> Nessuno è morto in vece mia. Nessuno.
> Ritornate alla vostra nebbia.

Non è mia colpa se vivo e respiro
E mangio e bevo e dormo e vesto panni.
(*Ad ora incerta* 576; lines 14–20)

Stand back, leave me alone, submerged people,
Go away. I haven't dispossessed anyone,
Haven't usurped anyone's bread.
No one died in my place. No one.
Go back into your mist.
It's not my fault if I live and breathe,
Eat, drink, sleep and put on clothes. (*Collected Poems* 64)

This dialogue is characterized by a repetition of negative clauses: "Non ho soppiantato nessuno"; "Non ho usurpato il pane di nessuno"; "Nessuno è morto. . . . Nessuno"; "Non è mia colpa." Not only is this negative structure an example of Freud's affirming negations (Rosato 425), but its repetitive cadence constitutes, in microcosmic form, the sort of traumatic repetition that Levi's use of Coleridge's *Rime* and his testimonial work represent on global levels. It is precisely this combination of repetition and negation that aids Levi in portraying the dialogue within a monologue between the two parts of a divided and conflicted survivor self. The affirming negations, in this context, have the striking effect of validating the accusations of the "sommersi," even while presenting the opposing—and seemingly dominant—point of view of the "salvati." Furthermore, the rhetorical strategy of redundancy forcefully suggests that this implicit dialogue is one that the surviving subject must enact over and over again.

But Levi makes two interesting changes to Coleridge's original in his own loose translation (in lines 4–5) that displace him with regard to this neatly divided dichotomy of the drowned and the saved and create, in effect, the gray zone that lies between them. The transitional segment that bridges the two introductory verses of faithful translation and the original verses beginning at line 6 represents a space of many ambiguities: between faithful and unfaithful translation, between the giving and the receiving of testimony, between survival and death. First, the focus on the first-person narrator's tale in Coleridge's line 584 ("And till my ghastly tale is told") has been shifted to the third-person narrator's and his listener in Levi's rewriting: "E se non trova chi lo ascolti" 'And if he doesn't find someone who might listen to him' (my trans.). By emphasizing the necessity of finding an interlocutor, a witness to the survivor's testimony, Levi establishes an interactive model of narrative responsibility, in which the living must speak for those who did not survive. As Levi will later explain in *I sommersi e i salvati*, in the chapter "La vergogna" ("Shame"), "Noi toccati dalla sorte abbiamo cercato, con maggiore o minore sapienza, di raccontare non solo il nostro destino, ma anche quello degli altri, dei sommersi, appunto. . . . Parliamo noi in loro vece, per delega" 'Those of us touched by fate have sought, more or less wisely, to tell not only our own story but also that of the others, the drowned. . . .

We speak in their stead, by proxy' (1056; my trans.). Implicit in this model is the fact that the weight of responsibility must be distributed among speakers and listeners alike at many different levels, as the "salvati" must become witnesses to the atrocities committed against the "sommersi" and the survivor's listener-reader must, in turn, bear witness to that which is recounted by the survivor. It is not enough merely to tell; the reader-listener must also be a willing witness, mirroring and repeating the narrative testimonial act of the survivor to create an infinite chain of witnessing and telling, listening and witnessing.[15]

For both the Holocaust survivor and the Ancient Mariner, each link in the transmission of the tale is simultaneously narrator and narratee, yet another example of the manner in which the representation *en abyme* of the transmissive act shines a particularly bright metanarrative light on the processes of witnessing. Coleridge's thematic doubling of the protagonist, in which "each person who hears the story becomes, like the Mariner, the teller of that story" (Murfin 277), is reflected in Levi's poem. Here, the persona of the poet proves to be only the outermost layer in the transmission of this poem, a poet who quotes Coleridge's original English text, who puts forward his own mistranslation of Coleridge, and then quotes a survivor, who, in his vehement denial of any wrongdoing against the "gente sommersa," implicitly cites the charges of his accusers. Even the final line of the poem constitutes another layer of this game of doubling through citation, as the survivor translates Dante ("e mangia e beve e dorme e veste panni" [*Inferno* [1977] 33.141]) into twentieth-century Italian, making changes of person and perspective to invoke the double of the traitor Branca Doria.

But in keeping with poetry's role as the space in which Levi works through his conflicted responses to his survivorhood, Levi's unfaithful translation in the fourth verse also subtly undermines this very narrative model whereby interlocutors, and therefore witnesses, are created within the textual space of testimony. While Coleridge's main verb is decidedly indicative and future-oriented, Levi's version is constructed on the first part of a hypothetical phrase, raising the disturbing specter of an audience in the subjunctive—possible, but far from certain. Levi's unfaithful translation of Coleridge, then, prompts us to question his faith in the very narrative-testimonial model that he has constructed.

The second change in Levi's reworking of the original poem involves a shift from the first person ("And till my ghastly tale is told / This heart within me burns") to the third ("E se non trova chi lo ascolti / Gli brucia in petto il cuore" 'And if he does not find someone who might listen to him, / His heart burns in his chest' [my trans.]). By displacing the subject position away from the lyric, authoritative first person, Levi problematizes his status as survivor and thus, in effect, his position in this interactive model of witnessing. Levi's decision to construct the survivor's voice in the third person would seem to place the poet at least one remove from the survivor's ostensibly authoritative position, which Levi begins to question in his later years. In the chapter "La vergogna," in *I sommersi e i salvati*, Levi discusses at length the feelings of guilt that he and his fellow survivors experienced after their liberation from the camps. Among other things, Levi asserts that the "salvati" who survived to tell about the horror of the Holocaust are a sheltered minority and that it was only the majority, those who "hanno toccato il fondo" 'had touched the bottom' that might have been able to testify fully to mankind's extreme capacity for evil: "sono loro, i 'mussulmani,' i sommersi, i testimoni integrali, coloro la cui deposizione avrebbe avuto significato generale" 'it is they, the "mussulmans," the submerged, the complete witnesses, those whose testimony would have had general meaning' (1056; 84 [my adapt.]). Instead, survivors like Levi must take on their role of witness even though that role's force—even its truth—is diminished by their survival.

This weakened view of the authority of survivorhood is confirmed later on in the poem, when Levi overtly quotes the survivor's defensive rebuke of the submerged. By taking the survivor's words out of the poet's mouth and citing them as the words of an ambiguous, unnamed survivor-speaker, Levi further develops the narrative duality that is set up by his translation of Coleridge's first-person stance to a third-person narrative position and positions himself definitively outside the neat drowned-versus-saved dichotomy that he has created. This rhetorical technique portrays a survivor-poet who is neither "sommerso" nor "salvato"—not subject to the true depths of the Nazi atrocities and yet not willing, in this moment of the poem, to accept the survivor's words, his responsibility, or his guilt. In effect, Levi establishes himself as a border figure who stands astride these two opposing zones of the moral system of Auschwitz: drowned (or better, submerged) and saved. This positioning points up the fact that it is his identification with both survivorhood and death that warrants his occupancy of an entirely different intermediary zone.

Just as Levi creates a more usable Ulysses through his corrupt translation of Dante's story, here he willfully mistranslates a passage from Coleridge's *Rime*. We are thus directed to consider the difficulties of survival and witnessing through the optic of translation, both as a potentially destabilizing textual practice and as a metaphor for traumatic transmission. In the Levi classroom, "Il superstite" functions well as a point of entry into Levi's later production by underscoring the complex centrality of the Ancient Mariner figure in his writing and thought from 1966 on. I have found it particularly rewarding to offer students the chance to look at the original Italian poem alongside Ruth Feldman and Brian Swann's English translation, to illustrate the translators' challenges in dealing with a multilayered text that unsettles our assumptions regarding the source or original (Insana, "Traumatic Translation"). This approach also gives students a strong preparation to view the essays in *I sommersi e i salvati* through the optic of its epigraph and to consider how Levi's unfaithful translation and forceful reshaping of the verses might give new insight to essays such as "The Grey Zone," "Shame," "Stereotypes," and even "Letters from Germans," where Levi discusses the complexity of having *Se questo è un uomo* translated into German. On a more macrocosmic scale, the trope of translation can have precisely the same function in our consideration of Levi's legacy, shedding light on the very process of its transmission to new languages, new testimonial contexts, and new expressive forms. As befits an oeuvre so defined by outward- and inward-looking intertextuality, these approaches allow students of Levi to sketch out interesting reconfigurations—beyond conventional generic and thematic parameters—of Levi's oeuvre. Moreover, they invite us to look toward recontextualizations and refractions of Levi's testimony (e.g., theatrical, musical, and cinematographic) that are no less conditioned by the demands and challenges of testimonial transmission.

NOTES

[1]For a more exhaustive examination of translation's function within Levi's testimonial production, see Insana, *Arduous Tasks*.

[2]One relevant translation studies–centered approach is the opposition, theorized by the German Romantic poet and translator Friedrich Schleiermacher, between leaving "the author in peace as much as possible and mov[ing] the reader toward him; or . . . leav[ing] the reader in peace as much as possible and mov[ing] the writer toward him" (49).

[3]For an interesting interpretation of *La vita è bella* in a translation studies context, see Alexander.

[4]Many of the afterlives of Levi's testimony are, not coincidentally, self-consciously indebted to the example of Lanzmann's *Shoah*, which is an extended reflection on the inherent distance of the testimonial gaze. On *Shoah* and the role of the translator, see Feldman, "Return," esp. 211–13. For further reading on *La strada di Levi*, see Belpoliti's "road diary," *La prova*. For an extended analysis of Ferrario and Belpoliti's *La strada di Levi*, see Insana, "In Levi's Wake."

[5]This and all citations from Levi's work are taken from Belpoliti's 1997 edition of Levi's *Opere*. Unless otherwise indicated, all translations from *Se questo è un uomo* refer to *Survival in Auschwitz* (trans. Woolf; Collier, 1961), and all translations from *I sommersi e i salvati* refer to *The Drowned and the Saved* (trans. Rosenthal; Summit, 1988).

[6]Not coincidentally, Levi opens his essay "Tradurre ed essere tradotti" ("Translating and Being Translated"; originally published in 1980 as "Lasciapassare per Babele" and reprinted in the 1985 collection *L'altrui mestiere* [730–34]) by establishing the translator as the noble but poorly paid agent of Babel's reversal.

[7]Levi's views on the fundamental importance of rendering the Holocaust in German are nowhere clearer than in the last chapter of *I sommersi e i salvati*. Discussing his hopes for the German translation of *Se questo è un uomo*, Levi writes, "In certo modo, non si trattava di una traduzione ma piuttosto di un restauro: la sua era, o io volevo che fosse, una *restitutio in pristinum*, una retroversione alla lingua in cui le cose erano avvenute ed a cui esse competevano. Doveva essere, piú che un libro, un nastro di magnetofono" 'In a certain sense, it was not a matter of a translation but rather of a restoration: [the translator's] was, or I wanted it to be, a *restitutio in pristinum*, a retroversion to the language in which events had taken place and to which they belonged. More than a book, it was to be a tape recording' (1128; 173–74 [my adapt.]).

[8]On the terminology and hierarchies of witnessing, see Felman and Laub, chs. 2, 3, and 7; Rothberg; Weissman.

[9]For scholars such as Langer, mediation is inherent to all written testimony, which thus presents certain obstacles of reception and interpretation to be overcome with respect to the more immediate medium of oral testimony (see esp. *Holocaust Testimonies*). There has been valuable work done on the oeuvre of Wiesel, in particular on the role of mediation in the production of his "first" memoir, *La nuit* (*Night*), which actually represented a filtering down from his original 862-page original manuscript and its 253-page published account entitled *Un di velt hot geshvign* ("And the World Remained Silent"), both in Yiddish. Seidman offers a detailed analysis of this matter and also considers the importance of the French Catholic writer Mauriac as a cultural mediator between Wiesel's testimony and the Western European, principally Christian, audience to whom he "introduced" it, both literally and editorially.

[10]On the notion of translation as "sur-vie," or survival, see Derrida.

[11]In the preface to *Se questo è un uomo*, Levi writes, "Il bisogno di raccontare agli 'altri,' di fare gli 'altri' partecipi, aveva assunto fra noi, prima della liberazione e dopo, il carattere di un impulso immediato e violento, tanto da rivaleggiare con gli altri bisogni elementari" 'The need to tell our story to "the rest," to make "the rest" participate in it, had taken on for us, before our liberation and after, the character of an immediate and violent impulse, to the point of competing with our other elementary needs' (5–6; 5–6).

[12]The discussion of Coleridge's *Rime* that follows is reprinted with permission from the journal editors from the article "Traumatic Translation: The Ancient Mariner's Voyage from English to Italian—and Back Again" (*Journal of Italian Translation* 1.1 [2006]: 23–35).

[13]Caruth's seminal work on trauma in literature, *Unclaimed Experience*, focuses on the essential unexpectedness of traumatic events. It is this element of surprise that compels the survivor to constantly reenact the event, expecting each time to gain a greater sense of preparedness for—and thus mastery over—its psychic reality.

[14]As McGann comments, underscoring the preoccupation in *Rime* with serial transmission and interpretation, "Coleridge means us to understand that the ballad narrative dates from the sixteenth century, that the gloss is a late seventeenth-century addition, and, of course, that Coleridge, at the turn of the nineteenth century, has provided yet another (and controlling) perspective on the poetic material" (50).

[15]This chain is also the impulse behind Levi's most famous poem (and one of his earliest), initially published as an untitled poetic epigraph to *Se questo è un uomo* and later republished as "Shemà."

TEACHING INDIVIDUAL WORKS

Adventures in Interdisciplinarity: Teaching *The Periodic Table*

Millicent Marcus

Though our students may not be conversant with C. P. Snow's landmark work on "the two cultures," they are certainly aware of the deep disciplinary divide that organizes academic life, institutionalized in the very label "arts and sciences" enshrined in course catalogs and imposed, with varying degrees of complexity, in area requirements throughout the curriculum. But they may be surprised to find such a disciplinary debate flaring up on the pages of a Holocaust memoir whose author is struggling to retell his story now for the fourth time (considering the ur-writing to be the *Auschwitz Report*, brought to scholarly attention by Robert Gordon's edition of its English translation [Levi with De Benedetti]). If we see each sustained recasting of Levi's Holocaust ordeal as an attempt to reinvigorate the testimonial process, beginning with the straightforward memoirs *Survival in Auschwitz* and *The Reawakening* and ending with the essayistic *Drowned and the Saved*, then *The Periodic Table* becomes an ingenious generic experiment in which the narrative is passed through the filter of an unexpected and seemingly incongruous interpretive grid—that of Dmitri Mendeleyev's tabulation of elements according to their atomic weight, in a layout that demonstrates a periodicity of properties. At its most obvious, Levi's decision to graft a chemical ordering device onto the unruly matter of human events sets Snow's two cultures on a collision course, pitting the sciences against the humanities, "hard" against "soft" knowledge, logic and reason against imagination and dream, fact against fiction, univocal truth and absolute certitude against ambiguity and interpretive pluralism, purity against contamination—in other words, activating all the binary oppositions to which the "two cultures" debate gives rise.

Of the greatest interest to teachers of *The Periodic Table*, however, is the way in which Levi invokes the science-humanities divide, only to show its systematic breakdown as the text unfolds. Our students have much to gain from examining Levi's reflections on the shifting and evolving interrelationship between scientific and literary thought in this chemical autobiography, both in its challenge to their unexamined assumptions about the truth-claims of academic disciplines and in its proposal of a "unified field theory" that fuses the objectivity of the chemist's proofs with the highly subjective and morally charged lessons of survivor testimony. Our pedagogical task, in leading the students through Levi's disciplinary metanarrative, is threefold: to demonstrate how the text foregrounds the gap between scientific and humanistic approaches to knowledge, then dismantles both disciplines' exclusionary claims to truth, and, finally, reveals the underlying complicity between them to promote the chemist-writer's testimonial mission.

Levi's organizing principle in *The Periodic Table* offers the most powerful of pedagogical tools for teaching this text. Taking our cue from the book's title, we can begin by asking our students to think about why Levi chose to name each chapter after a given element and what dictates the order of the elements' presentation in the text. It soon becomes clear that Mendeleyev has nothing to do with the logic behind such choices. Neither atomic weight nor atomic number nor periodicity of attributes determines the order and progression of the elementally named chapters, forcing us to look elsewhere for the book's principle of organization. What emerges is a series of explanations that range from the particulars of Levi's life story in any given chapter to the overarching pattern of human events that are mirrored in the progression of elements from argon to carbon, from textual beginning to end. The logic of Levi's choices are therefore to be found not in the principles of science but in those of literature and, more specifically, in those of the poetic imagination.

Exercises in Chemical-Poetic Interpretation

To demonstrate Levi's varied and evolving literary strategies in *The Periodic Table*, I ask each student to choose an element and analyze its link to the narrative of the chapter it names. Such poetic devices as personification, simile, metaphor, and allegory will emerge but will not exhaust the subtlety and complexity of Levi's strategy for "chemically" organizing any given chapter. Students should be invited to ponder the implications of the encounter between scientific and humanistic (in this case, literary) approaches to knowledge as they engage in this interpretive process.[1] The text sometimes gives explicit instructions on how to read its elemental imagery, as in the chapter on argon, one of the inert or noble gases, where Levi writes, "The little that I know about my ancestors presents many similarities to these gases" (4).[2] The comparison of Levi's Jewish-Piedmontese relatives with argon, expressed through the figure of spatial proximity (their *avvicinamento*, or vicinity) recalls the principles of contiguity that govern elemental resemblance for Mendeleyev. In rhetorical terms, we are in the realm of simile, and it is appropriate that the text begin with this simplest of figurative devices.

Only slightly more complex is the chapter on iron, which "bonds" with its subject matter through prosopopeia, or personification allegory, in the figure of Sandro, who literally "seemed to be made of iron [and who] was bound to iron by an ancient kinship" (43), thanks to the blacksmith trade of his forefathers. But the positive associations of iron are not without their negative counterparts—Sandro's metallic toughness will find its match in the toughness of the "iron future" that faces both Sandro and Primo and for which their wilderness exploits have helped Primo prepare (45). Toughness, however, is not the only attribute that renders iron the perfect vehicle for memorializing Sandro. "Some elements, such as iron and copper, were easy and direct, incapable of concealment" (38), Levi remarks in a passage preceding the portrait of Sandro and foreshadowing his eventual antifascist militancy. A man of deeds and not words, of openness and freedom, Sandro resisted the Salò regime through partisan combat, becoming the first to die in the resistance efforts of the Action Party's Piedmontese Military Command. In a kind of atrocious *contrappasso*, Sandro's openness in opposing fascism was punished by the enemy's insistence on leaving his body open to public view on the roadway. It is here that the writer gives his friend fitting burial, using his elemental rhetoric to construct for Sandro a funerary monument that portrays his ironness in words, despite Sandro's aversion to the medium of language. Acknowledging the daunting task of representing one who "was not the sort of person you can tell stories about, nor to whom one erects monuments" (49), Levi chooses to follow the example set forth by Sandro, who "spoke as no one speaks, saying only the core of things" (44). Paring down his own discourse to its essence, Levi chisels an epitaph for Sandro of ironlike economy, bringing his words into the closest possible alignment with their referents in the deeds of this extraordinary young man. It is worth noting that Sandro is the only character in *The Periodic Table* who is fully and authentically named—any suspicion that this too is a pseudonym, according to Levi's custom of renaming friends and acquaintances throughout the text, is dispelled toward the end of the chapter: "Sandro was Sandro Delmastro" (48), Levi announces in a formulation that gives this character's identity firm historical grounding and insists on the exact equivalence of words and the man they represent, when that man's ironlike actions literally speak for themselves.

In the chapters on argon, which cannot bond with other substances, and on iron, which Levi treats in its pure form, the rhetorical analysis can remain rather simple in its quest for direct correlations between elements and their human embodiments. Once elements join in compounds, Levi's poetic strategies become more complex, for he must use techniques that account for the running analogies between events as they unfold on both the chemical and human levels. And now we are in the realm of allegory, where one story stands for another, where the literal and figurative levels mirror each other not in static, one-to-one correspondence but in dynamic and simultaneous movement along parallel lines. In the chapter on zinc, meaning evolves in a three-tiered progression, at once chemical, sentimental, and political, where the element's self-protectiveness in the pure state and its readiness to combine with others once exposed to sulfuric acid yield a wealth of interpretive possibilities. Levi is quick to apply the lessons of zinc to fascist racial policy and to identify himself with the elemental impurity that the regime seeks to purge. It is in the unfolding of the romance plot that the allegory becomes "impure," for literal and figurative levels come to contaminate each other when Primo finds a "chemical" excuse to sidle up to Rita during a lull in his lab work. Though his experiment will ultimately fail at the level of chemistry ("[s]o my zinc sulfate ended up badly" [36]), Primo has nonetheless made a first shy advance toward Rita, herself doubly zinc-like in her emotional reserve and her racial purity. No sooner does he realize that "between Rita and myself there [had formed] a bridge, a small zinc bridge, fragile but negotiable" (35), than Primo feels emboldened to enact the meaning of the element's impurity by slipping his arm under Rita's as he accompanies her home from the lab. Acting on the model of his chemical exemplar, Primo is able to take a small step toward dispelling the isolation imposed on him by a racist regime from the outside and by neurotic shyness from within.

At the structural center of the book's twenty-one chapters stand "Gold" and "Cerium," the only elements whose narratives arise directly out of Levi's Holocaust experience. In "Gold," simple metaphor defines the elemental relation of this precious metal and the abstract notion of freedom so woefully denied Primo upon his arrest in December 1943. The chapter begins with an account of "a second history" concealed beneath the cover of official history (130)—a parallel chronicle of resistance activism, a golden history, which has only now come to the surface and which Primo, along with his cohorts, enthusiastically embraces. It is in a fascist prison, when Primo meets his cell mate, a gold prospector, that the elemental metaphor takes shape. Unlike Sandro Delmastro, whose full naming gave him the iron weight of his historical militancy, this character is nameless and weightless, unencumbered by the burdens of social belonging. Defying common associations of gold with financial wealth, Primo's cell mate extols his trade for its lightness—the mobility and autonomy it accords him. In so doing he subjects the precious metal to a process of resignification—he frees it of all material encrustations and, like the alchemists, purifies this element, restoring its primordial meaning of "worth" in an absolute sense. Here Levi locates the inestimable value of his previous golden existence, soon to be blighted by the series of incarcerations and dislocations that will lead him to Auschwitz.

In "Cerium," the second of the chapters dedicated to his Holocaust ordeal, Levi complicates the rhetorical strategy used already in "Iron." Both chapters serve an epitaphic function—they carve out beautifully wrought and deeply felt memorials to the men who bore so much responsibility for Levi's survival and his eventual power to bear witness. Whereas iron possesses inherent qualities that invited the workings of personification to represent Sandro, cerium requires more strenuous interpretive efforts to "become" Alberto. A man of infinite resourcefulness and miraculous good cheer, Alberto had an uplifting effect among the denizens of the Auschwitz netherworld. To cerium, then, Levi entrusted the daunting task of memorializing Alberto precisely because this element offered him a means to exercise his powers in the service of survival. Thanks to Alberto, Primo's theft of three mysterious "cilindretti" will start a transformational process that will convert rods meant for acetylene torches into flint for cigarette lighters (146), which in turn will be converted into the bread rations that will prolong the lives of two men awaiting liberation. To keep that process in motion, Alberto will have to defy not only the dreadful disciplinary machinery of the "universo concentrazionario" but also the temperamental makeup of Primo (146), whose skepticism and aversion to risk require Olympian efforts of persuasion. Under Alberto's aegis, the two men are able to whittle the rods down to size beneath the highly flammable cover of their blankets over the course of several nights, without literally or figuratively igniting a conflagration. A latter-day Prometheus, Alberto will incur the god's wrath only belatedly, when he loses his life on the forced march from Auschwitz. But Primo will survive to memorialize the friend who released the transformational power of cerium through his own elemental powers of inventiveness, perseverance, and love.

The complexity of Levi's multileveled poetic strategy reaches its zenith in "Chromium" and "Vanadium," the chapters in which his Holocaust past erupts into the present in profoundly destabilizing ways. "Chromium" is narrated from the perspective of a relatively comfortable and stable present tense: Levi is chatting with colleagues in the cafeteria of the paint factory where he has been gainfully employed for some time. A conversation about obsolete chemical practices that persist in current usage plunges him back in memory to 1946, to the immediate aftermath of his Auschwitz ordeal. Asked to solve the case of a mysteriously "livered" product (154)—batches of bright orange paint that had coagulated into useless gelatinous blobs—Levi traces the problem to an erroneous addition of twenty-three drops of a reagent, where only two to three drops had been required. The chemist's breakthrough discovery and its remedy coincide with two other breakthroughs of momentous personal import. Primo simultaneously overcomes his emotional paralysis through an encounter with the woman he will marry, and he is able to transform his futile and anguished writing attempts into a therapeutically effective process of memorialization. The symmetry between events on the personal and chemical levels becomes even more obvious when Levi discovers that the injuries done to the batches of livered paint date back to January 1944, the month that intervened between his arrest and his deportation to Auschwitz. But the fortunate outcome of the chemical narrative does not apply so easily to the story of human trauma that it allegedly mirrors. When Levi states, in the story's synthetic conclusion, "And so my ammonium chloride, the twin of a happy love and a liberating book . . . is religiously ground into the chromate anti-rust paint on the shore of that lake, and nobody knows why anymore" (159), the breezy and pat comparison of chemical, sentimental, and literary realms ends on a deeply disquieting note. The collective forgetfulness of past behaviors ("nobody knows why") does not bode well for the writer of Holocaust testimony. The worrisome implication is that *Survival in Auschwitz*, whose genesis is recorded in "Chromium," may not have succeeded in its double task of preserving memory and liberating the writer. Indeed Levi, like Samuel Taylor Coleridge's Ancient Mariner, referred to in the chapter (151), will never completely overcome the urge, "at an uncertain hour," to accost the unwary listener and tell his "ghastly tale."[3]

Return to the Disciplinary Divide

Lest the above exercises in rhetorical analysis lead to an unbalanced view of the "two cultures" debate within the pages of *The Periodic Table*, it is important to stress that Levi's poetic undermining of science's pretensions to logic and clarity is not the whole story. Chemistry is not merely a pretext, not simply a straw man set up by Levi to be defeated by the superior truth-claims of literature. Instead, chemistry serves to rein in the potentially escapist excesses of literary fantasy. It keeps Levi's writing anchored, grounded in the concrete world of matter, just as it provides a rich repository of rhetorical figures whose literal source in chemical processes—distillation, filtration, crystallization—serves to give dead metaphors new life and infuse them with the emotions of those who have experienced such processes in the lab (see Levi, "Ex-chimico").

In "Chromium," Levi offers the best explanation for why literature needs chemistry, why his writing, especially his Holocaust testimony, requires the discipline of scientific modeling to achieve its testimonial goal. In the immediate aftermath of Auschwitz, Levi had sought to bear witness in torrential outpourings of grievances: "I was writing concise and bloody poems, telling the story at breakneck speed . . . writing in a haphazard fashion page after page of the memories which were poisoning me" (151–52). But for these writings to become more than the ravings of an Ancient Mariner bent on imposing his "ghastly tale" on random passersby and capable of achieving only temporary peace from his agony, Levi had to forge a style capable of fulfilling two purposes: those of true catharsis and of engaging the "addressable other," so necessary to the course of testimony (Laub 68). For this reason, Levi turned to the model of chemistry, and as a result his "writing became a different adventure, no longer the dolorous itinerary of a convalescent, no longer a begging for compassion and friendly faces, but a lucid building, which now was no longer solitary: the work of a chemist who weighs and divides, measures and judges on the basis of assured proofs, and strives to answer questions" (*Periodic Table* 153). Through a writing process modeled on the example of chemistry, Levi is able to match the matter of his life experience with "the right word, that is, commensurate, concise and strong" (153), where the term *commisurare* conjures the scientific acts of measuring, equating, balancing that lie at the heart of the chemist's claim to analytic rigor.

But not just any chemistry has the power to inform the humanist project—Levi's scientific calling must involve a "militanza" 'militancy' ("Ex-chimico" 642; my trans.), an active enlistment in the struggle to make sense of the world of matter and men. Throughout *The Periodic Table*, Levi will return to the theme of "chimica militante" 'militant chemistry,' whose first explicit mention in the text defines the phrase by negation. While consigned to work in a remote asbestos cave to maintain his anonymity, Levi had written the fables of mercury and lead, both set in a primordial space of the imagination. Levi includes these stories in *The Periodic Table* but sets them apart from the others typographically, in italics, as well as ideologically—they bespeak "a prisoner's dream of escape, between these tales of militant chemistry" (78). This contrastive definition is rich with promise for an understanding of the chemical militancy that drives the rest of *The Periodic Table*, whose stories arise from lived experience, which in turn can generate concrete actions in the hic et nunc of our world. For Levi, the phrase "militant chemistry" becomes a redundancy, since the very rootedness of the chemical enterprise in the material world implies an engagement with the epic struggle that characterizes the human condition in its entirety. Already in "Zinc" Levi had drawn the battle plan of the encounter ("[t]he hour of the appointment with Matter, the Spirit's antagonist, had struck" [33]), and in "Nickel" Levi's weekly meetings with his supervisor "sounded like war plans" (75). But it is not until "Silver" that Levi's chemical militancy will reach full measure. In this chapter Levi reveals his intimate blueprint for collecting the stories that will make up *The Periodic Table*. Indirectly quoting his exchange with Cerrato, a classmate with whom he is reunited after twenty-five years and who is clearly a projection of Levi himself, the writer expresses his chemical militancy in a conceit of Psychomachian proportions. His "chemical events" give

> the impression of fighting an interminable war against an obtuse and slow-moving enemy, who, however, is fearful in terms of number and bulk; of losing all the battles, one after the other, year after year; and to salve your bruised pride you must be satisfied with the few occasions when you catch sight of a break in the enemy front and you pounce on it and administer a quick single blow. (203)

Despite the epic language of this passage, Levi's goal is a modest one: not to tell the stories of "the grand chemistry, the triumphant chemistry of colossal plants and dizzying output" but to tell "the stories of the solitary chemistry, unarmed and on foot, at the measure of man" (203). Such stories will be collected and lined up, like the elements of a periodic table, to reveal to noninitiates the workings "of [the chemist's] trade, which is only a particular instance, a more strenuous version of the business of living." And here we get at the heart of Levi's chemical militancy, where the individual, quiet, yet heroic struggle to make sense of the world of matter serves as a model for the human project writ large, and where "we transformers of matter," as the writer explains to Cerrato, can teach others the art of a transformational engagement with the real. It is here that science and literature must work hand in hand to fulfill this vital task in a relationship whose evolving interdependency can be traced from the very earliest pages of Levi's text.

As far back as "Hydrogen," Levi reports:

> [C]hemistry represented an indefinite cloud of future potentialities which enveloped my life to come in black volutes torn by fiery flashes, like those which had hidden Mount Sinai. Like Moses, from that cloud I expected my law, the principle of order in me, around me, and in the world. I was fed up with books, which I still continued to gulp down with indiscreet voracity, and searched for another key to the highest truths: there must be a key, and I was certain that . . . I would not get it in school. (23)

Through a kind of affectionate and parodic free indirect discourse, Levi has entered the mind of his sixteen-year-old self, whose mystified visions of chemistry take truly spectacular form: clouds, fiery flashes, black coils of smoke surround the revelation of "the highest truths." This stage setting, which could come right out of a Hollywood blockbuster or a Veronese painting, offers the perfect backdrop for Levi's youthful self-dramatizing, and, like the volutes of smoke, the prose has a baroque quality of surface excess, appropriate to this overwrought vision of scientific world mastery. Most obvious is the young man's claim to Mosaic grandeur, his view of himself as the chosen one to whom the revelation will be vouchsafed on a mountaintop. Like Moses, Levi will be the lawgiver, whose chemical decalogue will create order in the world of matter and men. This vividly depicted scene not only conjures settings of biblical superspectacles across the media but also alludes to a more intimate Jewish space, that of the Aron Hakodesh, or Holy Ark, whose facade is adorned with the tablets of the Ten Commandments and whose depths harbor the scrolls of the Torah.

From this passage in "Hydrogen" Levi then develops a web of imagery that extends throughout the course of *The Periodic Table*: that of the Temple of Wisdom, the inner sanctum of privileged knowledge, whose threshold can only be crossed by a small group of the elect, the initiates who are in possession of a key capable of unlocking its jealously guarded mysteries. Convinced that traditional schooling will not provide access to chemistry's "highest truths," Levi stocks his rhetorical arsenal with figures that express his extracurricular approach to learning. Using stealth or brute strength, Levi will force his way into the portals of knowledge: "I will make a lock-pick, I will push open the doors" (23).

The image of the key will recur strategically throughout the text, most momentously in "Nickel," when the fledgling chemist devises a method for the extraction of this metal from an asbestos cave and is convinced "of having opened a door with a key, and of possessing the key to many doors, perhaps to all of them. I was thinking of having thought of something that nobody else had yet thought, not even in Canada or New Caldeonia, and I felt invincible and untouchable even when faced by close enemies, closer each month" (77). The baroque prose of Levi's earlier quest for the key in "Hydrogen" has been replaced here by a technique of singsong repetition and parataxis that adds a note of breathless, childlike jubilation to Levi's satiric portrait of his youthful self. Not only has he found the key to unlock all doors, but the neochemist's triumphalism has achieved global dimensions, ranging from the North American hemisphere to the South Pacific, as a child would thumb through the pages of the family atlas. The young Levi's self-congratulatory effusions, however, are immediately countered by a bitter reflection in hindsight—that nickel would be put to the worst possible uses at the service of the Nazi-fascist war machine.

Chemistry could not forever maintain its exalted position in the young Primo's pantheon of disciplines. In the introduction to "Zinc," he announces, "[Professor] P.'s chemistry was not the motor-force of the Universe, nor the key to Truth" (29), and in "Potassium" astrophysics threatens to gain the upper hand. The inner sanctum of knowledge is now the province of the more abstract sciences, and errors such as those that led Levi to substitute potassium for sodium "happen to the profane, to those who dawdle and play before the portals of the temple instead of going inside" (59). Chemistry is tainted by its collusion with the world of matter, preparing compounds is little different from following a recipe from the Pellegrino Artusi's cookbook, and the discipline's ancestry can be traced back to a murky alchemical past:

> The origins of chemistry were ignoble, or at least equivocal: the dens of the alchemists, their abominable hodgepodge of ideas and language, their confessed interest in gold, their Levantine swindles typical of charlatans or magicians; instead, at the origin of physics lay the strenuous clarity of the West—Archimedes and Euclid. (53)

In disciplinary terms, this exaltation of physics at the expense of chemistry is of the greatest possible interest, for it replicates within the sciences the same split that characterized the "two cultures" debate from the start. Chemistry now occupies the "softer" humanities position with respect to the "harder" discipline of physics. It is the latter that emerges as cerebral, lucid, elegant, abstract, disinterested, and, most consequentially, as the apotheosis of all that Western culture, going back to its classical Greek antecedents, holds dear. Chemistry, instead, becomes its "orientalized" opposite—opaque, equivocal, venal, and unredeemably complicit in the fallen material world.

Even within the discipline of chemistry, the "two cultures" debate will flare up—this time in the rivalry between the organic and inorganic branches of the field. In "Chromium," when Levi finds the antidote to the livering of the orange paint by inorganic means, he celebrates his success using terminology reminiscent of the humanities-science dichotomy. Levi solves the problem by "drawing on good inorganic chemistry, that distant Cartesian island, a lost paradise, for us organic chemists, bunglers, 'students of gunks'" (157). Where the former partakes of the "hardness" of sound scientific method, while the latter reeks of the approximation and the blundering of those "pasticcioni" 'bunglers' who sink their hands into the "pastyness" of organic substances (162; 157).

Carbon

The conflict of disciplines at the core of Levi's project in *The Periodic Table* finds resolution in the chemical-poetic alliance forged by carbon in the book's final chapter. It is here that Levi lets his literary imagination take flight, but he can do so only because science provides the grounding for this exercise. In his selection of carbon for the finale of a text that is neither a "chemical treatise" nor an "autobiography" (224), Levi has reached the culmination and completion of his great experiment in genre. The structural logic of his choice is obvious—a memoir that began with argon, an inert substance incapable of bonding with others, ends with the combinatory element *per eccellenza*, "the only element that can bind itself in long stable chains without a great expense of energy, and for life on earth . . . precisely long chains are required" (226–27). Carbon also takes us back to an important textual midpoint. It was in the center of the book, in the chapter "Gold," that Levi first announced his impulse to recount "the saga of an atom of carbon," but he was only able to write it down "many years later, and it is the story with which this book concludes" (128). Acknowledging that in the days of "Gold" he was not yet ready to commit the story of carbon to paper, Levi has prepared us for the climactic positioning of this element as the summation of a life experience—one that cannot be comprehended until the experience has run its course. For Levi, that course will range from the solipsism of argon to the inclusiveness of carbon, with nineteen other elemental stops of crucial importance along the way.

From its earliest pages, "Carbon" is replete with moments of literary self-reflexivity, including the writer's expression of wonder at the possibility of recounting his tale: "But, precisely for the good fortune of the narrator, whose story could otherwise have come to an end, the limestone rock ledge of which the atom forms a part lies on the surface" (226). Thanks to its arbitrary position on the outside of the stone, the atom will be subject to displacement, movement, and hence to the workings of time: "To it, until this moment, the present tense is suited, which is that of description, rather than the past tense, which is that of narration." And now we are in the realm of eventfulness—a condition that can only begin once an equilibrium has been disturbed, once stasis has been shattered by the forces of change. For Levi's carbon atom, those forces coincide with the blows of a pickax, which detach the atom from its stony encasement and plunge it "into the world of the things that change. . . . Its story, which once was immobile, now turned tumultuous" (226).

In tracing the journey of this atom over land, sea, and air, what emerges is a second chemical virtue of great magnitude, for "Carbon" is not only about connectedness but also, like "Cerium," about transformation. And so our atom passes through environments ranging from limestone cliff to atmospheric gas to Mediterranean vineyard to human wine drinker to cedar bark to woodworm to insect eye to milk molecule to human bloodstream to dot on the written page. Of all the changes to which this atom is subject, the most consequential one is photosynthesis, ushering carbon into the "organic adventure" in 1848 (226, 227). And here we cannot escape the urgent sense that Levi is talking about twin developments in the human sphere—the entrance of the Italian Jews, the social other, into full *italianità* upon their emancipation from the ghetto, and Levi's reentry into the human condition, some hundred years later, after the trauma of Auschwitz. The atom's painstaking insertion into the chain of life, its fulfillment of the bonding capabilities unique to carbon, finds its equivalent in Primo's hard-won achievement of human connectedness. And it is writing, as he had recounted so movingly in "Chromium," that brings Levi into alignment with carbon, enabling him to overcome his "inorganic" condition as an emotionally paralyzed victim of trauma and to take his place in the chain of life.

Levi concludes *The Periodic Table* on a seemingly trivial note: a man drinks a glass of milk, and, of all the carbon atoms ingested, "[o]ne, the one that concerns us, crosses the intestinal threshold and enters the bloodstream: it migrates, knocks at the door of a nerve cell, enters" (232). Throughout *The Periodic Table*, we have seen Primo knocking on doors—the doors into the temple of privileged knowledge that science had promised to offer the young starry-eyed student in "Hydrogen," the frustrated experimenter of "Potassium," the neochemist of "Nickel," and so on. But by the end of his journey through the periodic table of life, Primo, in his aspiration to truth, arrives at a very different kind of doorway. The grandiose portals of cosmic wisdom and advanced scientific thought have given way to a humble, microscopic, and intensely personal doorway—that of an individual nerve cell within the human organism. As the atom of carbon knocks at the door of this miniscule barrier—the membrane surrounding a nerve cell—Levi's writing makes a leap of breathtaking proportions: "This cell belongs to a brain, and it is my brain, the brain of the *me* who is writing" (232). On a syntactic level, Levi's sentence is deceptively simple, but its straightforward movement from "a brain" to "my brain," from the indefinite article to the first-person possessive adjective, vastly understates the literary distance traversed in the interval. Not only has Levi owned up to the autobiographical significance of all that he has just written, but, even more momentously, he has shifted his focus from the story proper to the process of its telling. In other words, the act of writing has become its own privileged object of representation.

Now we are ready to consider the words with which Levi concludes his great scientific-literary experiment, for it is here that the text's focus on the literary process draws us decisively into the workings of testimony. We are at the point where Levi's atom of carbon has gained entrance into the cell, triggering a nerve impulse that, "at this instant, issuing out of a labyrinthine tangle of yeses and nos, makes my hand run along a certain path on the paper, mark it with these volutes that are signs: a double snap, up and down, between two levels of energy, guides this hand of mine to impress on the paper this dot, here, this one" (233). The use of the present tense and the recurrence of the demonstratives "this" and "these" deserve special notice as elements of Levi's testimonial strategy, for it is by such means that the author is literally taking us into his brain as he sits in his study during the act of writing the very sentence we are reading. We are with him in the process of bearing witness. Carbon has thereby collapsed the distance between author and reader, between giver and receiver of testimony—this element's place in the chain of life is now our place in the chain of witness. But there is one more point to be made, and it requires the boldest leap of them all. If we imagine that Levi's writing instrument in *The Periodic Table* is neither a fountain pen nor an Olivetti typewriter but a pencil, endowed with that soft form of carbon known as graphite, then the most solemn of all connections has been made: between the ashes of Auschwitz and the dot on the page that seals the text of witness.

NOTES

[1]For a more creative assignment, students could be asked to recount episodes from their own autobiographies, organized around some scientific principle (e.g., the spectrum of colors). In so doing, they should be required to construct a range of links, from literal to far more subtle and complex rhetorical or poetic associations, between the components of the principle and their corresponding autobiographical events. Further topics for discussion or written assignments include the following: consider the problem of genre in analyzing Levi's text; analyze the relation of the first and last chapters of *The Periodic Table* and its implication for the text as a whole; discuss Levi's affectionately ironic portrait of the self as a young scholar; trace the imagistic threads that traverse the text (e.g., the temple of wisdom, the portal, the key); identify the ways in which the dichotomy between "hard" and "soft" knowledge breaks down.

[2]All quotations from *The Periodic Table* are from Rosenthal's 1984 translation; when provided, quotations from *Il sistema periodico* are from the 1994 Einaudi edition.

[3]Coleridge's *Rime of the Ancient Mariner* constituted a veritable obsession for Levi, who used lines 582–85 of the poem—"Since then, at an uncertain hour, / That agony returns: / And till my ghastly tale is told / This heart within me burns"—as the epigraph for *I sommersi e i salvati* (*The Drowned and the Saved*). These same verses serve as the opening of Levi's wrenching poem "Il superstite" ("The Survivor") and are the source of the phrase with which Levi chose to entitle his volume of collected poems, *Ad ora incerta*. I am grateful to Lina Insana for pointing out this network of allusions.

The Humanity of the Elements: An Interpretation of Levi's *The Periodic Table*

Elisabetta Properzi Nelsen

What immediately strikes readers of Primo Levi's *The Periodic Table* is the title, which prompts them to ask whether the book belongs to the field of chemistry or literature. The table of contents presents readers with another surprise: a listing of elements of the periodic table. This list becomes a motif for Levi's deeply intimate and personal narrative style. Levi offers an explanation of the title and the idea surrounding his book in the last chapter, "Carbon." He warns the reader that *The Periodic Table* is neither a treatise nor an autobiography but a *microstoria*, a "micro-history" (224), whose pages of "indecipherable characters" outline the future of a young person that "will become clear 'afterwards.'"[1] Levi develops this assertion by affirming that "every element says something to someone . . . like the mountain valleys or beaches visited in youth" (225). The author therefore establishes a link between an individual's chemical makeup and personal memory, a memory made of valleys and beaches, places that eventually belong to and become essential components of memory, just as the body's chemical components make each individual unique. These remembered places must be identified and therefore described in words, made up from an alphabet that mirrors the molecules of the body's chemistry. In response to the question, "What is it about chemistry that interests you?" in an interview with Ferdinando Camon, Levi answered:

> I'm interested in human contact with matter, in understanding the world around me; I'm interested in the chemistry of the human body, biochemistry. In short, science: but the science of particles doesn't say much to me. However, I am thrilled by the discovery of genetic mechanisms, by the way each individual is coded, by the minuscule chain whose alphabet is made up of molecules. (*Conversations* 65)

Levi thus intended to create a text in which the author's literary uniqueness might combine with his childhood interest in chemistry, which eventually led him to pursue studies and a career in science.[2] At the same time, Levi's scientific background makes him a keen observer and expert of the human body's chemical constituents, enough to provide him with an interpretative tool for the various human behaviors whose consequences inform social changes and historical events. Such an interest in science is not necessarily exclusive to Levi's literary experience. The union of science and literature, which may be traced back to Galileo's *Dialogue Concerning the Two Chief World Systems, Ptolemaic and Copernican* and *The Assayer*, was mainly delineated during the Enlightenment and reached the scientific and literary conclusions of the French school of naturalism.

Levi's contemporary Italo Calvino also investigated the meeting of science and literature. From the beginning of his literary career, Calvino had a keen interest in botany and agriculture that was expressed in detailed descriptions of the woods that Pin crosses in *Il sentiero dei nidi di ragno* (*The Path to the Nest of Spiders*), the thick arboreal vegetation in *Il barone rampante* (*The Baron in the Trees*), or even the meteorological phenomena of city life in *Marcovaldo*. Calvino also explored space through the primordial, celestial narrative voice of Qfwfq in his science fantasy *Cosmicomiche* (*Cosmicomics*). Also in *Palomar* (*Mr. Palomar*), Calvino's eponymous protagonist attentively examines the movements of a wave breaking on shore—movements that, considered in terms of the physical coordinates of time and space, reveal intimate reflections on the human experience.

Why, then, is *The Periodic Table* considered such an original and particular book? Why does this work, first published in Italy in 1975, continue to stir such an interest that transcends "Italianness," enough to be widely accepted as a classic? We must again refer to Calvino, in particular to the third of fourteen answers that he provides to the question "Why read the classics?": "The classics are books that exert a peculiar influence both when they refuse to be eradicated from the mind and when they conceal themselves in the folds of memory, camouflaging themselves as the collective or individual unconscious" ("Why" 127). Calvino's response offers a consistent explanation of Levi's *Periodic Table* as a classic. It refuses to be eradicated from the reader's mind and, at the same time, conceals itself in the collective and individual unconscious. Calvino inserts the concepts of memory and unconsciousness in his answer. A classic, then, is personal, intellectual, and historical memory but also the written form of an individual psychological consciousness that contains desires, fears, phobias, and complexes; social, ethical, and religious norms; and taboos. It is a consciousness that Levi believes can be made accessible from a chemical-biological point of view but that is ultimately the unique and inimitable manifestation of human life. All this is exemplified in the Yiddish proverb that opens the book: "Ibergekumene tsores iz gut tsu dertseylin." The English translation gives us, "Troubles overcome are good to tell," but the Italian version provided by Levi reads, "È bello raccontare i guai passati," literally rendered in English as, "It's beautiful to tell stories of past troubles." Levi's translation of the proverb emphasizes the adjective *bello*, "beautiful," which in Italian also connotes a meaning of "good." Telling stories is simultaneously beautiful and good, enjoyable and therapeutic, precisely because, in doing so, one may recall troubles that fortunately have passed.

The Periodic Table is divided into twenty-one chapters named after the chemical elements, most of which may be grouped into three sections. The first, from "Argon" to "Nickel," refers to the author's youth and first work experience. The second section includes only three stories, "Phosphorous," "Gold," and

"Cerium." These three stories function to centralize the experience of so-called "past troubles," since they narrate Levi's arrest and deportation. The third part, from "Chromium" to "Vanadium," covers the postwar period, thus touching on the themes of return and reintegration into so-called normalcy.[3] The division of Levi's autobiographical account adapts itself well both to the novel's inspiration, the system of chemical elements, and to the reconstruction of the youth and early adulthood of the first-person narrator. The narrative units trace a human chronology determined by what came before, though, in terms of what comes after, the stories seem to identify moments, encounters, portraits, and words that are metaphorically transformed, in Nicholas Patruno's words, into "challenges, conflicts, victories and defeats" (*Understanding* 57).

The collection also indirectly addresses Levi's experience as a prisoner in the concentration camp. The use of the word *experience* to signify this captivity, physical and psychological torture, sense of terror, dehumanization, and force of survival is certainly reductive, especially if we think of the positive connotation more frequently associated with the term. Perhaps the only positive significance that Levi attempts to draw from the aberration of Auschwitz may be found in a question that is consistently present throughout the book, particularly in the stories that trace his return home: the suffused attempt to find, at all costs, a possible moral or a message that might make some sense of the atrocities suffered. For this reason, the author's Jewishness lies at the heart of *The Periodic Table*. From the first story, "Argon," Levi feels the need to tell the reader about his origins and ancestors, traced back to the Spanish communities that arrived in the Italian region of Piedmont from Provence around 1500. Levi even explains the meaning of their surnames, which, in Italian toponomy, identify families of Jewish descent, "such as Bedarida-Bédarrides, Momigliano-Montmélian, Segre (this is a tributary of the Ebro which flows past Lérida in northeastern Spain), Foà-Foix, Cavaglion-Cavaillon, Migliau-Millau" (4). Levi then continues to chronicle the settlement of these Jewish families in various areas of southern Piedmont, up until the end of the nineteenth century, acknowledging their constant condition of marginality and rejection from the local community. While narrating incidents of humiliation for the Jews that existed even in his father's childhood, Levi also admits that his ancestors refused to integrate into the community and instead completely rejected the Christian milieu, creating "a symmetrical barrier against all of Christianity." With an irony that also hints at the feeling of pride with which he differentiates his "chosen people" from the goyim or *narelim*, Levi recalls the "good-natured wit" of his aunts and uncles: "wise, tobacco-smelling patriarchs and domestic household queens, who would still proudly describe themselves as 'the people of Israel'" (5). In this first story, Levi affirms the religious and social diversity that his community of origin had experienced since its first settlement in Italy, consequently understood as an experience of *fondamentale sfasamento*—translated by Raymond Rosenthal as "fundamental displacement." "Displacement," however, does not completely fit the meaning of the Italian *sfasamento*, which also connotes a sense of confusion and bewilderment. In effect, the idea of displacement can evoke bewilderment and thus anticipate the feeling incarnated in Levi's attitude toward his Jewish identity, especially after his return to Italy after the liberation of Auschwitz.

"Argon" opens with a description of the inert or noble gases (of which argon is one), and Levi draws on the nexus of chemistry and humanity to consider the inertia that characterizes the noble gases as a fundamental quality for the life of the earth. He further develops the similarity among inert gases and his ancestors by endowing the latter with attributes of immobility, dignified abstention, and voluntary relegation, despite their extremely active and tenacious work ethic (3–4), as well as their sense of pride in belonging to and descending from a chosen people, particularly visible in the author's notion of conserving a distinctive kind of intellect that allows him to perceive a strong sense of identity in relation to the Jewish tradition.

The sense of belonging to a specific tradition is reflected in Levi's memory of the language spoken by the ancestral community, a tongue that succeeded in combining the Piedmontese dialect with the "language of the fathers," which Levi calls the *incastro ebraico*, the "Hebrew inlay" (9). This dialect is defined as "rugged, sober, and laconic," while the Hebrew language is "sacred and solemn, geologic, polished smooth by the millennia like the bed of a glacier." This union of dialect and traditional language, at once extremely fascinating and comforting, determines an intimate language made up of "family sayings," to recall Natalia Ginzburg's acceptation, and also yields a historical, classical, and authoritative language including religious truths and doctrines and, above all, a close relationship with the divine. This contrast between the Piedmontese dialect and classical Hebrew is stressed by the comical aspect of his Jewish community's linguistic expression, a humor that Levi considers both a defense mechanism as well as a way to balance a sense of the divine with a humble quotidian existence. Such reconciliation between the daily and the divine occurs in the human condition, as "man is a centaur, a tangle of flesh and mind, divine inspiration and dust" (9). This comic peculiarity, which Levi also attributes to Yiddish (9), is typical of the Jewish people as a direct result of their being dispersed and lacking a specific place to connect to their heritage.

As in his relation of his memory of his aunts and uncles, Levi presents a fairly colorful portrait, halfway between farce and comedy, of the women in his family. He begins with Nona Fina, or Grandmother Fina, wife of the legendary Uncle Barbaricô, who seems to best embody the typical characteristics of the inert gases. Grandmother Fina did splendid crochet work. At sixty-eight, after an illness, she was confined to her bedroom, only stepping out on the balcony on Saturday afternoons to greet neighbors as they left the synagogue. Nona Fina's comic life is evoked in an anecdote about her youth, when she apparently served pork chops to a learned and famous rabbi from Moncalvo, defending her action with the excuse that there was nothing else left in the pantry (15).

In describing his father's mother, Grandmother Malia, Levi highlights her as a matriarchal yet eccentric figure, a woman responsible for handing down the

Jewish religion and culture and capable of dealing with the challenging experiences that render her life extremely bizarre and extravagant. Grandmother Malia is represented according to opposing extremes of juvenility and maturity, young *Strasscœur* and rigorous teacher to her children. The ironic solution to this character lies in the fact that, when she became a widow in her old age, Malia married an elderly Christian doctor, completely estranging herself from the family as well as developing a vice of avarice in direct contrast to her past generosity (18). Levi endows his grandmother with a destabilizing trait with respect to tradition. If, according to Jewish custom, the woman has the task of preserving and passing on religious and cultural identity, Grandmother Malia complicates this function and situates herself between the Jewish and Christian traditions, referring to both with an ambiguous, rebellious, and essentially distrustful perspective—in other words, with no theological or spiritual concern.

The same unconventional tendency is evident in the figure of Levi's father, whom Levi recalls secretly tasting *prosciutto* during their Sunday visits to Grandmother Malia's house (19). Through these two characters, his grandmother and father, Levi gives us a typical model of the Jewish people—his people—and also situates them in the same Italian literary tradition as Giorgio Bassani's *Storie ferraresi*, with the intention of composing a sort of Jewish *comédie humaine* in the social and historical context of Italy from the 1960s onward. Levi has thus succeeded in sculpting unforgettable figures that belong to a Judaic world that has been only marginally explored in Italy. The evocative capacity of this stereotypical yet unconventional representation of his family seems to link Levi to the Yiddish rhythms of Saul Bellow or to the voices of Philip Roth or even to anticipate the radical images included in Alessandro Piperno's *Con le peggiori intenzioni* (*With the Worst Intentions*).

Patruno affirms that the stories in *The Periodic Table* are "gems of prose" (*Understanding* 57). Each chapter is a personal narrative account that is complete on both the stylistic and thematic levels of expression. At the same time, the reader must be aware of the difficulty presented by each story and of the intricate connection between narration and metaphor that exists in Levi's mode of storytelling. In this way, certain chapters might seem more easily accessible than others. Readers certainly tend to prefer those stories with more evident biographical references, which allow for deeper empathy with the events narrated. I am referring in particular to the first three: "Argon," "Hydrogen," and "Zinc," together with the trio of "Phosphorus," "Gold," and "Cerium."

"Lead" and "Mercury" the seventh and eighth chapters, exist as independent entities within the structure of the book, as might be inferred by their being printed entirely in italics. In the story "Nickel," which immediately precedes "Lead," Levi explains the autobiographical motive of his childhood interest in science fiction that lies behind the presence of these two atypical narratives in the text. Moreover, according to Levi, "Lead" and "Mercury" are two newly discovered stories that hark back to the misery of war and attest to the author's liberation and survival. Despite the existential significance of these recovered documents, which represent a preferred genre from Levi's youth, the two stories seem to distance themselves from the other narratives, almost as if they were out of place, for reasons other than those provided by the author.

Considered "a prisoner's dream of escape" inserted among these "tales of militant chemistry" (78), "Lead" and "Mercury" are first-person narratives of the fictional characters Rodmund and Corporal Abrahams, respectively. Rodmund says he comes from a faraway country inhabited by shepherds, hunters, and warriors that is still wild and completely different from that in which he now lives. He leaves his land and journeys to foreign countries in search of lead, which he hopes will make him wealthy and even gain him a wife. Anticipating the future storyteller Libertino Faussone in Levi's *La chiave a stella* (*The Monkey's Wrench*), published in 1986, Rodmund certainly symbolizes the natural and industrial man who produces labor, an essential theme in Levi's poetics.[4] On the other hand, "Mercury" is a lighter story, precisely in relation to the chemical element's characteristics of elusiveness and weightlessness (Patruno, *Understanding* 64). The narrator, Corporal Abrahams, tells us about a distant island called Desolation, where he lived in isolation with his wife, Maggie, until the arrival of other settlers. The island is pinpointed in the middle of the ocean on a map (97), which Levi feels the need to draw to make the place credible and real. The key theme of this story is the fragility of behavior and the awareness of a lack of human coherence that is parallel to the fleeting quality of mercury and the impossibility of forcing it into predetermined limits. The narration is made particularly mysterious and indefinable by its mix of allegorical and realistic elements, with which Levi creates a place halfway between terrestrial paradise and the island of the "noble savage" typical in eighteenth-century literature. The tales from Levi's youth thus focus on the two themes of work and ethical vagueness: the first as a metaphor for strength, human achievement, and creativity, the second as a sign of weakness, insecurity, and instability. It seems that Levi insists more strongly on these two opposing aspects, especially following his return home from the death camp, and that he prefers to face them by making them reemerge from a past in which both elements were present in a positive energy that nurtured hope and faith. Yet within *The Periodic Table* these elements suggest the limits of human potential: the energy of human activity that can be salvaged together with a sense of exhaustion after the return home and the memory of what the author has suffered.

Let us then take a closer look at one of these "gems of prose" and examine the third chapter, "Zinc," a story from Levi's youth. "Zinc" mainly deals with his apprenticeship and relation to the social world of the university. The suffused yet already painfully felt sociopolitical context of fascism envelops the author's youthful experiences, including his first love. The story follows a linear chronology that covers six distinct narrative moments: the introduction of Professor P., chair of the chemistry department at the University of Turin; the selection of eighty first-year students for the chemistry laboratory; the description of the lab; the figure of Caselli, the laboratory custodian; the preparation of zinc sulfate and the description of zinc's properties; Levi's first meeting with Rita. These six narrative nuclei break down to compose a single plot that contains both the anecdotal form that carries on the author's narrative of memory as well as the recollection of Rita that affirms itself as a lyrical and elegiac seal of personal life, Levi's youth, in relation to the historical period of fascism, synonymous with catastrophe and ruin.

Levi opens the story by setting the portrait of Professor P. against the dominant political regime. The author describes his professor in terms of his psychology, morality, and social relation to others: "P. was a skeptical, ironic old man, the enemy of all forms of rhetoric (for this reason, and only for this, he was an anti-Fascist), intelligent, obstinate, and quick-witted with a sad sort of wit" (29). Levi is fond of Professor P. precisely because of his low-profile, antifascist attitude, represented by the "comic black bib" that peeks out of his jacket when he moves (30).[5] When relating to his students, Professor P. is old-fashioned, authoritarian and severe, secular and anticlerical, opinionated and prejudiced, especially toward women interested in scientific studies: "His students handed down stories of his examinations conducted with ferocious coldness and ostentatious prejudice: his favorite victims were women in general, and then nuns, priests, and all those who appeared before him 'dressed as soldiers'" (29). In Levi's youthful imagination, Professor P. is a kind of savage hunter who performs brutal initiation rituals on students; for them to succeed, they must be exposed to humiliation and denigration (31). Yet Professor P. is also an extravagant, eccentric, exotic, almost maniacal character who uses the chemistry lab to conduct personal experiments based on the analysis of ashes and burned rags left in the basement. The description of the Chemistry Institute, decorated with what Levi calls "mysterious minarets" (30), works with this tone of exoticism to confound chemistry experiments with incomprehensible alchemic activities. In Levi's eyes, however, the laboratory is still "tidy and clean," dominated by the figure of Caselli, P.'s "faithful technician-beadle" (31, 30). Caselli is a symptomatic figure in Levi's human typology that can also evoke Pirandellian aspects for its psychological and social typicality. Levi lingers on the description of this character for almost a whole page, analyzing Caselli as a submissive figure with "vicarial functions," penetrating deeply into his interior life and innermost thoughts (32). Levi's portrait is thus an investigation of particular human personalities that do not necessarily have to be fixed in artistic form according to the typical Pirandellian acceptation but rather that evoke common psychological traits that conjure up opposing sentiments mixed with pity and comprehension, disdain and affection, which exemplify the weaknesses and limits of the human being. The description of Caselli is effective in the way it reproduces general considerations on his psychology, embodied in his own thoughts, which, according to Levi, could be read in his "sad but proud eyes" (32).

Once Caselli has been illustrated, Levi shifts his attention to the observation and processing of zinc. In the narrative economy, zinc works to connect Professor P. and Caselli with the young Primo but mainly with the female character who appears immediately after the description of the chemical element. Moreover, the thematic mechanism of zinc is crucial for Levi the narrator to expand his perspective beyond personal memory and face the historical and political problem of fascism and its resulting totalitarianism and racism. Zinc, in fact, facilitates the recrimination of fascism and anti-Semitism in the story. Although Levi recalls a past experiment with zinc and sulfuric acid, the addition of which makes zinc impure and thus nonresistant, the memory is narrated entirely in the present tense and thus effectively communicates Levi's philosophical considerations on purity and impurity. Just as purity must be praised because it protects from evil like "a coat of mail," impurity is also laudable because it "gives rise to changes, in other words, to life" (34). Levi even admits that he is attracted to impurity more than purity, which he recognizes as "disgustingly moralistic" but synonymous with dissent and diversity and necessary for the experience of life: "Dissension, diversity, the grain of salt and mustard are needed: Fascism does not want them, forbids them, and that's why you're not a Fascist; it wants everybody to be the same, and you are not" (34). The use of the second-person pronoun *you* here effectively reinforces the motifs of dissent and diversity affirmed above in relation to the meaning of impurity echoed in the Nazi-fascist ideas of the "pure race," considered superior to the diverse, contaminated, and inferior Jewish race. At the same time, "salt" and "mustard" may distantly evoke an evangelical message that is still assimilated into a secular acceptation. Thus zinc is better if modified, if it radically distorts its "immaculate virtue" (34).

Satisfied with having contributed to the impurity of zinc in his experiment, Levi then directs his attention toward his laboratory classmates. The description of the chemical reaction thus functions as a transition between scenes, so that the narration passes from the chemical event to the visualization of the human element. Literarily speaking, the shift from the experiment ("the zinc wakes up, it is covered with a white fur of hydrogen bubbles") to the group of other students ("you can . . . take a stroll around the lab and see what's new and what the others are doing") occurs in an abrupt, almost unexpected way, just like a chemical reaction (34). Among Levi's classmates, Rita emerges, "very thin, pale, sad, and sure of herself" (34). The feminine motif that suggests the theme of love seems situated in this passage with a precise narrative objective; in fact, the recollection of Rita gives rise to Levi's consideration and condemnation of a "perpetual masculine solitude": "I . . . am Jewish, and she is not: I am the impurity that makes the zinc react, I am the grain of salt or mustard" (35). Yet again, zinc works as a path—"a small zinc bridge"—to a possible negotiation of this issue. Levi's discovery that Rita and he are reading the same novel, Thomas Mann's *The Magic Mountain*, determines the encounter and acquaintance that strangely develops around literary and not scientific interests. All this is left nearly unsaid and revealed in fragments such as the final syllables of the title or the names of the main characters of the German novel. In the same way, in the story's chronology, Levi's sense of Jewish identity is still limited to religious differences and not to the theories expounded in the fascist journal *Difesa della razza* (*In Defense of Race*) and the subsequent promulgation of racial laws.[6] Only after Auschwitz will this youthful simplicity become the painful complexity that will afflict Levi's life as a chemist and writer up to his death.

Rita is represented as an elegiac memory of youth, as the hope nurtured during that prewar period that something could still have changed. For this reason, Levi's definition of memory as "a marvelous but fallacious instrument" (*Drowned* [Summit, 1988] 23) seems to break down in this recollection of Rita, which stands out and gains ground, while the experiment with zinc sulfate fades away against the background of the laboratory. In fact, the scene becomes almost synesthetic since Rita's image is noticed from a distance through the physical sensation of walking arm in arm (36). It is as if Levi, at the end of "Zinc," wishes at all costs to regain his humanity, which in this case is youthful, distressed, wounded, and metaphorically killed as a result of the atrocities suffered in the death camp. Levi also attempts to recover the humanity of others, as he offers—through the writing of memory—the image of the woman who could be a Dantean savior.

The last words of "Zinc" foreshadow the final part of the final chapter, "Carbon," which sums up the intent, randomness, and truthfulness of this last story and those that precede it. Considered, in Patruno's words, as a "hymn to life" and an "appreciation of the suffering of the Jews and of their ongoing ability to survive" (*Understanding* 77), "Carbon," like the other narrative units of *The Periodic Table*, is a song of praise to a humanity that has been wounded, killed, stolen, and torn away from its civil and cultural values only because it was deemed impure, diverse, and dangerous. Survival thus means continuing and enduring as a primary element of life, in its deepest, double chemical and human nature. The act of writing can obtain different results, like those that produce chemical reactions of all kinds—new, distorted, useless, essential, unexpected, threatening, happy and painful, hopeful or fatal. Storytelling, story writing, and poetic thought do not necessarily have to be autobiographical, even if Levi notes that all human work is autobiographical. What then is the humanity of the elements? Where can we find it? Is it separate from what constitutes the elements or innate to them? Perhaps the union between humanity and chemistry may be found in the admission of human failure, in the recognition of a sense of desperation inherent to the human and historical condition, and in the impossibility of interpreting and making sense of it. The barrier of ineffability also produces writing, and writing is memory, personal and collective, autobiographical and historical, imaginative and realistic. Writing has the task of redemption, accusation, personal comfort—in other words, the knowledge of mystery. Just as the Dantean vision of paradise is realized in the knowledge of the divine point of the sphere, so Levi's vision of human knowledge is realized in the imprinting of the atom with an individuality and humanity: "a double snap, up and down, between two levels of energy, guides this hand of mine to impress on the paper this dot, here, this one" (233).

NOTES

[1]All quotations from *The Periodic Table* are from Rosenthal's 1984 English translation.

[2]Levi's predisposition for science and decision to pursue this course of study began with his enrollment in the Faculty of Chemistry at the University of Turin in 1937, from which he graduated in 1941, despite the fascist racial laws promulgated in 1938 that impeded Jews from attending public schools and universities. As soon as he graduated, Levi was clandestinely hired in a Piedmontese asbestos cave, to then move to Milan to work at the Swiss pharmaceutical company Warden. After the liberation of Auschwitz, Levi was hired at the paint factory Duco-Montecatini, just outside Turin. In 1947 Levi worked as a chemist in another paint factory, SIVA, from where he resigned in 1972 to dedicate himself to writing. His capacities as a chemist were also a great resource for his survival in the concentration camp. Forced to work as a chemist in the Buna factory, Levi, in "Cerium" (the eleventh story in *The Periodic Table*), narrates how he would steal anything and everything from the laboratory, including a few bars of cerium with which he made wicks for cigarette lighters to sell at the *Lager*'s shop.

[3]Among the various but not numerous critical contributions to *The Periodic Table*, Patruno's "*The Periodic Table*," in his *Understanding Primo Levi*, offers particularly detailed, comprehensive, and useful analysis of each story, the novel's narrative structure, and the semantic significance between chemical element and autobiographical fact. Also worth noting is Scheiber's "The Failure of Memory and Literature in Primo Levi's *Il sistema periodico*," which elaborates the complex and delicate thematic structure of memory in Levi's poetics, focusing on "Vanadium" to recognize not only Levi's painful process of remembering Auschwitz but also the failure of memory since those past atrocities represent a concept impossible to comprehend.

[4]*La chiave a stella* narrates the many construction adventures of a specialized factory worker, Libertino Faussone, who tells them to a writer friend of his. The work is developed on the structure of the teller-listener relationship, typical of the oral novella and already present in Boccaccio's *Decameron* and in Calvino's *Le città invisibili* (*Invisible Cities*). Besides offering the reader a bridge that links real life with the imaginary, *La chiave a stella* celebrates the value of the human work ethic, considered by Levi to be a real source of happiness.

[5]Under the fascist regime, university professors had to wear a black shirt as a sign of respect and support for the party. Professor P. wore a surrogate shirt, a sort of bib underneath his coat that could easily be removed. University instructors also had to swear loyalty to the regime and enroll in the fascist party.

[6]The first issue of the *Difesa della razza* appeared on 5 August 1938. The journal, edited by Telesio Interlandi, was published until 1943 with the task of offering statistical and scientific data on the superiority of the Aryan race, which also included the Italian race. The propaganda was intended to push Italians to protect themselves from possible contaminations from inferior races. In "Zinc," Levi declares that, until the journal's publication and the emanation of the racial laws, the fact of his being Jewish was of little importance: "In truth . . . it had not meant much to me that I was a Jew: within myself, and in my contacts with my Christian friends, I had always considered my origin as an almost negligible but curious fact, a small amusing anomaly, like having a crooked nose or freckles; a Jew is somebody who at Christmas does not have a tree, who should not eat salami but eats it all the same, who has learned a bit of Hebrew at thirteen and then has

forgotten it. According to the above-mentioned magazine, a Jew is stingy and cunning; but I was not particularly stingy or cunning, nor had my father been" (35–36). Moreover, the choice of Thomas Mann as a link of interest between Primo and Rita may not be casual: the German author was against Nazism and decided to leave Germany and move first to Switzerland, then to California, and did not return to his homeland until 1945.

The Writing of History in Levi's and Francesco Rosi's *La tregua*

Gaetana Marrone

Teaching Primo Levi's *La tregua* (*The Truce*; 1963) offers instructors the opportunity to introduce the great memoirist of the Holocaust as well as one of the outstandingly moving novels of postwar Italy. Its cultural and political relevance inspired the filmmaker Francesco Rosi to work on a scenario with Tonino Guerra beginning in the early 1960s and finally realized in 1997, delayed by the expenses of production of the large-scale project, with John Turturro in the leading role. Rosi's *La tregua* champions Levi as the progressive counterpoise to the "static" view of the Holocaust found in established historical responses to Nazi atrocity. The critical and political debates over Rosi's film may attest to the director's commitment to fashioning a cinematic equivalent to Levi's novel: the true cost of a man's soul becomes the most shattering measure of surviving in a world where the ideology of evil is the ultimate historical drama. Hence, the teacher must illuminate two pedagogical aspects: that of comparing Rosi's adaptation to its literary source (subjective narration versus the dramatic representation of a writer-witness) and that of Holocaust representation in general. In his decision to make a film of Levi's text, Rosi faced a formidable challenge. If cinema is an eye on reality, as he believed, then the testimonial memoir of one of the most recognizable survivors of the Holocaust becomes a locus for documentation and denunciation, as well as storytelling. This essay focuses on cinema in its function of "come denuncia e come testimonianza della realtà" 'how to report and to witness reality' (Rosi, "Il mio modo" 103)[1] and as a medium to tell stories through which we, and our students, can learn how to judge events in the context of history. More important, we are confronted with the moral responsibility that Holocaust representation demands. As Millicent Marcus has perceptively remarked, *La tregua* exhibits an "almost biblical referentiality," and any nonliteral adaptation could elicit "charges of heresy" ("Filming" 253). On this point, Levi himself inscribes his autobiographical writing on Hebrew scripture (Deut. 6.4–9), in Primo/Turturro's closing lines, powerful and prophetic:

> Meditate che questo è stato:
> Vi comando queste parole.
> Scolpitele nel vostro cuore
> Stando in casa andando per via
> Coricandovi alzandovi
> Ripetetele ai vostri figli.
>
> Meditate that this has been:
> I command you these words.

Carve them in your hearts
Staying at home, going on the way
Upon going to bed, when rising up
Repeat them to your children.

La tregua is Levi's sequel to his classic memoir of his year of camp labor at the Buna-Monowitz chemical plant, *Se questo è un uomo* (*Survival in Auschwitz*; 1947), in which the above passage also appears. Written between December 1961 and November 1962, *La tregua* recounts his picaresque nine-month-long journey back to Turin after the liberation of Auschwitz by the Red Army on 27 January 1945 (a date that today commemorates the victims of the Shoah). The memoir details the daily life of a heterogeneous group of human beings (Jews and non-Jews alike) who travel through bombed-out towns and transit camps on their eventful journey home. There are petty thieves, farmers, gypsies, as well as intellectuals, coming from diverse ethnic backgrounds, speaking a multiplicity of languages (Italian, Polish, Czech, French, Greek, German), and obeying different social and moral codes.

The opening chapters of *La tregua*, entitled "Il disgelo" ("The Thaw") and "Il Campo Grande" ("The Main Camp"), describe the occurrences of January 1945, as Levi attempts to confront the Holocaust in its "matter," that is, "from the viewpoint of a chemist of history" (Lang, *Holocaust Representation* 33). He questions the memorable christening of a series of baths, "alla maniera russa, a misura umana, estemporaneo ed approssimativo" 'in the Russian manner, to human measure, extemporaneous and rough,' and underscores the liberators' unconscious desire "di spogliarci delle vestigia della nostra vita di prima, di fare di noi degli uomini nuovi, conformi ai loro modelli, di imporci il loro marchio" 'to strip us of the vestiges of our former life, to make of us new men consistent with their own models, to impose their brand on us' (*La tregua* 18–19).[2] But notwithstanding the spectrum of this "grande ombra simbolica" 'great symbolic shadow' (19), a change in tone has now taken place. Within this realm of oppressive experience there is the first-person narrator's desire to understand: after the escape from hell follows the euphoric stage of a difficult yet rejuvenating journey back to life. Levi returns to his roots for the ultimate survivor's story and revisits them from a writer's rather than from a witness's viewpoint: a triumph over the experience of the actual horrors committed in the tragic world of the *Lager*. *La tregua* invites discussion of the ways in which survival may foster a crisis in identity, one that bears the scars of irrefutable monstrosity with likely deep social consequences.

The ultimate difficulty that confronts anyone who survived the concentration camp is how to communicate a past that remains essentially memorial and real. How can one recount when the events defy language?[3] There are frightening truths that can only be transmitted by silence, and there are others that not even silence can express. And yet they must be told. For a long time, many survivors refused to talk, even if they continued to visit their sites of pain and horror while the world, in its haste to forget the tragedy that had taken place, continued to function as if nothing had happened. They feared that no one would understand the true price for having survived hell, for being a living witness of the spectral logic of annihilation. Some victims endured isolation and self-imposed exclusion. An ontological phenomenon, the Final Solution defies any understanding. "Let's be honest," argues Elie Wiesel, "[i]n this sense the enemy can boast of his triumph. Through the scope of his deadly enterprise, he deprives us of words to describe it" (Foreword xi). Thus the *Lager* becomes an object that haunts the survivor from the space of the unconscious: it is the guilt of the unthinkable, heightened by the fact that few are willing to confess it. The camps for the extermination of the Jews, such as Auschwitz, Treblinka, and Sobibor, seemed to belong to another time. The essential could remain unspoken, buried in the ashes that cover a dramaturgy of suffering, hence the drama of the witness. In images of the *Lager*, the new common language—the language of violence—that allows the victims to communicate with one another functions as a mechanism for coping with guilty memories. Levi spoke at length of the victim's compulsion to enact the past, a sort of voluntary repetition that compensates for a sentiment of loss and guilt. This famous Holocaust survivor felt compelled to metamorphose his experience into storytelling itself. In a 1977 interview, Levi confessed, "Ormai sono diventato un registratore; se mi si accende, comincio a ricordare per gli altri. Per quelli che non sono tornati ma fecero di tutto per lasciare una traccia. Sono il testimone di quel che esiste nel pozzo della notte" 'By now I am like a tape recorder; if you turn me on, I begin to remember for the others. For those who did not return but did everything to leave a trace. I am a witness of what exists at the bottom of the well of the night' ("Primo Levi, il testimone"). Thus while the multiplicity of languages in the prison camp seems to be the realization of a biblical curse (the story of Babel), with the newfound freedom celebrated by *La tregua* it becomes the starting point for recapturing a common bond that overcomes ethnic boundaries: as Cesare Segre has noted, Levi and his heterogeneous companions see their linguistic knowledge expand into a promising gamut of possibility ("Primo Levi" 93–94).

These are disturbing issues that both Levi and Rosi address with striking talent. Can the filmic image perhaps be more accessible and expressive than the word? A historicized discussion of the Holocaust through literature and cinema enables students to be informed and sensitized about its ideological and material infrastructures: how the unthinkable technocratic "solutions" to Germany's wartime problems were implemented and executed as a logical component of social modernization. By the end of 1943, the lack of manual labor becomes such a serious issue in Germany that the architects of annihilation saw fit to utilize everybody, including the Jews. It is out of this critical period that Auschwitz was constructed. In an interview with Ferdinando Camon, Levi recalled the circumstances that had given rise to this "hybrid *Lager*" and had encouraged rational production methods that matched extermination with exploitation or, better still, extermination through the process of exploitation:

> Io devo la sopravvivenza a questo: cioè al fatto di essere arrivato, come tutti gli ebrei italiani, abbastanza tardi, e di essere stato infilato in un sistema produttivo. . . . quello di un serbatoio di manodopera a basso prezzo, anzi prezzo nullo. Era stato calcolato in modo molto razionale questo fatto: si prevedeva una sopravvivenza di tre mesi. C'era un conflitto tra l'autorità politica, le SS, padrona dei *Lager*, e l'industria tedesca: a cui non piaceva questo sistema, non per ragioni umanitarie, ma perché un operaio che sta lì tre mesi e poi muore è un cattivo operaio, che non rende: infatti noi rendevamo poco, e questa cosa creava conflitti e faceva nascere proteste. Questa diarchia era visibile a occhio nudo, perché vivevamo di notte in *Lager*, sotto il dominio delle SS, e di giorno in fabbrica, sotto il potere dell'industria tedesca. (*Conversazione* 38–39)

> I owe my survival to the fact that I arrived rather late at the camp, as did all Italian Jews, and I was inserted in a productive system. . . . We were reserved for manual labor at a very low cost, in fact free. This plan was conceived in a very rational way: they could foresee a survival rate for a period of three months. There arose a conflict between the political authority, the SS who ran the *Lager*, and the German Industry who did not approve of the system, not for humanitarian reasons, but because a worker who is eliminated within three months is not a productive worker: indeed we produced little, causing conflicts and protests. This diarchy was clearly visible to the naked eye, because at night we were in the *Lager*, under the supervision of the SS, and during the day we worked in the factory, under the power of German Industry.

The concentration camp empire of Auschwitz, with its sinister strategy to balance the ratio between productive and unproductive prisoners (it had a capacity of about twenty thousand prisoners), exceeds all logic and documents the barbarity of our time. One entered the German camps in general never to emerge. Death was a byproduct of hunger, cold, and illness. As Levi describes the Nazi offense against humanity, he makes clear that there exists no rational explanation for what happened in the camps. Thus treatment in the camp can only be interpreted as a manifestation of inexplicable and wanton evil with no possible relation to the European cultural tradition and to history (Feinstein 337). In *La tregua*, Levi relates how the Polish command *Wstawàch* ("get up") still haunts the survivor on his reaching home on 19 October, despite his recapturing "il calore della mensa sicura, la concretezza del lavoro quotidiano, la gioia liberatrice del raccontare" 'the warmth of secure meals, the solidity of daily work, the liberating joy of recounting [his] story' (254). Evoked by a powerful surge of memory, a dream within a dream, the gelid dawn command of Auschwitz seals the concluding lines of "Il risveglio" ("The Awakening"), the book's final chapter. From such a point of view, *Wstawàch* becomes a recurrent act of symbolic communication: "Tutto è ora volto in caos: sono solo al centro di un nulla grigio e torbido, ed ecco, io so che cosa significa, edanche so di averlo sempre saputo: sono di nuovo in Lager, e nulla era vero all'infuori del Lager" 'Now everything has turned to chaos. I am alone in the center of a gray and turbid nothing, and then I know what it means, and I also know that I have always known: I am in the *Lager* once more, and nothing was true outside the *Lager*' (254). Here is a case of documented horror; the effect is visceral panic. Primo's pounding nightmare signals a revolt against the experience of the *Lager*. Students might be asked to pursue further the intricacies of how the crude biologistic formula of annihilation implemented in the death camps rejects interpretations that point only to Nazi officers as the perpetrators of the Holocaust.

The title of Levi's *La tregua* (first published in the United States in 1965 as *The Reawakening*) announces temporary stillness, not a permanent solution. An ironic resolution shapes the title selected for the American edition, borrowed from the closing chapter of the novel (Patruno, *Understanding* 29). Levi's journey proves to be an exemplary spiritual experience of hope, but the silence and the shadow of doubt that the infernal machine of Auschwitz cast on the inmates could only be overcome during short-lived respites from pain. The title can be extended to cover a broad spectrum of the generation marked by the war, perhaps of all survivors, entrapped in the dark space between historical tragedy and the burden of its legacy. Thus, the truce is an effective metaphor that attests to the recurrent nightly awakening of a shattered self, the period combining a primordial vitality with the poignant tone of reflective recollection.

Rosi's epical adaptation of the chaotic world in postwar Europe captures the very moment when civilization triumphs only through its flickering glimpses of hope and laughter. Because of its extraordinary moral weight, the subject demanded the largest effort of authenticity in any representation or judgment of it. We find before us a film that transcends the argument for viewing the Holocaust as a rupture in history, that is an event still beyond the reach of language, exceeding known words and concepts. *La tregua* attests at once to the continuity for Levi between the pre- and post-Holocaust existence. It detracts nothing from the challenge posed by that event and also reinscribes Primo's odyssey to ordinary experience, since the survivor speaks now with the authority of Auschwitz.

Through the recollection of his extraordinary adventures Levi conveyed the process of coming back to life and of the reawakening of hope by indulging in the small and big events of everyday life. Notwithstanding the palpable realities of the Holocaust, his discourse is fashioned by a strong belief in humanity. Working under tremendous pressures, on location in Eastern Europe, Rosi was able to create a moving story of survival, both physical and interior, at times irreducibly real and familiar, at others undeniably threatening and alien. The difficult shooting conditions in Ukraine (where *La tregua* was entirely filmed) meant that both actors and the crew had to be flexible, be dedicated, and make sacrifices. One of the strongest, most realistic aspects about this film is the director's use of real faces of Ukraine, faces that are intelligent, long-suffering, and very much aware of the poverty they have endured since World War II. Individual portraits of refugees introduce the viewer to a reality in its most haunting guise: the world seems to have reverted to primeval chaos. The film primarily translates the moral indignant tone of Levi's novel, dramatizing that thin line between the tragic and the grotesque through a series of unsettling and comic occurrences, intercut with flashbacks in Auschwitz. Among the novel features that attracted Rosi to this text was that, unlike other Holocaust stories that recounted the brutality committed during camp internment, *La tregua* focused on depicting the trials that freedom brings to the survivors. Indeed, freedom marks a turning point in the prisoners' existence. As Levi writes, "di fronte alla libertà ci sentivamo smarriti, svuotati, atrofizzati, disadatti alla nostra parte" 'face to face with freedom we felt ourselves lost, emptied, atrophied, unfit for our part' (*La tregua* 13). A second point is the recognition of what Levi (a scientist with a literary and philosophical formation) finds meaningful for us the readers: namely the requirements that have to be met to be human.

In the opening shots, we witness the Germans burning the *Lager* and trying to destroy all evidence of it. Rosi sets up the scene by superimposing a written text over these images, thus identifying the context of historical reference. Four Russian soldiers on horseback rise above the horizon set against a foggy gray sky, shot with a telephoto lens. They move toward the main camp and, in a low camera angle, are shown tearing down its front gates. The worn-out prisoners slowly make their way out to freedom. Soon afterward they spot the Red Army approaching with horses and tanks. At this confusing time, the frightened prisoners return to their camp for shelter. But Primo stands at the gate and witnesses this historical moment. At this point his voice-over is introduced, describing his inner thoughts, symptomatic of what is to come in the film: an eyewitness account of facts that follows a chronological order. From now on the spectator is constantly made to participate in a grave gaze that encompasses the character's reflective eye. We plunge into the past from the vantage point of its outcome and, more precisely, of its author's survival.

In reconstructing Levi's experience of the concentration camp, Rosi wanted to preserve a strong veneer of objectivity. He builds on a montage of images that suggest the tonality of news footage, intercutting the burning of documents with last-minute executions. As the Germans hastily evacuate Auschwitz, the deportees are left alone staring in silence; their long wait evokes a kind of sinister limbo that constitutes all existential interrogations. Rosi's realist mode of historical representation reveals a great capacity for invention. The stark contrast between atmosphere and violence toward humanity is what defines the film.

The film more fully characterizes a number of the memorable companions about whom Levi wrote incisively. Furthermore, it imaginatively portrays those moments when Holocaust survivors reexperience the beauty of nature and music, as well as such essential human needs as humor, love, sex, and brotherhood. The figurative balance and narrative economy of the film enhances the intense and yet measured emotion that Levi gives to his story—a breath of a narrative epic together with the minimalness of everyday characters. Primo's relationship with Galina, one of the girls who works for the Kommandantur in the transit camp of Katowice, is a perfect example: the shyness, sweetness, tenderness, and profound sentiments of a young man who falls in love, purely, without seeking the benefit from this encounter. The touching, delicate love story allows us to verify our own fragility and insecurity and to reflect on the attitudes and comportment of today's youth. Rosi represents the delicacy of an uncommon story without recourse to the usual, melodramatic canons. Levi writes fondly about Galina, whom he sketches very briefly as a sensitive, intelligent eighteen-year-old girl from Kazàtin; she eventually disappears, "risucchiata dalla vacuità dello spazio russo, per i cammini del suo paese sconfinato, lasciando dietro di sé un profumo aspro di terra, di giovinezza e di gioia" 'sucked up again into the emptiness of Russian space, along the paths of her endless country, leaving behind her a sharp scent of earth, of youth, and of joy' (*La tregua* 75). Her story with Primo in the novel is invented, and to carry it further in the film would have upset Rosi's desired equilibrium with the book. The director highlights, however, the moment when the train reaches the station with Galina, adding a few exchanges between Rovi and Ferrari (small-time criminals deported to German labor camps), who stick their heads out the windows as the train is pulling in. Primo and Galina's theme music fades up, and the two finally embrace and part.

Rosi does not need to literally show deportees on the brink of death, nor did he have to downplay music and songs in the name of historical authenticity, as Segre has argued in reviewing the film ("*La tregua?*"). Other critics have taken a polemical view of Rosi's cinematic adaptation. Goffredo Fofi finds fault in *La tregua* without even watching it: "I have not screened the film, and most likely I won't like it" (106). Writing in 1997, at the Cannes Film Festival, Didier Péron launched a ferocious attack, defining the film as "a truly fantastic expression of stupidity," whereas Claude Baignères, in a more positive light, praises the director by writing, "Rosi engages a dialogue between contemporary history and eternal man, and the result becomes magical."

Indeed, with reacquired freedom, a positive state of being embraces the survivors. Emotions such as happiness and unexplainable euphoria become inseparable from their natural state of inner rebirth. Moments of peace are possible whenever the mind is silenced, whether triggered by great beauty or physical exertion or impending danger. In the book, the picaresque Cesare, one of Levi's privileged companions, stands out because of his gift for daring, wit, and mimicry. This is not the case in the cinematic adaptation, where he is given less relevance, especially when compared with Mordo Nahum. The film is ever more focused on Primo. An exemplary case is the episode of the refugees trying to exchange some of their scarce belongings for a hen. Primo (Cesare in the novel) resorts to onomatopoeia (*coccodè* ["cluck, cluck"]) and gestures (crouching on the ground, pecking randomly using his hands as a beak) to reproduce the mannerisms of the chicken and easily fools the poor-witted peasants. But besides such scenes rich with a powerful comic force, Rosi's *La tregua* most prominently suggests a political allegory of the future. We can detect its earliest signs in Levi's description of organized life in the post-Auschwitz period as he introduces the Starye Dorogi settlement camp, the mysterious Red House, a sort of political fairyland. Mordo Nahum, known as *Il greco* ("The Greek"), embodies a kind of postwar cynicism. Levi carries on a lengthy conversation with this mesmerizing wise man and explicitly addresses the fact that, while Mordo is able to return to Greece, Primo must remain behind. Indeed, Greece was one of the founding countries of the United Nations; Italy only joined in 1955. This reference to the United Nations signals the author's shift from the emotional and existential transformation of the survivor to a global concern for the future. For Levi, his mission as a witness becomes a vital necessity, and the words of Mordo—"Guerra è sempre" 'There is always war' (*La tregua* 61)—ascribe the paradoxical historical situation to a suspended moment of truce.

La tregua is an autobiographical story, but Rosi translates it into something very personal, imbuing the literary text with his values and his world. There are scenes in the film in no way connected with Levi's memoir: among them, the potential sex scene between Levi and Flora in the woods or the German officer in the train station, who kneels in front of Primo as if to ask for forgiveness. Rosi reduces Primo/Turturro's dialogue to a minimum, as though to enhance the poetic power of the filmic image. It is in silence that one of the film's most talked-about reinvented scenes unfolds: the German kneeling before Primo at the Monaco train station, when he sees the Star of David shining out of Primo's jacket. If the writer schematizes his existential relation to what he describes as a "folla anomala di visi sigillati" 'anomalous crowd of sealed faces' with the suspension of a judgment (*La tregua* 251), for Rosi, this symbolic gesture falls within the contemporary milieu that underlies his film. The German officer kneels under the weight of the accusing gaze of Levi, a gesture that symbolizes an admission of guilt, what Vincent Remy has descried as "an absurd pardon" toward a forgetting of historical reality in the wake of the Holocaust. Rosi was inspired by a photograph of the German chancellor Willy Brandt in front of a memorial dedicated to the victims of the Warsaw ghetto. As Jean Gili has observed, the message of the film is exhausted here—in the figure of a man who takes upon himself the tragedy of an entire people, guilty, before history, of crimes against humanity (7).

At the end of his long journey, back home, Primo begins to write, staring at the camera lens. It is a moment of great emotion, of summing up. *La tregua*'s final scene sets in motion the mechanisms of identification with an ontological space. The closing shots come to question our responsibility to open our eyes and see, to open our hearts and recapture our ancient human soul. Levi, the author, is capable of defining his sentiments, his burden, only after his return, when he can start life anew and write for others. Ultimately, the slow, labyrinthine journey described in *La tregua*—the colorful railroad odyssey that carries Primo and other freed camp inmates back home—conveys a dream of peace, of freedom, of communication and human solidarity and the hope of discovering how beautiful, notwithstanding all that has happened, the world can be. Rosi asserts the importance of memory as a vehicle to construct the future on the basis of a transgenerational network: "Levi ci ha lasciato il dovere di ricordare, ed anche il dono della speranza" 'Levi has left us the duty of remembering, as well as the gift of hope' (qtd. in Colombo).

NOTES

[1] Unless otherwise noted, all translations from the Italian are mine.

[2] All references to Levi's *La tregua* are to the first edition (Einaudi, 1963).

[3] In *Se questo è un uomo*, Levi attempts to define the total loss of human dignity experienced in the *Lager* as the destruction of a man: "Allora per la prima volta ci siamo accorti che la nostra lingua manca di parole per esprimere questa offesa, la demolizione di un uomo. In un attimo, con intuizione quasi profetica, la realtà ci si è rivelata: siamo arrivati al fondo" 'Then for the first time we realized our language lacks adequate words for expressing this offense, the destruction of a man. In an instant, with almost prophetic intuition, the reality of our state is revealed to us: we have reached rock bottom' ([2005] 23).

If Not Now, When?
A Novel of Reconciliation and Becoming

Risa Sodi

If Not Now, When? is a complex novel that tells the story of a ragtag group of Eastern European Jewish partisans as they struggle through the last two years of World War II.[1] In it, Levi traces the lives, decisions, and motivations that drive a band of men and women to fight their way across the Soviet Union, Poland, and Germany, gaining freedom and dignity along the way and the chance to emigrate to Eretz Israel. Levi's complex motivations for writing *If Not Now, When?* include a desire to understand the Ashkenazi Jewish world and to present it to his Italian readership. Thus the backdrop of the novel, originally published by Einaudi in 1982, differs from his previous and subsequent works insofar as it centers not on Italy but on the Slavic and Germanic lands to the northeast. Unlike his previous works, the novel does not reflect Levi's personal war experience, nor does it unfold within the *univers concentrationnaire* of the Holocaust.

Primo Levi and the Ashkenazi World

As an Italian Jew of Sephardic origin, Levi was largely unaware of the existence of Ashkenazi Jewry until his deportation to Auschwitz in 1944 (Jesurum 98; Levi, *Drowned* [Summit, 1988] 100–01 and *If Not Now* 340). And yet the unfamiliar Eastern European Ashkenazi world was to become the central landscape of *If Not Now, When?*, Levi's homage to World War II Jewish partisans.

Italian Jewish culture was based on a mixture of Sephardic (Spanish) and Italki (native Italian) rites, whereas Ashkenazi culture was rooted in the Germanic and Slavic practices of northeastern Europe. Ashkenazi culture, in contrast with Italian Jewish culture, was characterized by strict religious observance, communal organization in small villages called shtetls, and near-universal use of Yiddish. Italian Jewry had a much different countenance from its Ashkenazi counterpart: by the late nineteenth century, Italian Jews were highly assimilated in terms of housing, occupations, and social and civic relations. They spoke not Yiddish but the Italian of their neighbors. By his own admission, Levi was hardly aware of his Jewish background until made so by the promulgation of the 1938 fascist racial laws.

Levi was fascinated yet puzzled by the differences between the Italian and Ashkenazi experiences. By re-creating the story of a band of Ashkenazi partisans, Levi sought to relay the story of Eastern European Jewry to an Italian audience and also to correct lingering moralistic judgments, according to which Jews did not do enough to resist the Nazis. On a personal level, the novel allowed Levi, through his fictional characters, to recast his own role in the Holocaust. *If Not Now, When?* signals Levi's only attempt to write a Holocaust novel or any sort of long-form fiction devoid (by and large) of Italian characters and set outside the Italian milieu.

The Genesis of If Not Now, When?

Levi's brainchild had a thirty-year gestation period. Its origin can be traced to three crucial elements: Levi's immersion in the Ashkenazi Jewish experience at Auschwitz; his encounter, a short time later, with a band of former partisans and Zionists on their way to Palestine; and the tales he heard from a friend who worked at a postwar Jewish refugee assistance center in Milan. These seeds, combined with intense debates in the late 1970s in Israel and elsewhere over the role of European Jews during the Holocaust and Levi's drive to put aside autobiographical prose and challenge himself to write a novel removed from his own experience, spurred Levi to begin the research that ultimately led to *If Not Now, When?*

Levi returned to Italy, after liberation from Auschwitz on 7 January 1945, via a fitful and exhausting ten-month journey from Poland through the Soviet Union, Romania, Hungary, Czechoslovakia, Austria, and Germany. He finally arrived home on 19 October 1945. At the Brenner Pass he encountered a group of "extremely self-confident and resolute people; they were young Zionists on their way to Israel. . . . They felt immensely free and strong, lords of the world and of their destinies" (*Reawakening* [Summit, 1986] 371). This encounter formed one of "i nuclei generative" 'the original nuclei' of *If Not Now, When?*; indeed, the lead character, Gedaleh, was modeled on the leader of that band ("Note ai testi" 1538; my trans.).

Another nucleus for *If Not Now, When?* was Levi's conversation in 1966 with his friend Emilio Vita Finzi about a particular group of male and female Jewish partisans Vita Finzi had observed as a volunteer at a Jewish refugee assistance center in Milan. Levi was particularly struck by Vita Finzi's tales of the group's compact solidarity and insistence on being recognized as combatants and not refugees. "Io mi sono annotato questa storia e l'ho lasciata per quindici anni nel cassette. Poi me venne l'idea che unendo questi due episodi poteva nascere un romanzo" 'I jotted down this story and I put it aside in a drawer for fifteen years. Then I got the idea that, by joining these two episodes [the encounter with the partisans at the Brenner Pass and Vita Finzi's stories of the partisans in Milan], a novel might be born' (1538; my trans.).

At least two other elements came to play in the genesis of *If Not Now, When?*—one external and one internal. In the late 1970s, debates simmered in Israel and elsewhere over the behavior of Jews during the Holocaust. As Levi wrote in "Itinerary of a Jewish Writer," the questions were, "Did they really let themselves to be led to slaughter without resisting? If so, why? If not, how many, when, where had they resisted?" (166). Also in the late 1970s and into the early 1980s, Levi, by then an accomplished and respected writer, was confronted with doubts by some—and probably even himself—that he was capable of writing fiction that was not connected to the Holocaust or his autobiography. Tackling the subject matter of Eastern European Jewish partisans, both men and women, fighting and loving their way through World War II was a way of answering his critics and his challenge to himself. Levi spoke frankly about these several motivating factors to Philip Roth in 1986:

> *If Not Now, When?* followed an unforeseen path. The motivations that drove me to write it are manifold. Here they are, in order of importance:
>
> I had made a sort of bet with myself: after so much plain or disguised autobiography, are you, or are you not, a full-fledged writer, capable of constructing a novel, shaping characters, describing landscapes you have never seen? Try it!
>
> I intended to amuse myself by writing a "Western" plot set in a landscape uncommon in Italy. I intended to amuse my readers by telling them a substantially optimistic story, a story of hope, even occasionally cheerful, although projected onto a background of massacre.
>
> I wished to assault a commonplace still prevailing in Italy: a Jew is a mild person, a scholar (religious or profane), unwarlike, humiliated, who tolerated centuries of persecution without ever fighting back. It seemed to me a duty to pay homage to those Jews who, in desperate conditions, had found the courage and the skills to resist. ("A Man" 20–21)

Levi goes on to reveal to Roth an additional motivation: he possessed "the ambition to be the first (perhaps only) Italian writer to describe the Yiddish world." By "exploit[ing]" his popularity in Italy, he hoped "to impose upon my readers a book centered on the Ashkenazi civilization, history, language, and frame of mind, all of which are virtually unknown in Italy, except by some sophisticated readers of Joseph Roth, Bellow, Singer, Malamud, Potok and of course yourself [Philip Roth]" (21).

Levi was in the process of drafting the series of essays on the concentration camp experience that ultimately would take shape as *The Drowned and the Saved*, which he put aside to do research for and write *If Not Now, When?* He first meticulously documented the story of Ashkenazi fighters in World War II—even going so far as to teach himself Yiddish and translate the little-known story of a group of Jews who fought in the Pripet Marshes and then wended their way to Italy—before beginning to write (Kahanovich).

What made *If Not Now, When?* "good fun" to plan and write, and why did Levi claim that the year he spent writing it was "a happy one" or that the end result was "a liberating book" ("A Man" 22)? Why did he say, "[F]or the first and only time in my life as a writer, I had the impression (almost a hallucination) that my characters were alive, around me, behind my back, suggesting spontaneously their feats and their dialogues"? Part of the answer lies with the protagonist, Mendel. Through his alter ego, Mendel, and through Mendel's contrasts with Gedaleh, Levi was able to explore and symbolically recast his role in the Holocaust; through their interactions, he attempted to reconcile his own (in)actions and to resolve the lingering shame he later wrote about so poignantly in *The Drowned and the Saved* ("Shame"; see also "The Last One," in *Survival in Auschwitz*). Finally, by writing about hope amid the massacre, Levi let fiction trump autobiography, permitted dignity to replace humiliation, and allowed the finality of the Holocaust to mutate into a tale of becoming.

Form and Style in If Not Now, When?

If Not Now, When? opens in medias res with Mendel's assertion, "In my village, there weren't many clocks" (19). This simple statement, together with crucial paratextual components, sets up the form of the novel and reveals much about important thematic elements and about the character of Mendel. Understanding Mendel, in turn, helps us understand Levi and his creation of an alter ego.

That the novel begins in medias res accentuates the sense of urgency conveyed in the title, an oft-quoted citation from the Pirke Avoth ("Ethics of the Fathers"), composed by the first-century Jewish scholar Hillel. These moral maxims represent part of the postbiblical codification of Jewish oral law called the Mishnah. In chapter 1, verse 14, Hillel asks, "If I am not for myself, then who will be for me? And if I am only for myself, then what am I? And if not now, when?"[2] As adopted by Levi, this maxim underscores the importance both of timely action and of compassion, humanitarianism, and service—all attributes of Mendel and the partisans of *If Not Now, When?*

In the Italian edition of the book, two important elements are interposed between the title and the beginning of the novel proper. The first is a bifold map—in place of an epigraph—that serves as a graphic representation of the theme of the journey and links *If Not Now, When?* to *The Reawakening* and to *The Search for Roots*, both works of literal or intellectual exploration and geographic and emotional discovery. Like *The Reawakening*, *If Not Now, When?* traces a Ulysses-like voyage of return and, like *The Search for Roots*, presents an exercise in cultural commonalities and genealogies. Moreover, one can posit that a search for roots lies at the core of Levi's opus as a whole and—for Levi as an Italian, a Jew, a partisan, and a survivor—very strongly in *If Not Now, When?* The second telling element between the title page and the opening words of the novel is the title of the first chapter, "July 1943." The simple calendrical framework Levi attaches to his chapter titles reprises a tendency he had shown in his earliest poems ("February 25, 1944," "February 11, 1946," "Monday," or "Another Monday") and in the chapter "October 1944" in *Survival in Auschwitz*. This time-based scheme differs substantially from the content-based chapter headings he adopted in his only previous novel, *The Monkey's Wrench*. Levi returned to a calendrical titling scheme for the poem "July 12, 1980"—written during the drafting of *If Not Now, When?* Thus, the geographic exactitude of Levi's map and the chronometric specificity of his chapter headings underscore Levi's concern for precise topography, dating, and historical convergences, even if grafted onto a fictional matrix. They also inform Mendel's first sentence and clarify Levi's intent that this novel and its characters—though fictional—be firmly grounded in time and place.

The July 1943 opening date of the novel is not accidental, as informed Italian readers would know, for it coincided with the Allied invasion of Sicily (and the beginning of the end for Mussolini and fascism). July 1943 also saw the crucial Battle of Kursk—staged not far from Mendel's hideout in the village of Valuets (today known as Walvez)—a precursor to the eventual Nazi defeat.[3] Similar juxtapositions of the exotic and the familiar, triumph and defeat, and carnage and rebirth thread their way through the novel. The calendrical chapter headings are signposts for historical events, and the chapters are populated with a vast array of ethnic and national groups (e.g., Byelorussians, Tatars, Tartars, Cossacks, Samoyeds, Ukrainian Baptists, Georgian Jews). Add in modern character types (e.g., Bundists, Mensheviks, nihilists, feminists, xenophobes, wise old leaders, brash young men, the lost, the alienated, the battle-crazed, the battle-weary), and one begins to realize the amplitude of Levi's ambition and the breadth of his anthropological, historical, and narrative project in *If Not Now, When?*

Some criticized the novel for a lack of narrative invention and for its conventional structure (see, e.g., Keffer with Ruch). Like most of Levi's previous works, it proceeds in strict chronological order, with few deviations for flashbacks or other sorts of narrative embellishments. Yet here Levi introduces a new element into his writing: the omniscient narrator. Levi had structured *Survival in Auschwitz* and *The Reawakening* as first-person narratives and had given *The Monkey's Wrench* a first-person narrator (couched in the guise of an alter ego, an unnamed writer and chemist). *If Not Now, When?* instead shifts the narrator duties to a bona fide outsider, an omniscient unnamed party who, akin to Alessandro Manzoni's narrator in *The Betrothed* and Elsa Morante's in *History*, occasionally speaks directly to the reader (96, 292, 330). This *io narrante* ("narrating I") also offers his own musings, as if reflecting patterns of oral history or simply muttering to himself (203, 317). Levi's readers eventually realize that they have become privy to the inner voice of Levi's primary alter ego, Mendel.

Primo Levi's Alter Ego(s)

Three candidates vie for the title of Levi's alter ego: Mendel, Gedaleh, and the unnamed narrator (who is also occasionally conflated with Mendel). Francine, a character present only in chapter 11, might also be advanced as an alter ego, though *doppelgänger* might a better term (Sodi, "Primo Levi's *If Not Now*").[4]

Alternatively, one might also advance Leonid as a nightmarish alter ego for Levi. A young man intent on pursuing his own destruction, he represents a type that the younger Levi had feared becoming.[5] While various candidates may present themselves, only Mendel elicits Levi's overt identification, and only Gedaleh consistently connects to Levi's belief set.

Mendel is the primary voice in *If Not Now, When?*, and he alone among its thirty-odd characters is present throughout its entire arc and in all its crucial moments. His character partakes of both the "quiet and rather private" interpersonal moments in Levi's tale and of its "fierce and exciting" episodes of partisan activity (Eberstadt 45; Howe 16). That Levi closely identified with Mendel was made explicit in a 1982 interview: "Deep down, I did identify with Mendel," Levi told Rosellina Balbi. "I mean that he does what I would have done, or rather what I should have done if I had been able" ("*If Not Now*" 105).

Mendel opens *If Not Now, When?* from Valuets, an alien location, not from his hometown of Strelka. We soon learn that his beloved shtetl has been decimated, his wife killed, and Strelka's other inhabitants consigned to a common grave. Mendel is on the run and consumed with a brittle nostalgia for a world he has lost. The crucial element in *If Not Now, When?*—time—is established on the spot as time lost, time interrupted, time gone awry, and time running out. Ironically, Mendel, a watch mender by profession, has been encumbered with witnessing that rift in time.

Mendel introduces himself with the words, "My name's Mendel, and Mendel is short for Menachem, which means 'consoler,' but I've never consoled anybody" (21). Despite his assertion to the contrary and in a case of temperament over agency, Mendel's calm presence does indeed lend comfort to many around him, not the least of whom are Leonid and Gedaleh. Leonid may tag him a "nebbish, a loser, a meshuggener" at first (54), but this emotionally scarred young man also opens his heart to Mendel in a way that he does not with anyone else. Mendel repays his trust by taking to Leonid as to a younger brother. He senses their existential kinship, springing perhaps in some small measure from Leonid's skewed relationship with time: after all, he had landed in a Nazi *Lager* in part for the crime of having stolen a watch.

When a year later Mendel unexpectedly betrays Leonid by bedding his lover, Mendel's shame and remorse over his failings, and later guilt over Leonid's suspected suicide, reveal the depths of his feelings of responsibility toward Leonid and, by extension, toward his fellow man. Mendel, imperfect though he may be, nevertheless most closely embodies the ancient virtue of *pietas*.[6] Haltingly, over the course of the novel, Mendel's compassion and humanity allow him to effect a degree of consolation and to witness a nascent reconciliation of the rift in time begun in Strelka—an embryonic *tikkun olam*, or "healing of the world."

How else is Mendel like Levi? Mendel the consoler has another virtue, prudence, which is especially appreciated by Levi. "You're not playacting," Gedaleh tells him. "You've remained a watchmender; and you haven't dressed in peacock feathers, or a hawk's either. Welcome to you, too; you'll be useful to us because you're prudent. You'll serve as a counterweight. With us here prudence has been somewhat forgotten" (161). Our author, too, was prudent. In fact, upon his arrest in 1943, it was his prudence that saved his life: if Levi had confessed to being a partisan and not to the "lesser crime" of being an Italian Jew, he would have been shot on the spot instead of having been imprisoned and later deported to Auschwitz.[7] His memoir of the eleven brutal months he spent in the Nazi *Lager* features ample episodes of prudence, just as prudence (linked to modesty) was a hallmark of Levi's later dealings with his publisher, Einaudi; his employer, SIVA; his German colleagues in the paint business; and his interviewers. His attitude may stem from an atavistic *torinesità*, or a Turinese mind-set, but prudence, modesty, and reserve can nevertheless be found in comments made by Levi and about Levi the man and the writer.[8]

Levi and Mendel also share the virtue of *pietas* (duty and responsibility). One cannot read about Levi's dealings in Auschwitz with Pikolo (Jean Samuel) or with Charles Conreau and others in the chapter "The Story of Ten Days," in *Survival in Auschwitz*, or of his loyalty and kindness to Lorenzo Perrone, in *Survival in Auschwitz* and in the short story "Lorenzo's Return," without noting Levi's sense of moral obligation. Indeed, one might characterize his entire narrative project, from *Survival in Auschwitz* to *The Drowned and the Saved*, as a sort of *tikkun olam* and a Jewish equivalent to the Latin *pietas*.

There is a third way in which Mendel can be read as Levi's alter ego: his adaptable technical skills. Just as Levi took great pride in his chemical training and technical know-how (it contributed to saving his life in Auschwitz, as recounted in "Chemical Examination," a chapter of *Survival in Auschwitz*, and brought him intellectual joy and challenge, as evidenced by *The Periodic Table*), so Mendel proves a most adaptable watch mender. Like Faussone of *The Monkey's Wrench*, Mendel parlays straightforward mechanical dexterity into a panoply of astonishing feats: repairing Red Army weapons, maneuvering an abandoned train, and operating an Italian truck. Gedaleh states that "there are only two defenses against despair: working and fighting" (80), and Mendel does both. Mendel is a *homo faber* and, as such, is a stand-in for Levi.

If Mendel represents the calm, prudent, comforting side of Levi, then Gedaleh Skidler represents the man of action Levi admired and, perhaps, in his far-off partisan days, had hoped to become. Like Sandro Delmastro from *The Periodic Table*, Gedaleh is brash and physical; like Lorenzo Perrone, he follows his personal moral compass, the world be damned. "I must say that thinking has never been my strong suit," Gedaleh readily confesses, and his men acknowledge that he was never "one of those men who reason too much" (246, 112). How strongly this contrasts with Levi's self-portrait in the opening lines of *Survival in Auschwitz*: "I was twenty-four, with little wisdom, no experience and a decided tendency . . . to live in an unrealistic world of my own, a world inhabited by civilized Cartesian phantoms" ([Simon, 1996] 13).

Both Mendel and Levi were survivors (of a pogrom and a *Lager*, respectively), but Gedaleh was a survivor of another order: he was "Gedaleh, the legendary leader, the one who had headed the revolt in the Kossovo ghetto, and whose life had been saved by a violin" (93). He stands in contrast to "the zhid . . . [who] follows his own incomprehensible and ridiculous precepts, armed only by his cleverness, rich and cowardly" (149). "Gedaleh's courage," Levi writes, "was extempore and varied; it didn't spring from a school but from a temperament that chafed at bonds and was hardly inclined to study the future; where [others] calculated, Gedaleh flung himself as if into a game" (159). If, as Levi suggested, *If Not Now, When?* was a Western at heart, then Gedaleh was its Ashkenazi hero.

Gedaleh and the "Gedalists" stand in contrast to the ineffectual *yeshiva bucher* stereotype that Pavel, for example, gently mocks in the novel (115–16). In particular, Gedaleh stands in contrast to the downtrodden, Muselmann-like Leonid,[9] who cannot stop "looking back to take account" (tellingly, Leonid was an accountant in a former life). Gedaleh, on the other hand, "flings everything behind him. Today's Gedaleh flings yesterday's Gedaleh behind him" (229). Like any gunslinger, he has simple beliefs—"vodka, women, and the submachine gun"—and simple goals—"survive, do the maximum damage to the Germans, and go to Palestine" (171, 160).

Yet Gedaleh and Mendel are also bound together like two complementary facets of an ideal man: brashness and prudence, vision and pragmatism, impetuousness and temperance. Levi admitted to Balbi that he identified with Mendel, but he also appears to marvel at Gedaleh ("*If Not Now*" 105). The centaur was a favorite symbol of the author's. Levi celebrated it as a union of opposites, the wild wedded to the rational, the thoughtful to the fierce.[10] Centaurs are the subject of one of his science fiction stories ("Quaestio di Centauris") and, on one occasion, of his self-analysis:

> I am amphibian, a centaur (I've even written stories about centaurs). It seems to me that the ambiguity of science fiction reflects my present destiny. I am split in two. One half of me is of the factory, is the technician and the chemist, but there is another, quite separate half that lives in the world of writing, giving interviews, working on my past and present experiences. ("Science Fiction I" 85)

The radical centaur-like union/disunion of Gedaleh and Medel can also be figured as a Moses/Aaron dichotomy. Levi writes that Mendel had the "happy-uneasy impression of being in another world and another period: perhaps in the midst of the desert, on the march for forty years towards the promised land" (*If Not Now* 75). In the novel's retelling of the Exodus story, Gedaleh will lead his band to the promised land, while Mendel will journey with them in the wilderness and comfort them during their leader's absences. To this end, Mendel and Gedaleh are each halves of a whole and both alter egos for Levi.

Language, Themes, and Leitmotifs

Although *If Not Now, When?* was originally written in Italian, Yiddish was foremost on Levi's mind during the drafting process:

> I don't know either Polish or Russian and my Yiddish is poor, so I had to study up on it, which I did. I studied Yiddish for eight months, so as to be able to give these characters an Italian speech that would sound plausible as a translation. I don't know if the average Italian reader is aware of these things. (*Conversations* 64)

Levi also takes care in his author's note to list the source material he used to "reconstruct a period, a setting, and a language that I knew only marginally" (*If Not Now* 348). The materials included grammars, compilations of Yiddish proverb, and Yiddish joke anthologies.[11] Levi translated the diary written by the Jewish partisan Moshe Kahanovic to get a feel for Yiddish syntax.

This meticulously acquired background worked its way into *If Not Now, When?* through a cache of Yiddishisms and references to Jewish practices. A representative list might include *Nu* (the quintessentially Yiddish, and predictably untranslatable, exclamation, as in "Nu, we're alive" [99]), *nebbish* ("fool"), *shokhet* ("kosher butcher"), *trayf* ("not kosher"), *yeshiva bucherim* ("yeshiva students"), and *L'khayim!* ("To life!," "Cheers!"). Yiddishisms also show up in Pavel Yurevich's skit (115–16), in sayings like "between one picket and the next, the piglet mustn't pass" (165) or "speckled and spotted and brown, like the sheep of Laban" (248), and in "Tumbala," a song the Gedalists sing about a *narische bucher* ("foolish boy") (265–66). The result is a book that reads quite differently from other works by Levi. All Levi's books are marked by polyglossia, but *If Not Now, When?* has an unusual focus on a single foreign, endoglossic idiom—Yiddish.

Levi's Italian also features distinct properties here. Pier Vincenzo Mengaldo remarks, for example, that figures of speech proper to repetition—like polysyndeton (the repetition of conjunctions in close succession), anaphora (the repetition of a word or expression at the beginning of successive phrases or clauses), epiphora (the repetition of a word or words at the end of successive phrases or clauses), and anadiplosis (the repetition of a prominent and usually the last word in a phrase or clause at the beginning of the next)—occur more frequently in *If Not Now, When?* than in any of Levi's other books, with the exception of *Survival in Auschwitz* (xi). Parataxis (the juxtaposition of clauses or phrases without the use of coordinating or subordinating conjunctions) appears to be Levi's guiding stylistic device in the novel, as seen in the following description of Leonid: "Leonid has to fight. He needs it the way he needs bread and the air he breathes. And we need him: he was a German prisoner; he knows how a Lager works. He's a paratrooper, he followed the course, he knows about sabotage and commando raids. And he's brave: he's showed that recently" (219). As in *Survival in Auschwitz*, Levi enjoys here the effect produced by concatenations of nouns ("He felt his chest swell in a flood of conflicting emotions: pride, remorse, resentment, respect, gratitude" [279]), adjectives ("too quick, too energetic, dirty, tattered, proud, unpredictable, primitive, too 'Russian'" [311]), or a combination of both ("During the day it seemed not so much a modern army going by but a horde, a migration: men of every race, Viking giants and squat Lapps, tanned Caucasians and pale Siberians, on horseback, in trucks, tractors, great ox-drawn wagons, some even riding camels" [278]). Mengaldo further notes examples of hylozoism (Levi extends this philosophical doctrine that all matter is in some sense alive to ascribe living properties to inanimate objects), oxymorons, and antithesis (lxxiv), and Maria Teresa Cinanni points out Levi's "admiration of linguistic mélanges and polyglotism" (evident also in his esteem for François Rabelais and Giuseppe Belli, both included in *The Search for Roots*) (53).

Levi, moreover, was a careful wordsmith who often tinkered with a specific Italian word set. A study of word frequency in Levi finds thirty-nine words common to all his works (Nystedt). Twenty, or slightly more than half, have special significance for *If Not Now, When?*: *adventure*, *blood*, *curiosity*, *destiny*, *enthusiasm*, *experience*, *hope*, *human*, *journey*, *man*, *memory*, *music*, *nature*, *patience*, *resistance*, *to tell*, *to understand*, *war*, *weariness*, and *woman*. *Light* is a recurrent word in the novel, and indeed *If Not Now, When?* contains nearly all the time words common to Levi's opus. Levi's attention to the passage of time (as shown by the calendrical structure of the novel and chapter headings) is accompanied by a similar chronocentric interest in the changing of the seasons. As in his *Survival in Auschwitz* observations of the onset and conclusion of the Polish winter, Levi charts the changing climatic environment affecting his band of partisans in *If Not Now, When?* His descriptions in chapters 3–5 of Novoselki (today known as Nowosselki)—"the republic of the marshes"—in summer, winter, and during the spring thaw are particularly graceful and inspired.

Many themes can be teased out of an analysis of *If Not Now, When?*, but Levi points out four in particular in a 1982 interview with Fiona Diwan: memory, *pietas*, the journey, and *il raccontare interno*, or telling the tale ("Sono un ebreo"). He continues: "In percentuale direi che il libro è il 40 per cento umoristico, ed epico, mentre non darei che il 20 per cento alla component lirica" 'In terms of percentages, I'd say the book is 40 percent humorous and epic, and I'd only give 20 percent to the lyrical component' (my trans.). When asked whether telling a tale is a typically Jewish practice, Levi responds:

> Ora, questi temi non hanno nulla di intrinsecamente ebraico, non sono da ascrivere a una specificità ebraica . . . appartengono a tutti e non sono esclusivamente appannaggio ebraico. Concordo con lei nel dire che la pietas, la memoria, il viaggio nel caso degli ebrei si carica di un retaggio di sofferenza, di un passato intriso di dolore. . . . È una memoria che ha tesaurizzato, cumulato la tragedia. La memoria italiana si ferma al Risorgimento e a Garibaldi. Quella francese alla Rivoluzione . . . la me-

moria ebraica va invece fino al Mar Rosso o ancor più indietro ai tempi di Abramo e dell'impero assiro-babilonese.

> Now, these themes aren't intrinsically Jewish; they can't be ascribed to a Jewish specificity. . . . [T]hey belong to everyone and they're not part of an exclusive Jewish heritage. I agree with you when you say that *pietas*, memory and the journey, in the case of the Jews, are themes that express a legacy of suffering, of a past overflowing with pain. Jewish memory is the memory of suffering. . . . It is a memory that has hoarded, amassed tragedy. Italian memory stops at the Risorgimento and Garibaldi. French memory stops at the Revolution . . . Jewish memory, on the other hand, goes back to the Red Sea, and even further back, to the days of Abraham and the Assyrian-Babylonian empire. (my trans.)

Memory and time are radically interlinked concepts, and the presence of one as a theme inevitably leads to the other. *If Not Now, When?* portrays time in the guise of time interrupted and time gone awry, but it also links it to "Jewish time"—for example, Mendel's recollection that Strelka "was left without time . . . , the only one who really cared was the rabbi: he needed to know the correct time so he could tell when the Sabbath began and ended" (19–20).

Furthermore, there is a clear association with two other particularly Jewish concepts of memory, *zachor* and *yizkor*. The biblical imperative to remember, or *zachor*, is found in Exodus in the fourth commandment ("Remember the Sabbath and keep it holy"). However, *zachor* is more closely associated with the story of Amalek and the Amalekites' attempt to destroy the Jewish people on their emergence from Egypt (Deut. 25.17–19). A special Purim Torah reading enjoins the Jewish people to "remember Amalek," or, in other words, to remember the iniquity of their enemies and obliterate them from common memory. Levi understood the parallels between *zachor* and the partisan's fight against the Nazi oppressors; in *If Not Now, When?* Gedaleh enjoins Mendel to observe the ancient command:

> "We have a poor memory, except for one thing."
> "What's that?" Mendel asked.
> Gedaleh solemnly put his forefinger beside his nose.
> "'Remember what Amalek did to you on the way, after you had come out of Egypt. He attacked you while you were on the road, he killed all the weak, the sick, the weary, who were straggling behind; he had no fear of God. And so, when your God grants you peace from your enemies, you will extinguish even the memory of Amalek: don't forget it.' Yes: this is what we don't forget." (161)

More recently, *zachor* has been used in the Holocaust context of "never again." Its related term *yizkor*, or memorial, has given rise to the phenomenon of "yizkor books," or Holocaust memorial books for Jewish life destroyed by Nazi barbarity. In this context, *If Not Now, When?* can be read as a prolonged *yizkor*.

Time also correlates to the partisans as men without tomorrows standing outside of time (151). It is similarly evoked through the cycle of life, which at the end of the novel conflates birth and death in one moment in time. Deaths had been abundant in *If Not Now, When?*, including the deaths of many of the Gedalists' enemies and of at least two of their own (Leonid and Black Rokhele). But only one birth takes place in the novel: White Rokhele delivers a son—a new Adam—just as news breaks that the United States has destroyed Hiroshima with an atomic bomb. As Nicholas Patruno explains, the juxtaposition of these two events—one private and one public, one life-affirming and one life-negating—implies that "life is a cycle in which at best we struggle against oppression and at worst we become the oppressor" (*Understanding* 109–10).

It is perhaps reductive to say that only one birth takes place in *If Not Now, When?* Rather, multiple (symbolic) births take place. Line says, "We were also born. . . . Born, expelled. Russia conceived us, nourished us, made us grow in her darkness, as in a womb; then she had labor pains, contractions, and threw us out; and now here we are, naked and new, like babies just born" (344). The partisan struggle has made new men and women out of the Gedalists. They learn, like Mendel hiding irresolutely in the woods in chapter 1, that "freedom without structure and purpose can be its own prison" (Patruno, *Understanding* 93). And so they chafe at the enforced lassitude in Novoselki, at their ineffectualness in Ulybin's gang, and at their semi-imprisonment under Captain Smirnov. Their true joy and freedom is found in working and in fighting. As fighters, they defeat their humiliation and regain their dignity; as Gedalists, they forge a tight bond of brotherhood.

Yet this fraternal bond (Cesare Segre calls it "cameratismo" ["comradeship"] and invokes it as the main positive value of the novel [Introduzione xi]) has come through the spilling of blood and, with it, the bittersweet taste of vendetta. The Hebrew Bible is once again Levi's referent as the leitmotifs of blood and vendetta appear and reappear in his novel. Mendel cites Exodus and the biblical first plague of blood (*dom* in Hebrew) set upon the Egyptian oppressors by the Almighty, while soon after, by way of implying that a gentile partisan is guilty of anti-Semitism, Mendel whispers that he suspects him, too, of having Dom Israel—the blood of Israel, or Jewish blood—on his hands (68, 86). Levi also brings in a character named Mottel the Throat-Cutter, part *shokhet* ("kosher butcher") and part hothead, who as a partisan sharpens his ritual knife for "other uses" (165, 226). The intersection between the literary depiction of the Ashkenazi world and the novel's weltanschauung shows up in this bloodthirsty Mottel, who has borrowed the name, though certainly not the nature, of Sholom Aleichem's meek tailor, Motel Kamzoil.[12] And Levi links the leitmotifs of blood, vendetta, and the Bible again when Mendel contemplates the revenge he is about to take on the German officials of Neuhaus, whom he blames for the sniper attack that killed his comrade Black Rokhele: "Simon and Levi who avenge with blood the Schechemites' insult to their sister Dinah. Had that revenge been just? Does a just revenge exist? It doesn't exist, but you're a man, and vengeance cries out in your blood, and then you run and destroy and kill. Like them, like the Germans" (304).

Gedaleh's Fiddle and the End of the Novel

As the partisans near the end of their journey, Levi briefly leaves their material quest to focus on an intriguing symbolic representation, Gedaleh's fiddle. We learned earlier in the novel that this fiddle is responsible for his surviving the Kossovo ghetto and is linked to Martin Fontasch, the putative author of the song whose refrain reprises the title of the novel. Fontasch—tellingly, a carpenter by trade—assumes vaguely Christological dimensions within Gedaleh's Midrash-like recitation of his life and death. As Gedaleh softly bows Fontasch's song, he describes it as a talisman for his band; its magic properties spring in part from its inclusion of Hillel's call to action, and in part from its inclusion of the most sacred Hebrew prayer, the "Shemà" ("You know the words: Hear, O Israel, the Lord our God, the Lord is one" [170]).

Later, as Gedaleh tells the story of his former self, he also plays his fiddle. His playing seems to speak the fitful tale as much as his words do, and it stops and starts along with the improbable stops and starts in his journey from young shoe clerk and amateur violinist to legendary leader. Gedaleh's fiddle is symbolic of an earlier stage of his life in a distant place. "If I hadn't found this job, maybe I would have remained a child," Gedaleh muses (249). The fiddle evokes the *homo ludens* that he clings to with some part of his soul, even as he knows that will have to be abandoned.

Gedaleh as a man-child with a fiddle is a literary manifestation of the "violin paintings" by Marc Chagall, another inspiration for Levi. In such works as "Violinist Blue," "The Green Violinist," or "La Mariée," the artist depicted violinists celebrating the life-cycle events in his native village (Vitebsk, located in today's Belarus). Chagall gave visual expression to the Ashkenazi shtetl life that Isaac Babel and Aleichem, Levi's other muses, described in words. For *If Not Now, When?*, Levi took Chagall's rural fiddler and thrust him into a maelstrom of modern fighting and personal transformation.

When we next see Gedaleh playing his fiddle, he's on a train headed for Italy. He is at the halfway point between his former juvenile existence in Jewish Bialystok and an as-yet-unknown mature existence in an as-yet-unknown place. Portentously, his band of Gedalists is on the verge of liberation from fighting and from their *tsores*. They are climbing, literally, over the Alps, and, figuratively, to a new life: "the climb, the *alia*, this was the word for the road when you are coming out of exile, out of the depths, and you climb towards the light" (318). *Alia* (or *aliyah*) means "the ascent" in Hebrew and is widely used to indicate a return to Israel from the Diaspora. At this moment, as Gedaleh is advancing toward his dream of Palestine and his tune rings out "lively, new, noble, filled with hope," his fiddle unexpectedly splinters (318). "*Fidl kaput*," Pavel snickers (319). Gedaleh is devastated. Judging no repairs possible, he tosses it from the train onto the gravel below. Just as a glass must be broken ritually and symbolically, to recall the sadness engendered by the 70 CE destruction of the Temple in Jerusalem, before a Jewish couple may enter into marriage, so Gedaleh's fiddle must break before he can enter a new state and a new land. It is not insignificant that he has also crossed through the Brenner Pass from the Ashkenazi world to the Sephardic world. The fiddle, symbolic of earlier times, must cease to exist because the old Chagallian past has also ceased to exist. Even if Gedaleh and his band of partisans are able to reconcile past and present, that dear but inert and suddenly anachronistic legacy abruptly shatters in the face of the promising vitalism of the future.

Conversely, in real life, Levi was able to return home to Turin after the bloodshed of the war. Two characters in *If Not Now, When?* share that same luxury: Dov, a Siberian man, and Francine, a Frenchwoman. They, with Levi, stand as testimony to the possibility of resumption of Jewish life at the margins of the Nazi Reich. But many of the Ashkenazi partisans in Levi's novel are stateless. Most have lost loved ones in the Shoah, and all suffer the ancestral weariness of Diaspora Jews. Gedaleh and his men have left the Holocaust—the Churban, the Destruction, "Gehenna" ("hell")—behind, but with their first taste of freedom they also realize how much they have lost.

If Not Now, When? concludes with an interlinked birth and death. "The story closes on [a] double, deliberately ambiguous sign," Levi wrote ("Itinerary" 169). On receiving the Campiello Prize, he noted:

> The [birth and death] are two opposite symbols because I didn't want to end the book on the purely optimistic note of a birth. I preferred to counter it with the events of Hiroshima out of a sense of honesty and loyalty. Our world is not made of optimism. . . . If there's optimism, there's also pessimism. I preferred to end it with two divergent signs to indicate the ambiguity we live with. (Poli and Calcogno 266)

These remarks, made shortly after the book's publication, have a negative pall and contrast with the more positive comments, quoted above, that Levi made four years later in his interview with Roth. Thus the ambiguous end of the novel offers both an instrument for cataclysmic human genocide (the bomb) but also the potential for new beginnings (a baby). To the son of Isidor and White Rokhele will fall the task of navigating the post-Hiroshima, post-Auschwitz world.

Reception and Prizes

In 1982, the year of its publication, *If Not Now, When?* won two of Italy's most prestigious literary prizes, the Viareggio Prize and the Campiello Prize (Levi had previously won the Campiello Prize in 1963 for *The Reawakening*). *If Not Now, When?* received high praise in the United States, helped immeasurably by a glowing review from the novelist Irving Howe that was included as the introduction to the 1986 Penguin Books American paperback edition of the novel ("Primo Levi").[13] The reading public was rather slow to embrace Levi, however, and Howe attributes this reaction to delays in translation and to America's general antipathy toward reading foreign books (3). He also points to the saturation of the United States market by books on the Holocaust or a saturation of novels grounded in the Eastern European Jewish experience by American Jewish writers, novels that, because of their authors' shared cultural background with most American Jews, were perceived as more authentic than Levi's novel.

NOTES

[1]The English title is a direct translation of Levi's Italian title, *Se non ora, quando?*

[2]Hillel's verse appears twice in *If Not Now, When?* In the first instance, it forms the refrain of a defiant march Gedaleh sings in May 1944 ("If I'm not for myself, who will be for me? / If not this way, how? If not now, when?" [168–69]). Gedaleh attributes the verses to Martin Fontasch, a martyr of the Kossovo ghetto. The line reappears in February 1945, when the Gedalists steal a truck in Wolbrom and make for freedom ("The truck went on its way in the night, and Gedaleh shouted, laughing, 'If not this way, how? And if not now, when?'" [286]).

[3]Levi makes this history explicit in chapter 2: "What? You haven't heard anything? The Americans have landed in Italy, we've recaptured Kursk, and Mussolini's in jail" (57).

[4]The idea of an alter ego, or doppelgänger, was dear to Levi, as shown by his comments on Conrad's "Youth," in *The Search for Roots* (63–73). In addition, each in his own way, Mordo Nahum, in *The Reawakening*, and Jean Améry, in *The Drowned and the Saved*, are alter egos—or foils—for Levi.

[5]See Levi's comments on Null Achtzehn in *Survival in Auschwitz* [Simon, 1996], esp. 42–43 but also 87–89.

[6]For more on the concept of *pietas*, see Levi's comments on Belli's *Sonnets* in "Pity Hidden beneath Laughter" in *The Search for Roots* (xvi–xxvi).

[7]Levi also mentioned to Camon that "at the end there was also an element of pride: I would have been sorry that it hadn't come out that I, a very bad partisan . . . but a partisan all the same, was a Jew—to show that even the Jews can make up their minds to fight back" (*Conversations* 8).

[8]For example, Levi once stated, "I guard my own privacy jealously" (Cases, "L'ordine"; Belpoliti, "I Am a Centaur" xxi).

[9]The Florida Center for Instructional Technology's *A Teacher's Guide to the Holocaust* defines *Muselmann* as a "German term meaning 'Muslim,' widely used by concentration camp prisoners to refer to inmates who were on the verge of death from starvation, exhaustion, and despair. A person who had reached the Muselmann stage had little, if any, chance for survival and usually died within weeks. The origin of the term is unclear" ("Muselmann").

[10]Levi's attention to oppositional forces is evident in *Survival in Auschwitz*, particularly in the chapter "The Drowned and the Saved": "But another factor seems to us worthy of attention: there comes to light the existence of two particularly well-differentiated

categories among men—the saved and the drowned. Other pairs of opposites (the good and the bad, the wise and the foolish, the cowards and the courageous, the unlucky and the fortunate) are considerably less distinct, they seems less essential, and above all they allow for more numerous and complex intermediary gradations" (87–88).

[11]*If Not Now, When?* marks the reappearance of two Yiddish proverbs that played central roles in previous works by Levi: "Redest keyn jiddisch, bist nit keyn jid" 'You're not a Jew if you don't speak Yiddish' (200; my trans.), used to much the same effect in *The Reawakening* (279), and "Ibergekumene tsores iz gut tsu dertseyln" 'It's good to tell your past troubles' (300; my trans.), which formed the epigraph to *The Periodic Table*.

[12]*The Search for Roots*, published a year before *If Not Now, When?*, revealed an author increasingly attuned to the Ashkenazi world. Indeed, this compilation contains chapters dedicated to the Yiddish writers Isaac Babel and Sholom Aleichem, the author of the Tevye the Dairyman stories in which Motel Kamzoil appears.

[13]Another favorable, high-profile review appeared in the *New York Times*, while *Newsweek* and the *Chicago Tribune* quibbled with some of Levi's characterizations. A strong dissenting view was put forth by Fernanda Eberstadt in *Commentary*, who criticized the novel for universalizing the Holocaust to the detriment of its particular German and Jewish aspects.

APPENDIX
CHAPTER-BY-CHAPTER SYNOPSES OF *IF NOT NOW, WHEN?*

CHAPTER 1: JULY 1943

Valuets / Leonid / Peiami

CHAPTER 2: JULY–AUGUST 1943

Venyamin / Novoselki

CHAPTER 3: AUGUST–NOVEMBER 1943

Novoselki / Adam / Dov / Line and Gedaleh introduced / train sabotage / skirmish with Germans / Greman assault on Dov's bunkers

CHAPTER 4: NOVEMBER 1943–JANUARY 1944

Piotr / Ulybin / telephone sabotage / Mendel kills prisoner

CHAPTER 5: JANUARY–MAY 1944

Leonid and Line / Mendel and Sissl / two airfield raids / Gedaleh returns

CHAPTER 6: MAY 1944

Ulybin and Gedaleh split up / Gedaleh makes camp by the Gorin River / Gedaleh sings song / Gedalists commandeer train and enter Sarny

CHAPTER 7: JUNE–JULY 1944

Mendel betrays his friendship with Leonid, with Line / Leonid shows signs of instability / Gedalists help Polish village

CHAPTER 8: JULY–AUGUST 1944

Mendel, Leonid, and others storm a *Lager*; Leonid dies / plans to go to Italy and then Palestine

CHAPTER 9: SEPTEMBER 1944–JANUARY 1945

Gedalists join forces with Edek's Polish partisans / battle takes place / White Rokhele pregnant and marries Isidor

CHAPTER 10: JANUARY–FEBRUARY 1945

Schmulek and underground shelter / detained by Soviets / departure in truck

CHAPTER 11: FEBRUARY–JULY 1945

Internment / Francine / Captain Smirnov / Neuhaus reprisal / departure in train for Italy

CHAPTER 12: JULY–AUGUST 1945

Gedalists cross into Italy; go to Milan / White Rokhele gives birth / atomic bomb dropped on Hiroshima

NOTES ON CONTRIBUTORS

Jonathan Druker is associate professor of Italian at Illinois State University, where he also teaches graduate and undergraduate courses on the literature and cinema of the Holocaust. He is the author of *Primo Levi and Humanism after Auschwitz* and, with Michael Rothberg, of two articles on Levi's reception in the United States. His current book project analyzes works of Holocaust literature with respect to trauma, time, and ethics.

Pietro Frassica is professor of Italian at Princeton University. His scholarship has focused on the early Renaissance, the eighteenth century (Baretti, Parini, Alfieri), and contemporary literature (Levi, Marinetti, Patti, Soldati, Lagorio) and theater (Pirandello). He is the author of *A Marta Abba per non morire*, *Romanzo europeo tra Otto e Novecento*, *Caro Maestro*, *Varianti e invarianti dell'evocazione*, and *Her Maestro's Echo*, as well as over eighty scholarly and popular articles.

Massimo Giuliani is professor of Jewish thought and head of the Philosophy Department at the University of Trento. Among his books are *Theological Implications of the Shoah*; *A Centaur in Auschwitz: Reflections on Primo Levi's Thinking*; *Il pensiero ebraico contemporaneo*; *Le tende di Abramo. Ebraismo, cristianesimo, islam: Interpretare un'eredità comune*; *Eros in esilio. Letture teologico-politiche del Cantico dei cantici*; and *Il giudaismo conservative*.

Nancy Harrowitz, associate professor of Italian at Boston University, teaches Italian literature and Holocaust studies. She is the author of *Antisemitism, Misogyny, and the Logic of Cultural Difference: Matilde Serao and Cesare Lombroso* and the editor of *Tainted Greatness: Antisemitism and Cultural Heroes* and, with Barbara Hyams, *Jews and Gender: Responses to Otto Weininger*, and she is finishing a book on Primo Levi.

Lina Insana is associate professor of Italian at the University of Pittsburgh, where she teaches twentieth-century Italian literature, Holocaust literature, the literature of fascism and resistance, Sicilian writers, and Italian American studies. She is the author of *Arduous Tasks: Primo Levi, Translation, and the Transmission of Holocaust Testimony*, and her current research project examines Sicilian cultural production at key moments spanning from Italian unification to the present day.

Massimo Lollini is Hatzantonis Distinguished Fellow in Italian and professor of Romance languages at the University of Oregon. He is the author of *Le muse, le maschere e il sublime. G. B. Vico e la poesia nell'età della "Ragione spiegata"* and *Il vuoto della forma. Scrittura, testimonianza e verità*; the principal investigator of the *Oregon Petrarch Open Book*; and the editor in chief of *Humanist Studies and the Digital Age*.

Millicent Marcus is professor of Italian and director of graduate studies at Yale University. Her specializations include medieval literature, Italian film, and the literature and cinema of the Holocaust. She is the author of several books, including *After Fellini: National Cinema in the Postmodern Age* and *Italian Film in the Shadow of Auschwitz*, and the editor (with Risa Sodi) of *New Reflections on Primo Levi: Before and After Auschwitz*.

Gaetana Marrone, professor of Italian at Princeton University, is the author of *La drammatica di Ugo Betti: Tematiche e archetipi* and *The Gaze and the Labyrinth: The Cinema of Liliana Cavani* (*Lo sguardo e il labirinto*), the editor of Ugo Betti's *Delitto all'isola delle capre*, and the general editor of *Encyclopedia of Italian Literary Studies*. She has been named to the Cavaliere dell'Ordine del Merito della Repubblica Italiana.

Letizia Modena is associate professor of Italian studies at Vanderbilt University. Her research interests include twentieth- and twenty-first-century Italian literature and culture, architecture in literature and film, place and identity in literature and film, utopianism and urban studies in Italy and France, and science and literature. She is the author of *Italo Calvino's Architecture of Lightness: The Utopian Imagination in an Age of Urban Crisis*.

Elisabetta Properzi Nelsen is professor of Italian literature at San Francisco State University. Her research focuses on baroque poetry and on Italian women writers, and she has published on Dacia Maraini, Elsa Morante, Marina Jarre, Clara Sereni, and Piera Sonnino. She is writing a book on Giacomo Lubrano and is the author of *Literary Florence*, a literary guide and celebration of her native city.

Nicholas Patruno is professor emeritus of Italian at Bryn Mawr College. In addition to his extensive research on Levi, women in the Holocaust, and immigration writers, he has published primarily on nineteenth- and twentieth-century Italian writers, including Giovanni Verga, Elio Vittorini, and Eugenio Montale. He is the author of *Language in Giovanni Verga's Early Novels* and *Understanding Primo Levi*, and he has commented on Levi's life and works for NBC's *Today Show*.

Roberta Ricci is associate professor and chair of Italian studies at Bryn Mawr College. She has published on philological issues connected with the *varianti d'autore*, paratextuality, commentary, reception, readership, and authorship, in reference to the manuscript tradition of early modern Italian literature and the Latin elegy. She is the author of *Scrittura, riscrittura, autoesegesi: Voci autoriali intorno all'epica in volgare: Boccaccio, Tasso* and is working on a book on Florentine humanism.

Risa Sodi is director of the Yale Teaching Center and director of academic advising at Yale University. She is the author of *A Dante of Our Time: Primo Levi and Auschwitz* and *Narrative and Imperative: The First Fifty Years of Italian Holocaust Literature, 1944–1994*. With Millicent Marcus, she is the editor of *New Reflections on Primo Levi: Before and After Auschwitz*.

SURVEY RESPONDENTS

Uri Cohen, *Columbia University*
Jonathan Druker, *Illinois State University*
Joseph Francese, *Michigan State University*
Nancy Harrowitz, *Boston University*
Patrick Henry, *Whitman College*
Ilona Klein, *Brigham Young University, UT*
Scott Lerner, *Franklin and Marshall College*
Massimo Lollini, *University of Oregon*
Millicent Marcus, *Yale University*
Gaetana Marrone, *Princeton University*
Letizia Modena, *Vanderbilt University*
Elisabetta Properzi Nelsen, *San Francisco State University*
Robin Pickering-Iazzi, *University of Wisconsin, Milwaukee*
Sharon Portnoff, *Boston University*
Sherry Rouch, *Penn State University, University Park*
Risa Sodi, *Yale University*

WORKS CITED

Adorno, Theodor W. "Kulturkritik und Gesellschaft." *Kulturkritik und Gesellschaft*. Ed. Rolf Tiedemann. Vol. 1. Frankfurt: Suhrkamp, 1977. 11–30. Print. Vol. 10 of *Gesammelte Schriften*.

Agamben, Giorgio. *Quel che resta di Auschwitz. L'archivio e il testimone*. Torino: Boringhieri, 1998. Print.

———. *Remnants of Auschwitz: The Witness and the Archive*. Trans. Daniel Heller-Roazen. New York: Zone, 1999. Print.

Alexander, Zaia. *Beyond Babel: Translating the Holocaust at Century's End*. Diss. U of California, Los Angeles, 2002. Ann Arbor: UMI, 2002. Print.

Angier, Carole. *The Double Bond: Primo Levi: A Biography*. New York: Farrar, 2002. Print.

Anissimov, Myriam. *Primo Levi, ou, la tragédie d'un optimiste*. Paris: Lattés, 1996. Print.

Antelme, Robert. *L'espèce humaine*. Paris: Gallimard, 1978. Print.

———. *The Human Race*. Trans. Jeffrey Haight and Annie Mahler. Pref. Edgar Morin. Marlboro: Marlboro, 1992. Print.

Archilochos. *Carmina Archilochi: The Fragments of Archilochos*. Trans. Guy Davenport. Berkeley: U of California P, 1964. Print.

Arendt, Hannah. *Eichmann in Jerusalem: A Report on the Banality of Evil*. New York: Penguin, 1964. Print.

Arrighetti, Graziano, and Franco Montanari. *La componente autobiografica nella poesia greca e latina fra realtà e artificio letterario: Atti del Convegno: Pisa, 16–17 maggio 1991*. Pisa: Giardini, 1993. Print.

Baignères, Claude. "*La trêve* de Franceso Rosi: L'homme qui était mort." *Le Figaro* 14 May 1997: 30. Print.

Bainbridge, Simon. Ad ora incerta*: Four Orchestral Songs from Primo Levi*. Perf. BBC Symphony Orchestra. BBC, 1999. CD.

Banner, Gillian. *Holocaust Literature: Schulz, Levi, Spiegelman and the Memory of the Offence*. London: Mitchell, 2000. Print.

Bassani, Giorgio. *Le storie ferraresi*. Milano: Einaudi, 1960. Print.

Battaglia, Salvatore, ed. *Grande dizionario della lingua italiana*. Torino: UTET, 1961–2002. Print.

Bauer, Yehuda. *The Holocaust as Historical Experience*. London: Holmes, 1981. Print.

Baumgarten, Murray. "Primo Levi: *Survival in Auschwitz* and the Meaningfulness of Everyday Life." *YouTube*. YouTube, 29 Aug. 2010. Web. 10 June 2013. <http://www.youtube.com/watch?v=D8feaNRnAIU&feature=related>.

Beccaria, Gian Luigi. "Other People's Trades." *Primo Levi: Memoria e invenzione*. Ed. Giovanna Ioli. San Salvatore Monferrato: Biennale Piemonte e Letterature, 1995. 157–63. Print.

Belpoliti, Marco. "Editoriale." Belpoliti, *Primo Levi* 6–12.

———. "I Am a Centaur." Levi, *Voice* xvii–xxiv.

———. "Io sono uno centauro." Levi, *Conversazioni* vii–xx.

———. "Nota" [Note on "Il Lager"]. Levi, *Conversazioni* 260–68.

———. *Primo Levi*. Milano: Marcos, 1997. Print. Riga 13.

———. *La prova*. Torino: Einaudi, 2007. Print.

———. "Se questo è un sogno. Sogni, incubi e risvegli nell'opera di Primo Levi." *Al di qua del bene e del male. La visione del mondo di Primo Levi*. Ed. Enrico Mattioda. Milano: Angeli, 2000. 59–74. Print.

Benchouiha, Lucie. *Primo Levi: Rewriting the Holocaust*. Leicester: Troubador, 2006. Print.

Benigni, Roberto, dir. *La vita è bella*. Miramax, 1998. Film.

Benigni, Roberto, and Vincenzo Cerami. *Life Is Beautiful*. Trans. Lisa Taruschio. New York: Hyperion, 1998. Print.

Benjamin, Walter. "The Task of the Translator." *Illuminations*. 1968. Trans. Harry Zohn. New York: Schocken, 2007. 69–82. Print.

Bernstein, Michael André. "Narrating the Shoah." *A Holocaust Reader: Responses to the Nazi Extermination*. Ed. Michael L. Morgan. Oxford: Oxford UP, 2000. 337–49. Print.

Bertoletti, Isabella. "Primo Levi's Odyssey: *The Drowned and the Saved*." Pugliese, *Legacy* 105–19.

Biasin, Gian Paolo. "The Haunted Journey of Primo Levi." Kremer 3–19.

———. "Till My Ghastly Tale Is Told: Levi's Moral Discourse from *Se questo è un uomo* to *I sommersi e i salvati*." Tarrow 127–41.

Boitani, Piero. *Ombra di Ulisse: Figure di un mito*. Bologna: Mulino, 1992. Print.

———. *The Shadow of Ulysses: Figures of a Myth*. Trans. Anita Weston. Oxford: Oxford UP, 1994. Print.

Borowski, Tadeusz. *This Way for the Gas, Ladies and Gentlemen*. Trans. Barbara Vedder. New York: Penguin, 1976. Print.

Calvino, Italo. *Il barone rampante*. Torino: Einaudi, 1958. Print.

———. *Le città invisibili*. Torino: Einaudi, 1972. Print.

———. *Le cosmicomiche*. Torino: Einaudi, 1965. Print.

———. *Lezioni americane: Sei proposte per il prossimo millennio*. Milano: Garzanti, 1988. Print.

———. *Marcovaldo*. Torino: Einaudi, 1963. Print.

———. *Palomar*. Torino: Einaudi, 1983. Print.

———. *Il sentiero dei nidi di ragno*. 1947. Torino: Einaudi, 2002. Print.

———. *Six Memos for the Next Millennium*. Cambridge: Harvard UP, 1988. Print.

———. "Why Read the Classics?" *The Uses of Literature: Essays*. Trans. Peter Creagh. London: Harcourt, 1986. 125–34. Print.

Campbell, Timothy. "The Object(s) of Memory: Models of Remembering in Primo Levi's *Se questo è un uomo*." Pugliese, *Legacy* 97–105.

Cannon, Jo Ann. "Chemistry and Writing in *The Periodic Table*." Tarrow 99–111.

Cargas, Harry. *The Holocaust: An Annotated Bibliography*. Chicago: Amer. Lib. Assn., 1985. Print.

Caruth, Cathy. *Unclaimed Experience: Trauma, Narrative, and History*. Baltimore: Johns Hopkins UP, 1996. Print.

Cases, Cesare. Introduzione. Levi, *Opere* [1987–90] 1: ix–xxxi.

———. "L'ordine delle cose e l'ordine delle parole." Levi, *Opere* [1987–90] 2: xii–xiv.

Cavaglion, Alberto. *Primo Levi e* Se questo è un uomo. Torino: Loescher, 1993. Print.

Cicioni, Mirna. "Moral Snares and Parables: Between Science Fiction and Midrash." Kremer 75–90.

———. *Primo Levi: Bridges of Knowledge*. Oxford: Berg, 1995. Print.

Cinanni, Maria Teresa. *Testimoni di voci sommerse: L'esperienza del nazismo in alcuni scrittori ebrei europei: Joseph Rother, Primo Levi, Jean Améry, Miklós Radnóti*. Cosenza: Periferia, 1997. Print.

Cliff, Brian. "On Language and Violence." Kremer 105–14.

Coleridge, Samuel Taylor. *The Rime of the Ancient Mariner: Complete, Authoritative Texts of the 1798 and 1817 Versions with Biographical and Historical Contexts, Critical History, and Essays from Contemporary Critical Perspectives*. Ed. Paul H. Fry. Boston: Bedford–St. Martin's, 1999. Print.

Colombo, Furio. "Primo Levi lo scrittore del silenzio." *La Repubblica* 21 Dec. 1996: 39. Print.

Crowe, David. *The Holocaust: Roots, History, and Aftermath*. New York: Westview, 2008. Print.

Dante Alighieri. *Inferno*. Ed. and trans. Charles Singleton. 2 vols. Princeton: Princeton UP, 1977. Print.

———. *Inferno*. *Princeton Dante Project:* Commedia, Inferno, Purgatorio, Paradiso. Dir. Lauren Seem, Robert Hollander, Frank B. Ordiway, Giorgio Petrocchi, and John D. Sinclair. *Princeton University*. Trustees of Princeton U and Hollander, 1997. Web. 26 Feb. 2014.

Dear, Ian. *The Oxford Companion to World War II*. Oxford: Oxford UP, 1995. Print.

De Felice, Renzo. *The Jews in Fascist Italy: A History*. Trans. Robert L. Miller. New York: Enigma, 2000. Print.

Dei, Luigi, ed. *Voci dal mondo per Primo Levi: In memoria, per la memoria*. Firenze: Firenze UP, 2007. Print.

De Luca, Vania. *Tra Giobbe e i buchi neri: Le radici ebraiche dell'opera di Primo Levi*. Napoli: Istituto Grafico Editoriale Italiano, 1991. Print.

Derrida, Jacques. "Des Tours de Babel." Trans. Joseph Graham. *Difference in Translation*. Ed. Graham. Ithaca: Cornell UP, 1985. 165–207, 209–48. Print.

Devoto, Giacomo, and Gian Carlo Oli. *Il Devoto-Oli: Vocabulario della lingua italiana: 2008*. Ed. Luca Serianni and Maurizio Trifone. Le Monnier, 2007. Web. 20 Mar. 2014.

Dini, Massimo, and Stefano Jesurum. *Primo Levi, le opere e i giorni*. Milano: Rizzoli, 1992. Print.

Druker, Jonathan. *Primo Levi and Humanism after Auschwitz: Posthumanist Reflections*. New York: Palgrave, 2009. Print.

Eberstadt, Fernanda. "Reading Primo Levi." *Commentary* 44 (1985): 41–47. *Primo Levi and the Holocaust*. Web. 7 Jan. 2007. <http://www.brynmawr.edu/Acads/Langs/italian/holoc/articleforfinal.htm>.

Edelheit, Abraham, and Hershel Edelheit. *Bibliography on Holocaust Literature*. New York: Westview, 1986. Print.

———. *Bibliography on Holocaust Literature: Supplement*. New York: Westview, 1990. Print.

Farrell, Joseph, ed. *Primo Levi: The Austere Humanist*. New York: Lang, 2004. Print.

Feinstein, Wiley. *The Civilization of the Holocaust in Italy: Poets, Artists, Saints, Anti-Semites*. Madison: Fairleigh Dickinson UP; London: Associated UPs, 2003. Print.

Feldman, Ruth. "The Return of the Voice: Claude Lanzmann's *Shoah*." Felman and Laub 204–83.

———. "Testimony: Primo Levi's Poetry: Darkness and Light." Tarrow 142–47.

Felman, Shoshana. *The Juridical Unconscious*. Cambridge: Harvard UP, 2002. Print.

Felman, Shoshana, and Dori Laub. *Testimony: Crises of Witnessing in Literature, Psychoanalysis, and History*. London: Routledge, 1992. Print.

Ferrario, Davide, dir. *La strada di Levi* [*Primo Levi's Journey*]. By Ferrario and Marco Belpoliti. Cinema Guild, 2007. Film.

Ferrero, Ernesto. Introduzione. Levi, *Racconti* [1996] vii–xx.

———. *Primo Levi: Un'antologia della critica*. Torino: Einaudi, 1997. Print.

Fofi, Goffredo. "Non l'ho visto e forse non mi piace." *Panoram* 16 Jan. 1997: 106–09. Print.

Frankel, Ari, comp. *To Scratch an Angel*. Amer. Opera Project, n.d. CD.

Gambetta, Diego. "Primo Levi's Last Moments." *Boston Review*. Boston Rev., 1 June 2009. Web. 13 June 2013. <http://bostonreview.net/BR24.3/gambetta.html>.

Garvin, Barbara. *The Jews of Italy: Memory and Identity*. Bethesda: UP of Maryland, 2000. Print.

Gilbert, Martin. *Atlas of the Holocaust in History*. London: Dent, 1993. Print.

———. *The Holocaust: A History of the Jews of Europe during the Second World War*. New York: Rinehart, 1986. Print.

Gili, Jean A. "*La trêve*." *Positif* Nov. 1997: 6–8. Print.

Gilman, Sander L. "The Special Language of the Camps and After." *Midstream* 35 (1989): 22–30. Print.

Girelli-Carasi, Fabio. "The Anti-linguistic Nature of the Lager in the Language of Primo Levi's *Se questo è un uomo*." Tarrow 41–59.

Giuliani, Massimo. *A Centaur in Auschwitz: Reflections on Primo Levi's Thinking*. Lanham: Lexington, 2003. Print.

Gordon, Robert, ed. *The Cambridge Companion to Primo Levi*. Cambridge: Cambridge UP, 2007. Print.

———. *Primo Levi's Ordinary Virtues: From Testimony to Ethics*. Oxford: Oxford UP, 2001. Print.

Grassano, Giuseppe. *Primo Levi*. Roma: Nuova Italia, 1981. Print.

Gutman, Israel, ed. *The Encyclopedia of the Holocaust*. London: Macmillan, 1990. Print.

Harrowitz, Nancy. "Autobiography and the Narrator: Primo Levi's *The Periodic Table*." Pugliese, *Answering* 177–90.

———. "Primo Levi's Science as 'Evil Nurse': The Lesson of Inversion." Kremer 59–74.

Hilberg, Raul. *The Destruction of the European Jews*. London: Holmes, 1985. Print.

———. "I Was Not There." Lang, *Writing* 17–25.

Howe, Irving. "Primo Levi: An Appreciation." Levi, *If Not Now* 3–16.

———. "Writing about the Holocaust." Lang, *Writing* 175–99.

Hughes, Stuart. *Prisoners of Hope*. Cambridge: Harvard UP, 1983. Print.

Insana, Lina. *Arduous Tasks: Primo Levi, Translation and the Transmission of Holocaust Testimony*. Toronto: U of Toronto P, 2009. Print.

———. "In Levi's Wake: Adaptation, Simulacrum, and Postmemory." *Italica* 86.2 (2009): 212–38. Print.

———. "Traumatic Translation: *The Ancient Mariner*'s Voyage from English to Italian and Back Again." *Journal of Italian Translation* 1.1 (2006): 23–35. Print.

Jakobson, Roman. "Aspects linguistiques de la traduction." *Essais de linguistique générale*. Paris: Minuit, 1963. 78–86. Print.

———. "On Linguistic Aspects of Translation." *On Translation*. Ed. and trans. R. A. Brower. Cambridge: Harvard UP, 1959. 232–39. Print.

James, Clive. "Books: Last Will and Testament." *New Yorker* 23 May 1988: 86–92. Print.

Jesurum, Stefano. *Essere ebrei in Italia: Nella testimonianza di ventuno protagonisti*. Milano: Longanesi, 1987. Print.

Kafka, Franz. *Il processo*. Trans. Primo Levi. Torino: Einaudi, 1983. Print. Trans. of *Der Prozeß*.

Kahanovich, Moshe. *Di milhome fun di Yidishe partizaner in Mizreh-Eyrope*. Buenos Aires: Tsentral-Farband fun Poylishe Yidn in Argentine, 1956. Print. Trans. as *Jewish Partisans of Eastern Europe*. Washington: US Holocaust Memorial Museum, 1981.

Keffer, David, with Allen B. Ruch. "Primo Levi." *The Modern Word: The Scriptorum*. Modern Word, 20 June 2007. Web. 16 Aug. 2013. <http://www.themodernword.com/scriptorium/levi.html>.

Kerbel, Sorrel, ed. *Jewish Writers of the Twentieth Century*. New York: Dearborn, 2003. Print.

Klein, Ilona. "Humor, Science and Technology in Levi's *Storie naturali*." Tarrow 112–26.

Kremer, Roberta, ed. *Memory and Mastery: Primo Levi as Writer and Witness*. Albany: State U of New York P, 2001. Print.

Kuon, Peter. "'Chi potrebbe dire che cosa sono?': Questioning Humanism in Concentration Camp Survivor Texts and the Category of the 'Muselmann.'" *Humanisms, Posthumanisms, and Neohumanisms*. Ed. Massimo Lollini. *Annali d'Italianistica* 26 (2008): 203–22. Print.

Lang, Berel. *Holocaust Representation: Art within the Limits of History and Ethics*. Baltimore: Johns Hopkins UP, 2000. Print.

———. *Post-Holocaust: Interpretation, Misinterpretation, and the Claims of History*. Bloomington: Indiana UP, 2005. Print.

———. *Writing and the Holocaust*. New York: Holmes, 1988. Print.

Langer, Lawrence L. *Art from the Ashes: A Holocaust Anthology*. New York: Oxford UP, 1995. Print.

———. *The Holocaust and the Literary Imagination*. New Haven: Yale UP, 1975. Print.

———. *Holocaust Testimonies: The Ruins of Memory*. New Haven: Yale UP, 1991. Print.

———. "Memory's Time: Chronology and Duration in Holocaust Testimonies." *Admitting the Holocaust*. By Langer. New York: Oxford UP, 1995. 13–23. Print.

Lanzmann, Claude, dir. *Shoah*. New Yorker Films, 2003. Film.

Laqueur, Walter, ed. *The Holocaust Encyclopedia*. New Haven: Yale UP, 2001. Print.

Laska, Vera. *Nazism, Resistance, and Holocaust in World War II: A Bibliography*. Metuchen: Scarecrow, 1985. Print.

Laub, Dori. "Bearing Witness or the Vicissitudes of Listening." Felman and Laub 57–74.

Lejeune, Philippe. *On Autobiography*. Ed. Paul John Eakin. Trans. Katherine Leary. Minneapolis: U of Minnesota P, 1989. Print.

Leshem, Dan. "The Question of Ethical Discourse: Emmanuel Lévinas, Primo Levi and Giorgo Agamben." Pugliese, *Legacy* 153–60.

Levi, Primo. *Ad ora incerta*. Levi, *Opere* [1997] 2: 517–82.

———. "Un'aggressione di nome Franz Kafka." Interview with Federico De Melis. *Il manifesto* 5 May 1983. Rpt. in Levi, *Conversazioni* 188–91.

———. *L'altrui mestiere*. Torino: Einaudi, 1985. Print.

———. *L'asimmetria e la vita. Articoli e saggi, 1955–1987*. Ed. Marco Belpoliti. Torino: Einaudi, 2002. Print.

———. "An Assault Called Franz Kafka." Interview with Federico De Melis. Levi, *Voice* 155–60.

———. *The Black Hole of Auschwitz*. Ed. Marco Belpoliti. Trans. Sharon Wood. Cambridge: Polity, 2005. Print. Trans. of *L'assimetria e la vita*.

———. "Capire e far capire." Interview with Milvia Spadi. Sept. 1986. Levi, *Conversazioni* 242–59.

———. "Chemistry." Interview with Enrico Boeri. Levi, *Voice* 65–69.

———. "Chimico." Interview with Enrico Boeri. 1983. Levi, *Conversazioni* 19–24.

———. *Collected Poems*. Trans. Ruth Feldman and Brian Swann. London: Faber, 1988. Print.

———. *Conversations with Primo Levi*. Ed. Ferdinando Camon. Trans. John Shepley. Marlboro: Marlboro, 1989. Print.

———. "A Conversation with Primo Levi." Levi, *Voice* 121–35.

———. "Conversazione con Anthony Rudolf." Belpoliti, *Primo Levi* 102–10.

———. *Conversazione con Primo Levi*. Ed. Ferdinando Camon. Milano: Garzanti, 1991. Print. Rpt. of *Autoritratto di Primo Levi*. 1987.

———. "Conversazione con Primo Levi." Interview with Giuseppe Grassano. Levi, *Conversazioni* 165–84.

———. *Conversazioni e interviste, 1963–1987*. Ed. Marco Belpoliti. Torino: Einaudi, 1997. Print.

———. "Credo che il mio destino profondo sia la spaccatura." Interview with Giovanni Tesio. Levi, *Conversazioni* 185–87.

———. *The Drowned and the Saved*. Trans. Raymond Rosenthal. New York: Summit, 1988. Print.

———. *The Drowned and the Saved*. Trans. Raymond Rosenthal. New York: Vintage, 1989. Print.

———. "The Essential and the Superfluous." Levi, *Voice* 167–76.

———. "Ex-chimico." Levi, *Opere* [1997] 2: 641–43.

———. *If Not Now, When?* Trans. William Weaver. New York: Penguin, 1986. Print.

———. "*If Not Now, When?*" Interview with Rosellina Balbi. Levi, *Voice* 103–08.

———. *If This Is a Man*. Trans. Stuart Woolf. London: Vintage, 1996. Print.

——— "Intervista a Primo Levi." Interview with Giorgio Segrè. Levi, *Conversazioni* 274–81.

———. "Un'intervista con Primo Levi." Interview with Risa Sodi. Levi, *Conversazioni* 223–41. Trans. as "An Interview with Primo Levi." *Partisan Review* 54.3 (1987): 355–66.

———. "Itinerary of a Jewish Writer." Levi, *Black Hole* 155–68.

———. "Levi: L'ora incerta della poesia." Interview with Giulio Nascimbeni. *Corriere della sera* 28 Oct. 1984. Rpt. in Levi, *Conversazioni* 135–41.

———. "Lilith." Trans. Ruth Feldman. *Short Stories in Italian*. Ed. Nick Roberts. London: Penguin, 1999. 57–69. Print. New Penguin Parallel Texts.

———. "A Man Saved by His Skills." Interview with Philip Roth. Levi, *Voice* 13–22.

———. "Mendel, il consolatore." Interview with Rosellina Balbi. *La Repubblica* 14 Apr. 1982: 20–21. Rpt. in Levi, *Conversazioni* 129–35.

———. *Moments of Reprieve*. Trans. Ruth Feldman. New York: Penguin, 1987. Print.

———. *The Monkey's Wrench*. Trans. William Weaver. New York: Penguin, 1987. Print.

———. "Il necessario e il superfluo: Primo Levi e l'economia nella narrazione." Interview with Roberto Di Caro. Levi, *Conversazioni* 195–205.

———. "Note ai testi: *Se non ora, quando?*" Levi, *Opere* [1997] 2: 1537–42.

———. *Opere*. 3 vols. Torino: Einaudi, 1987–90. Print.

———. *Opere*. Ed. Marco Belpoliti. 2 vols. Torino: Einaudi, 1997. Print. Nuova universale Einaudi 225.

———. *L'osteria di Brema*. Milano: Scheiwiller, 1975. Print.

———. *Other People's Trades*. New York: Summit, 1989. Print.

———. *The Periodic Table*. Trans. Raymond Rosenthal. New York: Schocken, 1984. Print.

———. "Per Primo Levi, questo è un modo di dire io." Interview with Aurelio Andreoli. *Paese sera* 21 Aug. 1981: 3. Rpt. in Levi, *Conversazioni* 123–28.

———. "Primo Levi and Philip Roth: A Conversation." Afterword. Levi, *Survival* [1996] 175–87.

———. "Primo Levi, il testimone di quelli che non tornarono." Interview with Pasquale De Filippo. *La gazzetta del mezzogiorno* 10 Dec. 1977: 3. Print.

———. "Primo Levi: *La chiave a stella*." *YouTube*. YouTube, 4 June 2010. Web. 10 June 2013. <http://www.youtube.com/watch?v=VQe_CUgjyUk&feature=fvwrel>.

———. "Primo Levi: La memoria da rinfrescare." *YouTube*. YouTube, 22 Mar. 2010. Web. 10 June 2013. <http://www.youtube.com/watch?v=akbeEdx-cU4>.

———. "Primo Levi si racconta." Interview with Alberto Gozzi. *YouTube*. YouTube, 14 Apr. 2012. Web. 6 Mar. 2014. <https://www.youtube.com/watch?v=MouwDHXpLt0>.

———. *I racconti*. Introd. Ernesto Ferrero. Torino: Einaudi, 1996. Print.

———. *Racconti e saggi*. Torino: Stampa, 1986. Print.

———. *The Reawakening*. Trans. Stuart Woolf. New York: Collier, 1986. Print.

———. *The Reawakening*. Survival in Auschwitz *and* The Reawakening*: Two Memoirs*. Trans. Stuart Woolf. New York: Summit, 1986. 175–374. Print.

———. *La ricerca delle radici*. Torino: Einaudi, 1981. Print.

———. "Science Fiction I: *Storie naturali*." Interview with Edoardo Fadini. Levi, *Voice* 84–86.

———. *The Search for Roots: A Personal Anthology*. Trans. Peter Forbes. London: Lane, 2001. Print.

———. *Se questo è un uomo*. Levi, *Opere* [1997] 1: 3–201.

———. *Se questo è un uomo*. Torino: Einaudi, 2005. Print.

———. *Se questo è un uomo–La tregua*. Torino: Einaudi, 1989. Print.

———. *Il sistema periodico*. Torino: Einaudi, 1994. Print.

———. *Il sistema periodico*. Levi, *Opere* [1997] 1: 839–94.

———. *"The Sixth Day" and Other Tales*. Trans. Raymond Rosenthal. London: Joseph; New York: Penguin, 1990. Print.

———. *I sommersi e i salvati*. Levi, *Opere* [1997] 2: 997–1153.

———. *I sommersi e i salvati*. Torino: Einaudi, 1986. Print. Gli struzzi 305.

———. "Sono un ebreo ma non sono mai stato sionista." Interview with Fiona Diwan. Levi, *Conversazioni* 157.

———. *Storie naturali*. Levi, *Racconti* [1996] 3–184.

———. *Survival in Auschwitz*. Trans. Stuart Woolf. New York: Macmillan, 1987. Print.

———. *Survival in Auschwitz*. Trans. Stuart Woolf. New York: Touchstone, 1996. Print.

———. *Survival in Auschwitz*. Trans. Stuart Woolf. New York: Collier, 1987. Print.

———. *Survival in Auschwitz (If This Is a Man)*. Trans. Stuart Woolf. New York: Collier, 1961. Print.

———. *Survival in Auschwitz: The Nazi Assault on Humanity*. Trans. Stuart Woolf. New York: Simon, 1996. Print.

———. "Tradurre ed essere tradotti." Levi, *Altrui mestiere* 109–14.

———. *A Tranquil Star: Unpublished Stories*. Trans. Ann Goldstein and Alessandra Bastagli. New York: Norton, 2007. Print.

———. *La tregua*. Levi, *Se questo è un uomo–La tregua* 155–325.

———. *La tregua*. Torino: Einaudi, 1963. Print.

———. *The Truce*. Trans. Stuart Woolf. London: Vintage, 1996. Print.

———. *Vizio di forma*. Torino: Einaudi, 1971. Print.

———. *The Voice of Memory: Primo Levi: Interviews, 1961–1987*. Ed. Marco Belpoliti and Robert Gordon. Trans. Gordon. New York: New, 2001. Print. Trans. of *Conversazioni e interviste, 1963–1987*.

Levi, Primo, with Leonardo De Benedetti. *Auschwitz Report*. Trans. Judith Woolf. Ed. Robert Gordon. London: Verso, 2006. Print.

Levi, Primo, and Tullio Regge. *Dialogo*. Princeton: Princeton UP, 1989. Print.

Lévinas, Emmanuel. *Quelques réflexions sur la philosophie de l'hitlérisme*. *Les imprévus de l'histoire*. Saint-Clément-la-Rivière: Fata Morgana, 1994. 27–41. Print. Rpt. of *Esprit* 26 (1934): 199–208.

Lollini, Massimo. "Perché si scrive? Primo Levi e Paul Celan." *Rivista di letterature moderne e comparate* 52.2 (1999): 149–66. Print.

Losey, Jay. "'The Pain of Remembering': Primo Levi's Poetry and the Function of Memory." Pugliese, *Legacy* 119–25.

Magavern, Sam. *Primo Levi's Universe: A Writer's Journey*. New York: St. Martin's, 2009. Print.

Marcus, Millicent. "Filming the Text of Witness: Francesco Rosi's *The Truce*." *After Fellini: National Cinema in the Postmodern Age*. Baltimore: Johns Hopkins UP, 2002. 253–67. Print.

———. "'Me lo dici babbo che gioco è?': The Serious Humor of *La vita è bella*." *Italica* 77.2 (2000): 153–70. Print.

Marcus, Millicent, and Risa Sodi, eds. *New Reflections on Primo Levi: Before and After Auschwitz*. New York: Palgrave, 2011. Print.

Marrus, Michael. *The Holocaust in History*. New York: Penguin, 1987. Print.

McClellan, William. "Primo Levi, Giorgio Agamben, and the New Ethics of Reading." Pugliese, *Legacy* 147–53.

McGann, Jerome. "The Meaning of the Ancient Mariner." *Critical Inquiry* 8.1 (1981): 35–67. Print.

Megnaghi, David, ed. *Primo Levi: Scrittura e testimonianza*. Venezia: Marsilio, 2005. Print.

Mellone, James T. "A Bibliography of English and Italian Scholarly Writings on Primo Levi, 1985–2002." Pugliese, *Legacy* 233–66.

———. "Primo Levi: A Bibliography of English and Italian Scholarly Writings, 2003–2010." Pugliese, *Answering* 220–40.

Mendel, David. "Primo Levi and the Jews." Pugliese, *Legacy* 61–73.

———. "Primo Levi and Translation." *Bulletin of the Society for Italian Studies* 31 (1998): 11–17. Web. 20 Mar. 2014. <http://italianstudies.org.uk/wp-content/documents/bulletin1998.pdf>.

Mengaldo, Pier Vincenzo. "La lingua e la scrittura." Introduction. Levi, *Opere* [1987–90] 3: vii–lxxxiii.

Michaelis, Meir. *Mussolini and the Jews*. Oxford: Claredon, 1978. Print.

Millu, Liana. *Smoke over Birkenau*. Trans. Lynne Sharon Schwartz. Evanston: Northwestern UP, 1991. Print.

Molino Signorini, Franca. "The Duty and Risk of Testimony: Primo Levi as Keeper of Memory." Kremer 173–97.

Moliterni, Fabio, Roberto Ciccarelli, and Alessandro Lattanzio. *Primo Levi: L'a-topia letteraria, il pensiero narrative, la scrittura e l'assurdo*. Napoli: Liguori, 2000. Print.

Murfin, Ross C. "Deconstruction and *The Rime of the Ancient Mariner*." Coleridge 261–82.

"Muselmann." *A Teacher's Guide to the Holocaust. Florida Center for Instructional Technology*. U of South Florida, 1997–2013. Web. 10 Mar. 2014. <http://fcit.usf.edu/holocaust/DEFN/musel.htm>.

Neiger, Ada, ed. *Mémoire oblige: Riflessioni sull'opera di Primo Levi*. Trento: Dipartimento di Studi Letterari, Linguistici e Filologici, U degli Studi di Trento, 2009. Print.

Nelson, Tim Blake, dir. *The Grey Zone*. Lionsgate, 2002. Film.

Niri, Luciano, ed. *Profili Novecenteschi*. Firenze: Atheneum, 2010. Print.

Nystedt, Jane. *Le opere di Primo Levi viste al computer: Osservazioni stilolinguistiche*. Stockholm: Almqvist, 1993. Print.

Ozick, Cynthia. *Metaphor and Memory*. New York: Knopf, 1989. Print.

Pallotta, Augustus, ed. *Italian Novelists since World War II*. Detroit: Gale, 1997. Print. Dictionary of Literary Biography 177.

Parussa, Sergio. "A Hybridism of Sounds: Primo Levi between Judaism and Literature." Pugliese, *Legacy* 87–94.

Patai, Raphael. *The Jewish Mind*. Detroit: Wayne State UP, 1977. Print.

Patruno, Nicholas. "At an Uncertain Hour: The Other Side of Primo Levi." Kremer 91–102.

———. "Primo Levi: Auschwitz and After." *YouTube*. YouTube, 29 Oct. 2010. Web. 11 June 2013. <http://www.youtube.com/watch?v=jsMlPV45fng>.

———. *Understanding Primo Levi*. Columbia: U of South Carolina P, 1995. Print.

Patterson, David, Alan Berger, and Sarita Cargas. *Encyclopedia of Holocaust Literature*. Westport: Oryx, 2002. Print.

Péron, Didier. "Comment Rosi trahit Levi." *Liberation* 14 May 1997: 4. Print.

Philippe, Antoine. "The Drowned as Saviors of Humanity: The Anthropological Value of *Se questo è un uomo*." Pugliese, *Legacy* 125–33.

Piperno, Alessandro. *Con le peggiori intenzioni: Romanzo*. Milano: Mondadori, 2005. Print.

Pirandello, Luigi. *Six Characters in Search of an Author. Naked Masks: Five Plays by Luigi Pirandello*. Ed. Eric Bentley. New York: Dutton, 1965. 209–76. Print.

Poli, Gabriella, and Giorgio Calcogno. *Echi de una voce perduta: Incontri, interviste e conversazioni con Primo Levi*. Milano: Mursia, 1992. Print.

"Primo Levi: Back to Auschwitz (Part 1 of 2)." *Sorgente di vita*. RAI, 1983. *YouTube*. YouTube, 26 Jan. 2011. Web. 10 June 2013. <http://www.youtube.com/watch?v=cPOKXfHOuw4&feature=related>.

"Primo Levi: Back to Auschwitz (Part 2 of 2)." *Sorgente di vita*. RAI, 1983. *YouTube*. YouTube, 26 Jan. 2011. Web. 10 June 2013. <http://www.youtube.com/watch?v=lA7Xa2ANx2c>.

"Primo Levi: Periodic Table of Videos." *YouTube*. YouTube, 2 Sept. 2010. Web. 10 June 2013. <http://www.youtube.com/watch?v=uHcYfP6Ce0E>.

"Primo Levi ritorna ad Auschwitz." *Sorgente di vita*. RAI. Rai2, 25 Apr. 1983. Television.

Pugliese, Stanislao, ed. *Answering Auschwitz: Primo Levi's Science and Humanism after the Fall*. New York: Fordham UP, 2011. Print.

———, ed. *Italian Fascism and Anti-fascism: A Critical Anthology*. Manchester: Manchester UP, 2001. Print.

———, ed. *The Legacy of Primo Levi*. New York: Palgrave, 2004. Print.

Remy, Vincent. "L'impossible pardon." *Télérama* 19 Nov. 1997: 96. Print.

Rosato, Italo. "Poesia." Belpoliti, *Primo Levi* 413–25.

Rosenbaum, Thane. *The Golems of Gotham*. New York: Harper, 2002. Print.

Rosenfeld, Alvin H. *A Double Dying: Reflections on Holocaust Literature*. Bloomington: Indiana UP, 1980. Print.

Rosi, Francesco. "Il mio modo di fare cinema." *La cittànuova* 10 (1996): 103–10. Print.

———, dir. *La tregua* [*The Truce*]. Miramax, 1998. Film.

Ross, Charlotte. *Primo Levi's Narratives of Embodiment: Containing the Human*. New York: Routledge, 2010. Print.

Roth, Cecil. *The History of the Jews of Italy*. Philadelphia: Jewish Pub. Soc. of Amer., 1946. Print.

Rothberg, Michael. *Traumatic Realism: The Demands of Holocaust Representation*. Minneapolis: U of Minnesota P, 2000. Print.

Rothberg, Michael, and Jonathan Druker. "A Secular Alternative: Primo Levi's Place in American Holocaust Discourse." *Shofar: An Interdisciplinary Journal of Jewish Studies* 28.1 (2009): 104–26. Web. 13 June 2013.

Santagata, Marco, Laura Carotti, Alberto Casadei, and Mirko Tavoni. *Il filo rosso. Antologia e storia della letteratura italiana ed europea*. Bari: Laterza, 2009. Print.

Sarfatti, Michele. *The Jews in Mussolini's Italy: From Equality to Persecution*. Madison: U of Wisconsin P, 2006. Print.

Sargon, Simon A., arr. *Shemà: Hear: Five Poems of Primo Levi*. Gasparo, 1996. CD.

Sayre, Patricia, and Linnea Vacca. "On Language and Personhood: A Linguistic Odyssey." Kremer 115–30.

Scheiber, Elizabeth. "The Failure of Memory and Literature in Primo Levi's *Il sistema periodico*." *MLN* 121.1 (2006): 225–39. Print.

Schleiermacher, Friedrich. "On the Different Methods of Translating." Trans. Susan Bernofsky. *The Translation Studies Reader*. Ed. and introd. Lawrence Venuti. 2nd ed. London: Routledge, 2004. 43–63. Print.

Schlink, Bernhard. *The Reader*. Trans. Carol Brown Janeway. New York: Vintage, 1997. Print.

Segre, Cesare. Introduzione. Levi, *Opere* [1987–90] 2: vii–xxxv.

———. "Primo Levi nella Torre di Babele." *Primo Levi as Witness*. Ed. Pietro Frassica. Florence: Casalini, 1990. 86–97. Print.

———. "*La tregua*? Caro Rosi, proprio non ci siamo." *Il corriere della sera* 28 Feb. 1997: 31. Print.

Segre, Cesare, and Carlo Ossola. *Antologia della poesia italiana*. Torino: Einaudi, 2003. Print.

Seidman, Naomi. "Elie Wiesel and the Scandal of Jewish Rage." *Jewish Social Studies* 3.1 (1996): 1–19. Print.

Slings, S. R., ed. *The Poet's I in Archaic Greek Lyric*. Amsterdam: Vale UP, 1990. Print.

Snow, Charles Percy. *The Two Cultures and the Scientific Revolution*. Cambridge: Cambridge UP, 1959. Print.

Sodi, Risa. *A Dante of Our Time: Primo Levi and Auschwitz*. New York: Lang, 1990. Print.

———. *Narrative and Imperative: The First Fifty Years of Italian Holocaust Writing, 1944–1994*. New York: Lang, 2007. Print.

———. "Primo Levi's *If Not Now, When?*." *The Dictionary of Literary Biography: The Holocaust Novel*. Ed. Efraim Sicher. Detroit: Gale, 2004. Print.

Speelman, Raniero. "Primo Levi's Short Stories: A Modern Midrashim." Pugliese, *Legacy* 23–32.

Spielberg, Steven, dir. *Schindler's List*. Universal, 1993. Film.

Sungolowsky, Joseph. "The Jewishness of Primo Levi." Pugliese, *Legacy* 75–86.

Swaffar, Janet, and Katherine Arens. *Remapping the Foreign Language Curriculum: An Approach through Multiple Literacies*. New York: MLA, 2005. Print. Teaching Languages, Literatures, and Cultures 4.

Szonyi, David. *The Holocaust: An Annotated Bibliography and Resource Guide*. New York: Ktav, 1985. Print.

Tarrow, Susan, ed. *Reason and Light: Essays on Primo Levi*. Ithaca: Cornell Studies in Intl. Affairs–Western Socs., 1990. Print.

Telushkin, Joseph. *Jewish Literacy*. New York: Morrow, 2001. Print.

Tesio, Giovanni, ed. *Diffusione e conoscenza di Primo Levi nei paesi europei: La manutenzione della memoria*. Torino: Centro Studi Piemontesi, 2005. Print.

Thomson, Ian. *Primo Levi: A Life*. New York: Holt, 2003. Print.

Todorov, Tzvetan. *Facing the Extreme: Moral Life in the Concentration Camps*. Trans. Arthur Denner and Abigail Pollak. New York: Metropolitan, 1996. Print.

Usher, Jonathan. "'Libertinage' Programmatic and Promiscuous Quotation in Primo Levi." Farrell 91–116.

Venuti, Lawrence. *The Translator's Invisibility: A History of Translation*. London: Routledge, 1995. Print.

Vincenti, Fiora. *Invito alla lettura di Primo Levi*. Milano: Mursia, 1987. Print.

Vittorini, Elio. *Men and Not Men*. Trans. Sarah Henry. Marlboro: Marlboro, 1985. Print.

———. *Uomini e no*. Milano: Mondadori, 1966. Print.

Weissman, Gary. *Fantasies of Witnessing*. Ithaca: Cornell UP, 2004. Print.

Wiesel, Elie. Foreword. *Indelible Shadows: Film and the Holocaust*. Ed. Annette Insdorf. 2nd ed. Cambridge: Cambridge UP, 1989. xi–xii. Print.

———. *Night*. Trans. Marion Wiesel. New York: Hill, 2006. Print.

———. *La nuit*. Paris: Minuit, 1958. Print.

———. *Un di velt hot geshvign*. Buenos Aires: Tsentral-Farband fun Poylishe Yidn in Argentine, 1956. Print.

Wilson, Richard, dir. *Primo*. Perf. Antony Sher. Kultur Video, 2005. DVD. Adapt. of *If This Is a Man*, by Primo Levi, trans. Stuart Woolf.

Wouk, Herman. *This Is My God*. New York: Wouk Foundation, 1988. Print.

Young, James E. *Writing and Rewriting the Holocaust: Narrative and Consequences of Interpretation*. Bloomington: Indiana UP, 1990. Print.

Zuccotti, Susan. *The Italians and the Holocaust: Persecution, Rescue, and Survival*. New York: Basic, 1987. Print.

INDEX

Modern Language Association of America

Approaches to Teaching World Literature

Achebe's Things Fall Apart. Ed. Bernth Lindfors. 1991.
Arthurian Tradition. Ed. Maureen Fries and Jeanie Watson. 1992.
Atwood's The Handmaid's Tale *and Other Works*. Ed. Sharon R. Wilson, Thomas B. Friedman, and Shannon Hengen. 1996.
Austen's Emma. Ed. Marcia McClintock Folsom. 2004.
Austen's Pride and Prejudice. Ed. Marcia McClintock Folsom. 1993.
Austen's Mansfield Park. Ed. Marcia McClintock Folsom and John Wiltshire. 2014.
Balzac's Old Goriot. Ed. Michal Peled Ginsburg. 2000.
Baudelaire's Flowers of Evil. Ed. Laurence M. Porter. 2000.
Beckett's Waiting for Godot. Ed. June Schlueter and Enoch Brater. 1991.
Behn's Oroonoko. Ed. Cynthia Richards and Mary Ann O'Donnell. 2014.
Beowulf. Ed. Jess B. Bessinger, Jr., and Robert F. Yeager. 1984.
Blake's Songs of Innocence and of Experience. Ed. Robert F. Gleckner and Mark L. Greenberg. 1989.
Boccaccio's Decameron. Ed. James H. McGregor. 2000.
British Women Poets of the Romantic Period. Ed. Stephen C. Behrendt and Harriet Kramer Linkin. 1997.
Charlotte Brontë's Jane Eyre. Ed. Diane Long Hoeveler and Beth Lau. 1993.
Emily Brontë's Wuthering Heights. Ed. Sue Lonoff and Terri A. Hasseler. 2006.
Byron's Poetry. Ed. Frederick W. Shilstone. 1991.
Works of Italo Calvino. Ed. Franco Ricci. 2013.
Camus's The Plague. Ed. Steven G. Kellman. 1985.
Cather's My Ántonia. Ed. Susan J. Rosowski. 1989.
Cervantes' Don Quixote. Ed. Richard Bjornson. 1984.
Chaucer's Canterbury Tales. First edition Ed. Joseph Gibaldi. 1980.
Chaucer's Canterbury Tales. Second edition. Ed. Peter W. Travis and Frank Grady. 2014.
Chaucer's Troilus and Criseyde *and the Shorter Poems*. Ed. Tison Pugh and Angela Jane Weisl. 2006.
Chopin's The Awakening. Ed. Bernard Koloski. 1988.
Coetzee's Disgrace *and Other Works*. Ed. Laura Wright, Jane Poyner, and Elleke Boehmer. 2014.
Coleridge's Poetry and Prose. Ed. Richard E. Matlak. 1991.
Collodi's Pinocchio *and Its Adaptations*. Ed. Michael Sherberg. 2006.
Conrad's "Heart of Darkness" and "The Secret Sharer." Ed. Hunt Hawkins and Brian W. Shaffer. 2002.

Dante's Divine Comedy. Ed. Carole Slade. 1982.
Defoe's Robinson Crusoe. Ed. Maximillian E. Novak and Carl Fisher. 2005.
DeLillo's White Noise. Ed. Tim Engles and John N. Duvall. 2006.
Dickens's Bleak House. Ed. John O. Jordan and Gordon Bigelow. 2009.
Dickens's David Copperfield. Ed. Richard J. Dunn. 1984.
Dickinson's Poetry. Ed. Robin Riley Fast and Christine Mack Gordon. 1989.
Narrative of the Life of Frederick Douglass. Ed. James C. Hall. 1999.
Works of John Dryden. Ed. Jayne Lewis and Lisa Zunshine. 2013.
Duras's Ourika. Ed. Mary Ellen Birkett and Christopher Rivers. 2009.
Early Modern Spanish Drama. Ed. Laura R. Bass and Margaret R. Greer. 2006.
Eliot's Middlemarch. Ed. Kathleen Blake. 1990.
Eliot's Poetry and Plays. Ed. Jewel Spears Brooker. 1988.
Shorter Elizabethan Poetry. Ed. Patrick Cheney and Anne Lake Prescott. 2000.
Ellison's Invisible Man. Ed. Susan Resneck Parr and Pancho Savery. 1989.
English Renaissance Drama. Ed. Karen Bamford and Alexander Leggatt. 2002.
Works of Louise Erdrich. Ed. Gregg Sarris, Connie A. Jacobs, and James R. Giles. 2004.
Dramas of Euripides. Ed. Robin Mitchell-Boyask. 2002.
Faulkner's As I Lay Dying. Ed. Patrick O'Donnell and Lynda Zwinger. 2011.
Faulkner's The Sound and the Fury. Ed. Stephen Hahn and Arthur F. Kinney. 1996.
Fitzgerald's The Great Gatsby. Ed. Jackson R. Bryer and Nancy P. VanArsdale. 2009.
Flaubert's Madame Bovary. Ed. Laurence M. Porter and Eugene F. Gray. 1995.
García Márquez's One Hundred Years of Solitude. Ed. María Elena de Valdés and Mario J. Valdés. 1990.
Gilman's "The Yellow Wall-Paper" and Herland. Ed. Denise D. Knight and Cynthia J. Davis. 2003.
Goethe's Faust. Ed. Douglas J. McMillan. 1987.
Gothic Fiction: The British and American Traditions. Ed. Diane Long Hoeveler and Tamar Heller. 2003.
Poetry of John Gower. Ed. R. F. Yeager and Brian W. Gastle. 2011.
Grass's The Tin Drum. Ed. Monika Shafi. 2008.
H.D.'s Poetry and Prose. Ed. Annette Debo and Lara Vetter. 2011.
Hebrew Bible as Literature in Translation. Ed. Barry N. Olshen and Yael S. Feldman. 1989.
Homer's Iliad *and* Odyssey. Ed. Kostas Myrsiades. 1987.
Hurston's Their Eyes Were Watching God *and Other Works*. Ed. John Lowe. 2009.
Ibsen's A Doll House. Ed. Yvonne Shafer. 1985.
Henry James's Daisy Miller *and* The Turn of the Screw. Ed. Kimberly C. Reed and Peter G. Beidler. 2005.
Works of Samuel Johnson. Ed. David R. Anderson and Gwin J. Kolb. 1993.
Joyce's Ulysses. Ed. Kathleen McCormick and Erwin R. Steinberg. 1993.
Works of Sor Juana Inés de la Cruz. Ed. Emilie L. Bergmann and Stacey Schlau. 2007.

Kafka's Short Fiction. Ed. Richard T. Gray. 1995.
Keats's Poetry. Ed. Walter H. Evert and Jack W. Rhodes. 1991.
Kingston's The Woman Warrior. Ed. Shirley Geok-lin Lim. 1991.
Lafayette's The Princess of Clèves. Ed. Faith E. Beasley and Katharine Ann Jensen. 1998.
Writings of Bartolomé de Las Casas. Ed. Santa Arias and Eyda M. Merediz. 2008.
Works of D. H. Lawrence. Ed. M. Elizabeth Sargent and Garry Watson. 2001.
Lazarillo de Tormes *and the Picaresque Tradition*. Ed. Anne J. Cruz. 2009.
Lessing's The Golden Notebook. Ed. Carey Kaplan and Ellen Cronan Rose. 1989.
Works of Primo Levi. Ed. Nicholas Patruno and Roberta Ricci. 2014.
Works of Naguib Mahfouz. Ed. Waïl S. Hassan and Susan Muaddi Darraj. 2011.
Mann's Death in Venice *and Other Short Fiction*. Ed. Jeffrey B. Berlin. 1992.
Marguerite de Navarre's Heptameron. Ed. Colette H. Winn. 2007.
Works of Carmen Martín Gaite. Ed. Joan L. Brown. 2013.
Medieval English Drama. Ed. Richard K. Emmerson. 1990.
Melville's Moby-Dick. Ed. Martin Bickman. 1985.
Metaphysical Poets. Ed. Sidney Gottlieb. 1990.
Miller's Death of a Salesman. Ed. Matthew C. Roudané. 1995.
Milton's Paradise Lost. First edition. Ed. Galbraith M. Crump. 1986.
Milton's Paradise Lost. Second edition. Ed. Peter C. Herman. 2012.
Milton's Shorter Poetry and Prose. Ed. Peter C. Herman. 2007.
Molière's Tartuffe *and Other Plays*. Ed. James F. Gaines and Michael S. Koppisch. 1995.
Momaday's The Way to Rainy Mountain. Ed. Kenneth M. Roemer. 1988.
Montaigne's Essays. Ed. Patrick Henry. 1994.
Novels of Toni Morrison. Ed. Nellie Y. McKay and Kathryn Earle. 1997.
Murasaki Shikibu's The Tale of Genji. Ed. Edward Kamens. 1993.
Nabokov's Lolita. Ed. Zoran Kuzmanovich and Galya Diment. 2008.
Works of Ngũgĩ wa Thiong'o. Ed. Oliver Lovesey. 2012.
Works of Tim O'Brien. Ed. Alex Vernon and Catherine Calloway. 2010.
Works of Ovid and the Ovidian Tradition. Ed. Barbara Weiden Boyd and Cora Fox. 2010.
Petrarch's Canzoniere *and the Petrarchan Tradition*. Ed. Christopher Kleinhenz and Andrea Dini. 2014.
Poe's Prose and Poetry. Ed. Jeffrey Andrew Weinstock and Tony Magistrale. 2008.
Pope's Poetry. Ed. Wallace Jackson and R. Paul Yoder. 1993.
Proust's Fiction and Criticism. Ed. Elyane Dezon-Jones and Inge Crosman Wimmers. 2003.
Puig's Kiss of the Spider Woman. Ed. Daniel Balderston and Francine Masiello. 2007.
Pynchon's The Crying of Lot 49 *and Other Works*. Ed. Thomas H. Schaub. 2008.
Works of François Rabelais. Ed. Todd W. Reeser and Floyd Gray. 2011.
Novels of Samuel Richardson. Ed. Lisa Zunshine and Jocelyn Harris. 2006.

Rousseau's Confessions *and* Reveries of the Solitary Walker. Ed. John C. O'Neal and Ourida Mostefai. 2003.
Scott's Waverley Novels. Ed. Evan Gottlieb and Ian Duncan. 2009.
Shakespeare's Hamlet. Ed. Bernice W. Kliman. 2001.
Shakespeare's King Lear. Ed. Robert H. Ray. 1986.
Shakespeare's Othello. Ed. Peter Erickson and Maurice Hunt. 2005.
Shakespeare's Romeo and Juliet. Ed. Maurice Hunt. 2000.
Shakespeare's The Taming of the Shrew. Ed. Margaret Dupuis and Grace Tiffany. 2013.
Shakespeare's The Tempest *and Other Late Romances*. Ed. Maurice Hunt. 1992.
Shelley's Frankenstein. Ed. Stephen C. Behrendt. 1990.
Shelley's Poetry. Ed. Spencer Hall. 1990.
Sir Gawain and the Green Knight. Ed. Miriam Youngerman Miller and Jane Chance. 1986.
Song of Roland. Ed. William W. Kibler and Leslie Zarker Morgan. 2006.
Spenser's Faerie Queene. Ed. David Lee Miller and Alexander Dunlop. 1994.
Stendhal's The Red and the Black. Ed. Dean de la Motte and Stirling Haig. 1999.
Sterne's Tristram Shandy. Ed. Melvyn New. 1989.
Works of Robert Louis Stevenson. Ed. Caroline McCracken-Flesher. 2013.
The Story of the Stone (Dream of the Red Chamber). Ed. Andrew Schonebaum and Tina Lu. 2012.
Stowe's Uncle Tom's Cabin. Ed. Elizabeth Ammons and Susan Belasco. 2000.
Swift's Gulliver's Travels. Ed. Edward J. Rielly. 1988.
Teresa of Ávila and the Spanish Mystics. Ed. Alison Weber. 2009.
Thoreau's Walden *and Other Works*. Ed. Richard J. Schneider. 1996.
Tolstoy's Anna Karenina. Ed. Liza Knapp and Amy Mandelker. 2003.
Vergil's Aeneid. Ed. William S. Anderson and Lorina N. Quartarone. 2002.
Voltaire's Candide. Ed. Renée Waldinger. 1987.
Whitman's Leaves of Grass. Ed. Donald D. Kummings. 1990.
Wiesel's Night. Ed. Alan Rosen. 2007.
Works of Oscar Wilde. Ed. Philip E. Smith II. 2008.
Woolf's Mrs. Dalloway. Ed. Eileen Barrett and Ruth O. Saxton. 2009.
Woolf's To the Lighthouse. Ed. Beth Rigel Daugherty and Mary Beth Pringle. 2001.
Wordsworth's Poetry. Ed. Spencer Hall, with Jonathan Ramsey. 1986.
Wright's Native Son. Ed. James A. Miller. 1997.